The Last Conquistador

THE OKLAHOMA WESTERN BIOGRAPHIES
RICHARD W. ETULAIN, GENERAL EDITOR

"Juan de Oñate" by José Cisneros. (From *Riders Across the Centuries,* by José Cisneros, El Paso: Texas Western Press, p. 22; reproduced courtesy José Cisneros)

The Last Conquistador

JUAN DE OÑATE AND THE SETTLING OF THE FAR SOUTHWEST

By Marc Simmons

UNIVERSITY OF OKLAHOMA PRESS : NORMAN AND LONDON

Library of Congress Cataloging-in-Publication Data

The last conquistador : Juan de Oñate and the settling of the far
Southwest / by Marc Simmons.
    p.   cm.—(The Oklahoma western biographies ; v. 2)
Includes bibliographical references and index.
ISBN 0-8061-2338-9 (alk. paper)
    1. Oñate, Juan de, 1549?–1624.   2. Explorers—Southwest, New—
Biography.   3. Explorers—Spain—Biography.   4. Southwest, New—
History—To 1848.   I. Title.   II. Series.
F799.O587   1991
979'.01'092—dc20   90-50697
    [B]   CIP

The Last Conquistador: Juan de Oñate and the Settling of the Far Southwest is
Volume 2 in *The Oklahoma Western Biographies.*

The paper in this book meets the guidelines for permanence and durability
of the Committee on Production Guidelines for Book Longevity of the
Council on Library Resources, Inc. ∞

For my brother Hal

Contents

Illustrations

Figures

Maps

Series Editor's Preface

MARC Simmons has written a superb biography of Spanish Southwesterner Juan de Oñate, a stirring story that weaves Oñate's notable life story into the rich tapestry of sixteenth- and seventeenth-century New Spain and New Mexico. Throughout his book Simmons provides illuminating glimpses of sociocultural backgrounds that shaped Oñate and propelled him onward to the far northern reaches of New Spain.

Taking the lives of Oñate and his father as his initial focus, Simmons radiates outward to Spanish and New World influences that encircled the Oñate family and directed their thoughts and activities. Particularly revealing are discussions of the family's position among the Spanish elite of Mexico and its economic rise in that region. Simmons's treatment of Oñate's complicated maneuverings to gain and finally launch his pathbreaking expedition into New Mexico in 1598 is especially engrossing.

Over the last two decades, historian Marc Simmons has gained a national reputation as an authority on Spanish institutions and Mexican and American economic developments in the Southwest, and as a specialist on the Santa Fe Trail and the rise of Albuquerque. The present work illlustrates his equally significant talents as a biographer. Unflinching and balanced in his treatment of Oñate, Simmons paints a provocative and absorbing portrait of this stalwart Spanish conquistador. Boldly Basque, Oñate was by turns understanding and sympathetic, and yet arbitrary and dogmatic. Committed to looking after the livelihoods of his settlers, he used his mailed fist of authority against those who opposed his policies. Simmons blends the brilliant colors of Oñate's Spanish Basque ambition and fortitude with darker flashes of his anger, especially as exhibited in New Mexico, where extraordinary pressures often transformed Oñate into an oppressor rather than a leader.

As he has done in his numerous other books and essays, Simmons here tells a stimulating story without eschewing interpretation. Following Oñate on several expeditions through New Mexico and to the outer frontiers of New Spain, Simmons concurrently explains the significance these dramatic events hold, for a larger understanding of Oñate's life and character as well as for a clearer explanation of Spanish policy and culture.

In short, Simmons has produced a model volume for the Oklahoma Western Biographies series: a well-written biography that captures the life of a notable Westerner even while it illuminates the sprawling story of early Spanish entry into the American Southwest.

RICHARD W. ETULAIN

University of New Mexico

Preface

THE name of Juan de Oñate is scarcely a household word. Unlike his famous predecessors, explorers Francisco Vázquez de Coronado and Hernando de Soto, the colonizer Oñate remains a mystery man to most Americans. Yet, known or not, his pioneering work set the stage for the development of a vast section of what is now the southwestern United States. In 1598, at great personal cost, he led a formidable party of settlers with wagons and livestock on an epic march northward from Mexico to the upper reaches of the Rio Grande Valley, there to establish the first European settlement west of the Mississippi.

Earlier the Spaniards had called this remote frontier simply *La Tierra Nueva*, the New Land. But by Oñate's day it was referred to as *Nuevo México*, New Mexico reflecting the hope that it would somehow yield riches rivaling those Fernando Cortés had plundered from the Aztecs in the original Mexico far to the south. The dimensions of this country, so distant from Mexico City, were little understood. Spanish officials thought that New Mexico stretched as far as Newfoundland and bordered on the North Sea. Oñate himself asked permission from the king to bring two ships annually to the new colony unaware that the closest arm of the ocean was hundreds of miles away.

Today, the boundaries of the state of New Mexico, forming a near square between Texas and Arizona, do not in any way correspond to the broader limits of colonial Nuevo México, as recognized by the Spaniards. The present boundaries were created at the convenience of the United States following the end of its war with the Republic of Mexico in 1848 and subsequent Gadsden Purchase of 1853. But even though modern New Mexico is much reduced in size, it still retains the heartland along the Rio Grande that Oñate seized and settled nearly four centuries ago.

In his life and story several themes can be found that help illuminate the history of western America. As a conquistador, he epitomizes the stock image of the sixteenth-century Spanish adventurer who expanded the boundaries of the empire, but at the expense of Indians who chanced to be in the line of advance. As it happens, Oñate was probably among the best of the lot when it came to his treatment of the native peoples. By this time strict royal laws were in place to prevent the horrors so commonly reported during the first conquests. However, there were still instances where he bloodied his hands, in a fashion reminiscent of episodes fifty years before.

In a very real sense, Juan de Oñate represented the end of a tradition. He was the last conquistador, the final knight in burnished armor who sallied northward under authority of Cross and Crown to find wealth, glory, and fame. In that sense he was a medieval figure, confirming the old observation that the Middle Ages drew its last breath in the New World. On the other hand, some of his behavior and attitudes show him to have been, at the same time, a man of the New Era, one grappling with changes rapidly overtaking his society.

Oñate's career, to focus on another prominent theme, can serve as a reminder that in the growth of the United States there were not one but two frontiers—the well-known westward movement by English-speaking and a few French-speaking, peoples, and a less publicized northward advance by Hispanic pioneers out of the Caribbean and Mexico, or New Spain as it was initially called. The latter effort resulted in a thin peopling of what we now term the Spanish Border-lands, that is, the southern tier of states reaching from Florida across Texas and New Mexico to California. In varying degrees, the imprint of Spain remains on this region today.

What many people seem to forget is that events that transpired in the old Borderlands are as much a part of American history as what happened in the thirteen English colonies. Thus an account of Juan de Oñate, and his activities in New Mexico, should not be written off as foreign to our national story. Rather his chronicle can be taken as an authentic and integral chapter in our country's history. Indeed, that it has not been so taken perhaps explains why no biography of the man has appeared before now.

But there is another reason as well for the lack of books on Oñate. The beginning of his New Mexico venture occurred in 1595 when Oñate was about forty-three years of age. Before that date, so far as we know, there was little in his successful but unspectacular career that deserved more than a footnote in the history books. The exploits that won him lasting fame were all crowded into a fifteen-year period, ending in 1610 with his final exit from New Mexico. This means that the first two-thirds of his life, when his character and habits of mind were formed, stands largely outside the grasp of a biographer.

The situation is not unique to Oñate. France V. Scholes, who spent a half century studying Cortés, confessed that everything he knew about the conqueror's early life could be summed up in a few pages. Donald Chipman, in researching the personal history of Nuño de Guzmán, a rival of Cortés, acknowledges that he could learn hardly anything about his subject's physical appearance, and that his boyhood, adolescence, and young adulthood remain a total blank. The reasons for such a scarcity of information are several. One has to do with the loss and destruction of documents that are to be expected in the passage of four hundred troubled years. For another, certain records—of the kind biographers usually depend upon to fathom and explain motives, attitudes, and inner life—probably never existed in the first place for most of the *grandes capitanes,* great captains, of sixteenth-century New Spain. None of them kept intimate diaries or personal journals, that not being a practice congenial to the Spanish temperament of that time. Few seem to have penned long, newsy letters to family and friends. Almost none in their grandfather years wrote down recollections or memoirs of their early adventures—a conspicuous and practically solitary exception being the aged foot soldier Bernal Díaz del Castillo, participant in the overthrow of the Aztecs.

What we are left with as source materials are mainly the official government records, voluminous it is true in the case of Spaniards, but not altogether satisfactory since too often they merely skim the surface of events. Oñate's New Mexico reports to the king and viceroy, for example, clearly present himself and his actions as he wished to be seen, not as things actually were. To find the hidden side, the real Oñate who was a mix of strengths and flaws, requires much reading between the lines.

Does all this mean that little or nothing can be said about Juan de Oñate's life before 1595? Not exactly, because some data can be gleaned by following indirect paths. One of those paths leads to his father, Cristóbal de Oñate, who in some ways was more prominant than the son. A close look at Cristóbal in his roles as a frontier governor, Indian campaigner, and member of the silver aristocracy can suggest much about the influences that shaped the young Juan and the pattern that his early life must have followed.

A second path to understanding Oñate's formative period is revealed by reference to Spanish character in general and to the Spaniards' outlook or what historians are fond of describing as "the spirit of the times." There is no reason to think that Oñate was anything but an exemplary product of his national culture or that he failed to be thoroughly indoctrinated in the Hispanic world view. Repeatedly, by his words and actions, he provided clues to personal traits and to the direction of his thinking that leave no doubt he was struck from a recognizable mold.

A rounded biography requires careful selection and interpretation. A wise historian has to get beyond the screen of all that people said and did to discover what really happened. In the re-creating of a central character, like Juan de Oñate, one must aim not only at understanding him but at perceiving his physical reality—the sense that he was once alive and walked in full sunlight. In attempting to do this, I am conforming to the purposes of the Oklahoma Western Biographies series. Its stated intent is to spotlight the lives of notable persons, men and women whose experiences contributed in some significant way to the history of the American West. Oñate, as I have indicated, went north rather than west to settle new lands, but that happenstance of geography in no way diminishes his stature as a substantial figure in America's frontier saga.

In the preparation of this book, I have incurred a number of debts. Peter J. Bakewell provided the exact date of Cristóbal de Oñate's death, and clarified several other points concerning the early history of Zacatecas. Joseph P. Sánchez generously shared with me a document he had found in Spain that established an interesting detail regarding Juan de Oñate's death. David J. Weber also furnished me a number of useful references. I was able to refine my views on Spanish thinking through discussions with John L. Kessell and Trinidad R. Padilla. My thanks go as well to Evelyn Vinogradov and Danita Ross, and to the photographer L. A. Mitchell, who helped assemble the illustrations. As always, when dealing with the Spanish colonial period, I benefited from the expert advice of José Cisneros. Richard Etulain shepherded the manuscript along its way, gracefully and with tact.

Finally, a brief note of clarification: The word *Pueblos* when capitalized refers to the Indians, while the lower case *pueblos* following Spanish usage, refers to their villages.

MARC SIMMONS

Los Cerrillos, New Mexico

The Last Conquistador

CHAPTER 1

Introduction

ON the morning of September 21, 1595, Don Juan de Oñate y Salazar hurried through the streets of Mexico City, headed for the viceregal palace and the most important meeting he had ever faced. Indeed, it probably occurred to him that all of his life up to this moment had been a preparation for what was to follow later that day. Don Juan had won the fierce competition for the right to pacify and colonize the provinces of the proposed kingdom of New Mexico, as ordered by His Majesty King Philip II.

Don Luís de Velasco, viceroy of New Spain, had summoned Oñate to appear before him, amid the pomp and splendor of his court, so the formal negotiations could be completed and a contract signed. Acting on behalf of the king, Velasco had chosen Juan de Oñate for the important task ahead because of his record of service, aristocratic family connections, and personal wealth. Moreover, it seems the viceroy may have been motivated by friendship. He was well acquainted with Don Juan and had actively encouraged him to apply for the New Mexico prize.

Although accompanied by the usual stiff ceremony, Oñate's reception in the great palace radiated warmth, as the genial viceroy made him welcome. Discussions had been going on for some time, and Velasco was thoroughly familiar with the proposals that Oñate brought with him. However, protocol demanded that these now be read aloud, permitting the viceroy to rule for or against each item requested. In this time-honored way, legal-minded Spaniards made binding contracts, or *capitulaciones*.

Columbus himself had established the precedent for New World exploration when in the spring of 1492 he signed the Capitulations of Santa Fe with Ferdinand and Isabella, rulers of Aragon and Castile. That document spelled out his titles, powers, and authority over lands that might be discovered, and set the percentage of revenues he could keep if his venture turned a profit. Later on, other soldiers of fortune neglected the formality of making a contract and instead went off independently to discover and topple Indian kingdoms in both North and South America. Men such as Fernando Cortés and Francisco Pizarro achieved such stunning success and brought so much wealth to the royal treasury that the Spanish crown hesitated to reprimand them. But it moved gradually to assert control over all upstart conquistadors, as much to protect the native peoples, who had suffered frightfully in the first conquests, as to force the haughty and vain conquerors to heed the king's authority.

The movement in that direction culminated in passage of the Colonization Laws of 1573. Those were the very laws that Oñate used as a guide in writing up his proposals for the settlement of New Mexico, and they fixed the standard by which Viceroy Velasco decided what should be included in the final contract. The new code required future expansion to be carried out peacefully and charitably, carefully avoiding force except in self-defense or in cases where Indians who had submitted and been converted later rebelled. In addition, the laws established a strict supervisory role for the government over activities of private explorers and colonizers, like Oñate, and obliged them to adhere scrupulously to the articles of their capitulaciones.

Oñate's proposals, written in tight script on rag paper, were read out loud, probably by the court's royal notary. On each one, Velasco made a judgment, recorded in marginal notes. Many of Oñate's requests he accepted unconditionally. Others he modified. And a few he rejected outright as not being in conformity with the Colonization Laws of 1573. But all in all, when the reading was done Don Juan had cause for satisfaction. The viceroy had been as generous as he dared, and with the contract signed, plans for the occupation of New Mexico could get under way.

A summary of several of the important provisions of this key document reveals something of the way Spaniards carried out pioneering enterprises. Conspicuous was the requirement that Oñate bear the lion's share of the enormous expense involved in the New Mexico project. That gave the king a wonderful bargain. He saw the realm expanded, shared any rewards, and invested very little. Moreover, all the risk was shifted to the contractor.

As to specifics, Oñate proposed to equip and arm two hundred men who were to serve in the dual role of soldier and colonist. Many of them would have families, and he agreed to purchase the food, clothing, and other supplies they would need on the trip north and during the period of building new homes. He further pledged to take mining and blacksmithing tools, medicines, Indian trade goods, seeds, plows, and other assorted necessities—all to be transported in his wagons or carts, or on pack mules.

By the contract Oñate received titles, concessions, and honors from the crown as compensation for his large investments in energy and money. The political title of governor was his, as well as the designation of *adelantado* (an honorific office left over from the Middle Ages) and the supreme military rank of captain-general, together with rights to exercise all civil and criminal jurisdiction in New Mexico. These were important titles and sweeping powers, which would make him, as he surely knew, practically a frontier potentate. With that in mind he had asked that the titles be granted for life with the privilege of passing them on to his heirs. Evidently, he was envisioning a long line of Oñates, a dynasty to rule over the gleaming kingdom of New Mexico that he meant to build on the frontier. Here we find the chief motive that prompted Don Juan to wager so much on this ambitious endeavor.

For the rest, he was granted a salary of six thousand ducats annually as governor and the loan of three artillery pieces from the royal arsenal. He was empowered to make land grants to his settlers and permit them to collect tribute from the Indians under a system known as *encomienda*. He could name his own officials, set up a royal treasury office, build forts, exploit mines, and divide the colony into governmental districts. The crown, as a patron of the Spanish Catholic Church, agreed to underwrite the expenses of five priests and a lay brother to minister to the colonists and convert the Indians. And it promised to award all Oñate's men, after five years' residence in New Mexico, titles of *hidalgo* (the lowest rank of nobleman), as a way of attracting volunteers to the colonizing expedition.

Lastly, the contract incorporated a highly significant provision that placed Oñate directly under the Council of the Indies, the king's chief advisory body in Seville. That left him and his proposed government in New Mexico virtually independent of the viceroy and Mexico City's ponderous bureaucracy. Only the Council of the Indies, which was far away indeed, could hold him accountable for his actions.

Juan de Oñate brought high expectations to the meeting with Viceroy Velasco that September day four hundred years ago. Although now bound by the Colonization Laws, he still aspired to be an empire builder in the tradition of Cortés. His knowledge of recent

history, which was studded with spectacular Spanish feats, led him
to believe that New Mexico offered a theater for some brilliant accomplishment. In fact, Luís Navarro García, who is one of Spain's leading
historians, contends that from the start Juan de Oñate was looking
toward the creation of a new viceroyalty, centered upon New Mexico
and with himself at the head. For Oñate in 1595 that possibility would
not have seemed out of reach.

In one sense, the conclusion of contract negotiations at day's end
and the conditional approval granted by Viceroy Velasco (subject to
confirmation of the king) stand as a milepost in Oñate's life. He had
been given license to carry out a grand project of the kind every high-
reaching Spaniard hungered for. Behind him were wealth, experience,
family backing, and the benevolent if frugal support of the viceroy
and king. Success, in all of the dimensions measured by Spaniards,
seemed assured. But at that moment of elation he could have no
inkling of the unending series of reverses that lay ahead and the
battering his dreams would take. His fortitude and persistence in
confronting setbacks and misfortune during the fifteen years that
followed constitute the centerpiece of Juan de Oñate's story.

Oñate's occupation of New Mexico became part of a vast movement
by Spaniards into remote and hostile precincts of the New World.
Modern writer Claudio Sánchez Albornoz has called the American
experience "the great historic achievement of the Iberian peoples."
Their expansion was carried out beneath a pennant emblazoned with
the Latin words *Plus Ultra,* meaning "More Beyond," which served
as a fitting motto for sixteenth-century explorers. Gaspar Pérez de
Villagrá, Oñate's officer and historian, bragged that his companions
shouted, "*Plus Ultra!*" as "with strong arm and mighty courage" they
plunged ahead. "To the Castilian the discovery and settlement of the
entire universe would not be too great a task," he added, with the
cockiness that characterized Spaniards of that period.

As often noted, the Spanish owed their penchant for exploration,
settlement, and evangelization in the Indies to the eight-centuries-
long crusade, or *reconquista,* waged against the Moors, Islamic invaders out of Africa. Ferdinand and Isabella's final defeat of the infidels
early in 1492 released men, energy, and resources for new conquests
that would soon open abroad. Through the drawn-out course of
Moorish warfare, Spanish character and point of view had assumed
a distinctive stamp, promoting among other things an uncompromis-

Viceroy Luís de Velasco II, who signed the original contract with Oñate to colonize Mexico. (From Manuel Rivera Cambas, *Los Gobernantes de Mexico*, Mexico, 1872.)

ing devotion to the crown and church. A militant Christianity had
served as the rallying force behind the crusade, with the result that
priests emerged as one of the most respected and powerful classes in
society. Their natural allies were the Christian soldiers, who furnished
manpower for the holy wars and who thereby came to regard themselves as defenders of the faith. When men like Coronado and Oñate
invaded the wilderness of northern New Spain with priests marching
at their sides, they were perpetuating an alliance and union of aims
that reached far back in Spanish history.

The ideal of the Christian warrior drew inspiration from the figure
of Santiago, or Saint James the Apostle, patron of Spain. In Catholic
art he was depicted as a bearded, sword-welding knight astride a
white charger whose hooves trampled the lifeless bodies of Moors.
On occasion, it was said, he miraculously appeared upon the fighting
field to inspirit Spanish forces and lead them to victory. His interven-
tions were later extended to the New World and battles with hostile
Indians. The writings of Oñate's men speak of one such startling
appearance, during the assault on Acoma pueblo in 1599. The image
of Santiago, the equestrian saint, appealed irresistibly to the Spaniard.
In him the *caballero,* or warrior knight, found a model who displayed
an admirable combination of strength and religious zeal.

Spain, then, emerged from the Middle Ages with its crusading
spirit intact and harboring a strong sense of mission. In the new age
of discovery, which coincided with the rise of Protestantism, it tried
to defend Catholic orthodoxy in Europe while mounting an enormous missionary effort in its transatlantic colonies. The conquistadors, carrying the crusade through the Indies and to the Indians,
functioned as an arm of both church and state. They went after glory,
riches, and the souls of the natives, and that, united with their abiding
sense of history, gave them a distinctive style. Above all, Spaniards
of the sixteenth century had style.

Writers ascribed to them a good deal more, of course, in the way
of character traits. Dignity. Acute sense of honor, with refusal to
accept affronts. Fearlessness, even a contempt for death. Outward
simplicity. Disregard for comforts. Good manners, manifested in an
elaborate courtesy. A sense of fatalism, which is merely resignation
in the face of tragedy. Aloofness. Self-pride, of the kind that borders
on conceit and fosters the view that to work with one's hands is
demeaning. And extreme individualism, sometimes mentioned as the
universal Spanish trait.

Here individualism means each man living and thinking in his own way, functioning poorly in a group, showing distaste for compromise and concession. Or as the Greek geographer Strabo said of the Spaniards at the dawn of their history, "They would never put their shields together." The best scholars of Spain acknowledge that, but then declare that defects of national character aside, the Spaniard is vindicated because, unlike others, he knows how to live and die in the grand manner. Some of all of this can be discerned in the lives and experiences of Juan de Oñate and his generation. There was much done with style and in the grand manner, even in such an undertaking as the settlement of a remote land like New Mexico. Through many of his inward qualities, Oñate personified both the time and the culture in which he found himself. And through definition of his "Spanishness" the pattern of his conduct becomes comprehensible.

Philip II came to the Spanish throne in 1556 upon the abdication of his father Charles V. Little Juan de Oñate in far-off New Spain was then four years old. When Philip's long reign ended with his death in 1598, Oñate was on the Rio Grande just beginning his effort at colonization. In the nearly one-half century between those dates, Spain had become the most powerful nation in Western Europe. At least part of the reason lay in Philip's skill as a monarch. Grave, retiring, devoutly pious, a man of few words who habitually dressed in clerical black, the king was thoroughly committed to the principles of empire.

Continuing a process begun by his great-grandmother, Queen Isabella, he deepened and expanded royal power, centralizing a huge bureaucracy and devoting much of his personal energy to the mechanics of ruling. But a large part of his treasure and time went into fighting wars on several European fronts—for instance, against imperialistic Turks advancing across the Mediterranean, and against "Lutherans," as he termed all Protestants. His buildup of Spain's military machine and revival of the navy produced some successes, but could not avoid a spectacular defeat—the shattering of the Great Armada he sent against England and Queen Elizabeth in 1588.

Government expenditures constantly threatened to bankrupt the Spanish economy. In fact they did so in 1575 when the external debt produced a panic and financial collapse. That year the fleet bound for the Indies could not be provisioned for lack of ready money. And the renowned trade fair at Medina del Campo had to be suspended.

Philip spent countless hours alone at his desk in the Escorial, his huge palace, devising ways to resolve the crises. For relief from his anxiety, he paced the courtyards and listened to the nightingales that nested there. The brightest spot in his reign was the continuing expansion in the New World and its uninterrupted flow of gold and silver, which, if insufficient to pay all Spain's bills, at least furnished a basis for economic revival. New Spain, encompassing the future Mexico and much else to the north and south, was flourishing. Indeed, it was on the road to becoming what has sometimes been judged the Western Hemisphere's most successful colony. Half the Spanish inhabitants of Mexico City were rich enough to own gilded, mule-drawn carriages, adorned with jewels and curtained in silks. Their homes, claims the historian Lesley Byrd Simpson, were veritable palaces studding the fashionable streets of the capital. The splendor of these households, in his words, transcended vulgarity, for they were overflowing with luxury goods brought by galleons from Europe and China.

Mexico City's central plaza, breathtaking in size, was graced with palatial government buildings and a towering cathedral whose construction went on for decades. Scattered through the rest of the city were dozens of churches and chapels, not to mention cloisters and convents. Hospitals maintained by the religious orders offered health care, along with a government hospital for Indians. Numerous schools provided instruction. The Royal and Pontifical University of Mexico, having opened its doors in 1553, was conferring bachelor's and advanced degrees in law and theology. That began a half century before the founding of the Jamestown colony in Virginia and more than eighty years in advance of Harvard's establishment in Massachusetts. There were libraries, too, their books combed from shelves in Europe, and printing presses, the first introduced in 1539. The Mexico City of Philip II's day—the viceregal capital so familiar to Juan de Oñate—sparkled architecturally, socially, and culturally, at a time when most of the continent still lay under a mantle of wilderness, unexplored.

The city and the colony also basked in the refracted glitter of another sort, its source the prodigious output of silver in the hinterlands. A royal mint had commenced operation at Mexico City in 1535, the year the first viceroy took office, and later additional mints were added in provincial cities as needed. They stamped out lustrous pieces-of-eight, to the value of two billion dollars by the end of the colonial era, and another two billion worth of ingots was exported to Spain. The northern mining city of Zacatecas, residence of the Oñates, is said to have yielded one-fifth of the world's silver by the close of the eighteenth century. The treasure of all the Indies, as it filtered through Spain, played a decisive role in the birth of the commercial age. Little wonder then that Philip placed a high priority on protection of his empire in America, especially the viceroyalty of New Spain.

That concern was reflected in the stringent controls exercised over immigration, the aim being to permit only loyal, orthodox Spaniards to settle the king's overseas lands. Those even suspected of Protestant, Jewish, or Moslem leanings were rigorously excluded, as were most foreigners, even if they were Catholic. The policy stood in sharp contrast to the practice of the English, who later used their Atlantic seaboard colonies—and still later, Australia—as a dumping ground for religious dissenters, debtors, criminals, and other categories of social outcasts.

The real threat to the Indies, however, came not from within but from without, as the king knew only too well. Foreign corsairs, mainly English and French, poached upon Spanish waters, seizing treasure vessels and sacking coastal cities. Prominent among these seadogs was Francis Drake, "Draque" to the Spaniards, whose name inspired terror. In 1579 he sailed and raided up the Pacific shore of South America and continued as far north as the California coast. From there he returned to England by steering west and circumnavigating the globe. But Spaniards somehow got the idea that he had discovered the Strait of Anián, a legendary inter-oceanic waterway cutting through the upper reaches of North America to unite the Atlantic and Pacific, and believed that he had returned to England by that route.

For three centuries belief in such a strait was to prove a durable myth, even for English explorers, who called it the Northwest Passage. All European seamen knew that the nation controlling the continental strait, giving ships access to the Pacific and the Far East, would reap unparalleled commercial and military advantages. Since Philip's Spain was bitterly at odds with England, the mere possibility that Drake had stumbled upon this elusive wonder was enough to cause profound alarm in Madrid. It may even have sparked the king to begin thinking of occupying New Mexico, for he, along with his advisers, assumed that the outer fringes of that faraway country must touch upon waters of the strait. At any rate, it is known that a search for the passageway figured later in Oñate's New Mexican project.

The reign of Philip II is usually considered a pinnacle in the early modern history of Spain. Historians have long been in the habit of dating the beginning of the empire's decline from the day of his death by a painful blood disease, September 14, 1598. He was laid to rest in a marble casket placed in the Pantheon of the Escorial, but not before funeral services were delayed several months by quarrels of protocol over the seating arrangements for counselors and clergy. It was so typical of sixteenth-century Spaniards to be uncompromising on points of personal honor.

The degree of respect and affection those same Spaniards held for their king was truly remarkable. The crown always embodied, in the eyes of its subjects, the loftiest motives and highest virtues, a belief that eased the process of accepting the king's word as law. Juan de Oñate, writing to Philip II in 1595, voiced the standard refrain of his fellow countrymen of that time, when he pledged "to serve Your Majesty . . . to the full extent of my strength and resources and [willingly] endure the greatest hardships and difficulties in the royal service." Such commitment sprang from authentic devotion to "our sainted sovereign," as Oñate's officer Villagrá referred to him.

The crown, sad to say, did not always treat its subjects in a saintly manner. Indeed, it used men unmercifully, wearing them out in extravagant explorations and conquests, rewarding them with empty titles and ill-paid offices, and finally crushing them if they showed independence. Oñate himself would be victimized by his own too steadfast devotion to the king. But without a dogged determination to serve the sovereign, he would have made no splash and his name would have sunk like a rock, unnoticed, into the bottomless gulf of the past.

As it was, Don Juan de Oñate in the fall of 1595 was a man with a grandiose dream, and his contract, newly signed by Viceroy Velasco, served as a ticket, he believed, to renown in the history of Philip II's empire. But as an old Spanish proverb had it: *De decir a hacer hay mucho que ver,* which loosely translates, "Between dream and reality lies a vast distance." It was a bit of folk wisdom that could very well have been on Oñate's mind as he commenced plans for an expedition to his new kingdom on the Rio Grande. Now the great adventure began—to transform his vision of success into physical reality.

CHAPTER 2

Origins

THE Juan de Oñate who founded New Mexico was heir to strong blood and a rich cultural legacy. The Oñates were Basques, and in that simple fact much concerning the dynamism of individual family members is explained. The Basques inhabited the cool, wet mountains of north-central Spain, having lived there even before the ancient Iberian tribes found their way into the peninsula. Where the Basques originated no one knows. To this day, they speak a language, Euskera, unrelated to any other in Europe, one so difficult for outsiders to learn that it is said the Devil once tried for seven years but finally gave up in disgust.

The three small all-Basque provinces hang in a cherry-like cluster off the southwestern end of the Pyrenees Mountains. Two of them, Viscaya and Guipúzcoa, border on the stormy Bay of Biscay and the third, Alava, lies inland. It is a hard land of misty heights, luxuriant vegetation, and pitched-roof villages, quite unlike the sunny Spain celebrated in song and travel books. As the countryside is distinctive, so are its people.

A handsome race, the Basques tend to have slender bodies, long faces, prominent and curved noses, and slightly jutting chins. Overall they possess a rugged appearance, reminiscent of their homeland and history, that makes them recognizable from other Spaniards. Hardy, self-reliant, stubbornly strong, they are, French author Voltaire once declared, "a fearless lot who dance upon the tops of mountains." These qualities are summed up in the Basque word, *indarra*, which roughly means fortitude combined with forbearance.

Above all these people cling to a fierce pride in their Basque heritage. For centuries they successfully fought off invaders—Celts, Romans, Germans, and Moors—so that high-spirited resistance became part of their physical make-up. Basques were in the habit of boasting that they had never been conquered, although in fact their provinces were absorbed by the kingdom of Castile in the thirteenth and fourteenth centuries. They were staunch, even rigid, Catholics, leaders in the crusades to drive the Moors back into Africa, and they learned to speak Castilian with an odd and harsh accent.

An ill-concealed sense of superiority marked them as well, something fellow Spaniards found galling. And it was another boast of the Basques that they were all nobles. That was true! They retained ancient privileges and rights, known as *fueros*, and claimed crown recognition as hidalgos. The historian J. Lloyd Mecham has written that some Basque villages went so far as to refuse permission for foreigners to live among them unless they too were of noble rank.

Love of home was so pronounced with the Basques that only small numbers immigrated to the Spanish Indies in search of fortune. But those who did go gained influence far out of proportion to their numbers. In New Spain, for example, they won distinction as explorers, soldiers, and discoverers of mines on the frontier; and in the cities they achieved prominence in business and the civil bureaucracy. Others rose in the church hierarchy to the positions of bishop and archbishop. Wherever opportunity drew them, they had the habit of joining with one another to form a small but conspicuous minority.

In all things that Basques did can be seen a kind of dogged persistence, an unwillingness to admit defeat until every avenue leading to a difficult goal had been exhausted. A case in point is furnished by Fray Juan de Zumárraga, a Basque and the first bishop of New Spain. When he opposed Nuño de Guzmán, ruler of the colony after Cortés and merciless slayer of Indians, Guzmán threatened him with the gallows. Letters of protest to the king were intercepted by Guzmán's agents on the coast, until Zumárraga managed to get one out by hiding it in a cake of wax and entrusting it to a Basque sailor. Guzmán's crimes were thus exposed, and he was recalled in disgrace. We can imagine that at the news Bishop Zumárraga danced on the summit of his personal mountain.

One additional Basque trait casts light on their behavior abroad. That was pride in family, notable among all Spaniards but nowhere more so than among these northern mountaineers. They held the home sacred and remained strict in loyalty to family members. Ties of kinship stretched across the Atlantic, and whenever a Basque was involved in any great enterprise usually he could be found surrounded by relatives.

In the country districts of Spain, individuals were often identified by the name of their native village. Juan de Oñate's paternal great-

FRANCE

Basque Country

•Vitoria

•Burgos

OLD CASTILE

•Madrid

PORTUGAL

SPAIN

NEW CASTILE

•Guadalcanal

Guadalquivir River

Cartagena•

Seville•

•Granada

ANDALUSIA

Cadiz•

MOROCCO

Spain in the Time of Juan de Oñate

grandfather, Cristóbal Pérez de Narriahondo, was a resident of the hamlet of Oñate in Guipúzcoa. (*Oñate* was a Basque word meaning "at the foot of the mountain pass.") When his son, Juan Pérez, married and moved south across the Zadorra River to live in Vitoria, the principal city of Alava province, he became known as Juan Pérez de Oñate, literally Juan Pérez from Oñate. In that simple manner was the new family name created.

Juan Pérez, with his wife Osaña González, had three children: Juan, named after himself; Cristóbal, for the grandfather; and a daughter, María Pérez de Oñate. From this point forward the Juan and Cristóbal names would proliferate in the Oñate line, giving headaches to historians and genealogists who would try to sort them out. Here our interest focuses upon Juan Pérez's son Cristóbal, born

Basque countryside. (Courtesy Basque Studies Program, University of Nevada, Reno)

about 1504 or 1505. He was the future father of another Juan, the one destined to become governor of New Mexico.

Unhappily, nothing is known of Cristóbal de Oñate's upbringing or early experiences. In 1524, perhaps through the influence of his father or of some important relative, young Cristóbal obtained a choice job in public service overseas. He became assistant to the newly appointed accountant of the royal treasury of New Spain, Rodrigo de Albornoz, who had been secretary to the king. Surely, strings were pulled in his favor, because Cristóbal was only twenty years old. Still, candidates for office, even youthful ones, were expected to be persons of sound education and ability, so his employment, at least in part, must have been based on merit. When in the autumn of that year he took ship with the accountant Albornoz for New Spain, Cristóbal, we can suppose, was overflowing with boyish enthusiasm. Spaniards of that time embarked for the Indies filled with hope that wealth and fame awaited them on the far side of the ocean.

In due course, Cristóbal's ship cast anchor at the gulf port of Vera Cruz, and he went on land with Rodrigo de Albornoz, other treasury officials, and their entourage. One member of this party, whom Cristóbal had gotten to know well on the voyage, was Gonzalo de Salazar, the royal factor, or business manager for the treasury. In all respects, Salazar proved to be an unsavory character, described by contemporaries as a master of subtle duplicity. That depiction is amply borne out by his conduct as a political schemer during the succeeding months. He is a man of more than passing interest to us, since his daughter, who later followed him from Spain, would wed Cristóbal de Oñate, making the unlikable Gonzalo de Salazar maternal grandfather of Juan de Oñate.

The new arrivals did not linger in the unhealthy tropics at Vera Cruz but immediately started for Mexico City by a high road that took them past the snow-capped volcanic cone of eighteen-thousand-foot Mount Orizaba. It was the same route that Fernando Cortés had used scarcely five years before when he marched inland to subdue the Aztecs. Now Cortés was the governor of New Spain, ruling with an iron hand and vigorously attempting to expand the boundaries of the colony. His assumption of princely trappings had not gone unnoticed by the Spanish crown, which was already formulating plans to clip the wings of arrogant conquistadors. In fact, there is reason to believe that the new treasury officials whom Cristóbal de

Oñate accompanied were spies for the government, commissioned to send home reports of the doings and sayings of Cortés. Treasury officers of the empire had lofty status and broad powers, so they would have been in an excellent position to collect incriminating evidence.

Once in Mexico City, Salazar fawned upon Cortés in an effort to win his favor and confidence. But failing in that, he dispatched secret letters to Spain attacking Cortés's loyalty and libeling his character. Unaware of this, Cortés readied plans for an expedition deep into the jungles of Central America. Upon departure in late 1524, he left the top treasury officials in charge as a collective body of lieutenant governors. Salazar and another officer, Pedro Almindez Cherino, quickly usurped power, virtually taking over the entire government. Professor Lesley Byrd Simpson has called the pair New Spain's first dictators and characterized their rule as one of "unashamed hijacking."

Salazar seized and appropriated for his own use the immense estates of the governor. He also dispossessed Cortés's followers, the original soldiers and settlers, of their lands and petty offices in government. To consolidate his hold, he circulated rumors that Cortés had perished in the jungles. And so it seemed, for the governor was absent for more than a year and a half. In May 1526, however, Cortés made a sudden return, and Salazar and Cherino lost their authority. But the mischief they had committed was not so easily undone.

During the interval of Salazar's tyranny, Cristóbal de Oñate's employer, the accountant Albornoz, had remained in the background. After the governor came back from his Central American expedition, Albornoz wrote the Council of the Indies recommending that Cortés be replaced in office by someone who was not so greedy and that an *Audiencia,* a council of magistrates, be sent to share power and protect the king's interests. Guessing that his job was insecure, Cortés hurried to Spain and received a warm reception at the imperial court. Although Charles V informed Cortés of his removal from the governorship, as compensation he granted him the title of marquis and permission to build a fleet for exploration along the Pacific coast of New Spain.

In the welter of intrigue surrounding these events, Cristóbal de Oñate managed to keep his job with the treasury accountant. Our impression of him is that he was an amiable youth whom other people found congenial company, and that he maintained his position by

steering clear of the partisan politics that wracked the colony. His boss
Albornoz, for example, opposed and disliked Salazar, but Cristóbal
somehow contrived to stay in the good graces of both men. His
association with the rascally Salazar, though, was certainly not to his
credit.

Cristóbal de Oñate soon tethered his star to another scoundrel, the
notorious Beltran Nuño de Guzmán. Simpson defines him as "one
of those rare characters whose exclusive role seems to be that of
destroyer," a judgment most historical sources fully support. In 1528
Guzmán received word of his appointment as president of New
Spain's first Audiencia, a body created by the crown to rule the colony
following removal of Cortés as governor. When he reached Mexico
City and assumed power, Guzmán at once aligned himself with the
anti-Cortés faction against the old partisans of the conqueror, who
as first-comers considered themselves a privileged class. Among the
president's new allies were Gonzalo de Salazar and his favorites,
including the youth, Cristóbal de Oñate. Evidently through his
friendship with Salazar, Cristóbal gained first the ear and then the
confidence of Guzmán, so much so that when Cortés's men were
despoiled of their possessions and lands, he received some of the
property as a gift from the president.

By 1529 Guzmán's misdeeds, particularly his cruelty toward Indians,
had come to the attention of the Council of the Indies (through the
letter smuggled out by Bishop Zumárraga). Upon learning of his
pending dismissal from office, Guzmán decided to launch a new
conquest as the best means to regain crown favor and refurbish a
tarnished reputation. Therefore, he assembled a rag-tag army of four
hundred Spaniards, mainly idlers and soldiers of fortune off the
streets, and set forth to subdue unknown lands that stretched northwest from Mexico City to the Pacific shore. Over the next seven years
he carved out the province of Nueva Galicia, an achievement worthy
enough to win pardon for his past crimes, and the governorship as
well. But in the course of his exploration and campaigning, Guzmán
advanced to a new plateau of barbarity. He tortured and hanged
Indians. He pillaged and burned native towns and left vast expanses
of the countryside depopulated. Hundreds of captives were enslaved
and branded on the cheek. In his wake, beleaguered pockets of
survivors nursed a bitter hatred for all Spaniards. His arrest and
imprisonment in 1537 came too late to repair the damage.

At the age of twenty-four, Cristóbal de Oñate was one of those who embarked with Guzmán upon the conquest of Nueva Galicia. The decision to go marked a turning point in his life, for henceforth his fortunes would be made on that far frontier. What prompted him to follow a man of so dismal a reputation? We can only speculate that the prospect of adventure and the chance to win riches outweighed any reservations he might have held about the morality of his leader. Guzmán, for his part, saw in Cristóbal a promising and loyal young man, far superior in every way to most of the other recruits in his rapacious army. At once he granted him the rank of captain over a troop of cavalry.

Up to that moment Cristóbal de Oñate's one job in life had been clerking in the treasury office. His military experience was nonexistent. Still, he was beneficiary of the long Spanish tradition of militarism that grew from the centuries of conflict with the Moors. Noble, merchant, artisan, peasant, and even clergyman had learned to provide for his own defense. Every man in his home and fields became a warrior. To leave one's shop or lay down one's plow on short notice and go soldiering became as natural to a Spaniard as breathing. Certainly, there is nothing to indicate Cristóbal entertained qualms about his ability to lead men into battle. Mexican historian José López Portillo y Weber claims that he quickly mastered the arts of war and emerged as one of Guzmán's most trusted and energetic subordinates.

That claim is confirmed by reference to some of Cristóbal's documented accomplishments. He was one of the founders of Culiacán, northernmost in a string of new municipalities that emerged from the rubble of Guzmán's conquests. In the early 1530s he headed a wing of the army that crossed eastward over the forbidding Sierra Madre to explore the plains of the future Mexican state of Durango. Afterward he retired south to become the key figure in establishing the city of Guadalajara, named after Guzmán's birthplace in Spain.

The extraordinary thing in all this activity is that Cristóbal rejected the brutality of Guzmán, choosing instead to deal with the Indians in a respectful manner and trying to enforce royal laws that protected them. Historical accounts consistently identify Cristóbal as a moderating influence in what otherwise was a grim chapter in the expansion of New Spain. The first viceroy, Antonio de Mendoza, spoke of him in glowing terms, and at a later day the residents of western Mexico chose to credit Oñate, rather than Nuño de Guzmán, as the true father and architect of Nueva Galicia. Being a man of proven decency and honor, his protracted association with Guzmán seems all the more puzzling.

Cristóbal's honorable conduct also stands in sharp contrast to that of his brother, Juan, who followed him from Spain, arriving in Nueva Galicia about 1531. An individual without apparent scruple or restraint, Juan found in Guzmán a man of kindred spirit. He gleefully participated in the torture and slaughter of Indians, and on occasion he fed their corpses to his mastiffs. A whole litany of crimes was attributed to him at the time of Guzmán's trial, but by then Juan (with Cristóbal's help) had fled to Peru to escape punishment. There he died in exile, blind and penniless. Two brothers of strict Basque upbringing, raised in the same household in Vitoria, yet they stood poles apart in character. Their case exemplifies one of the imponderables in the human condition.

In the aftermath of Nuño de Guzmán's disgrace and removal from office, Cristóbal de Oñate, who had been filling the lieutenant-governorship, was made acting governor of Nueva Galicia. He served responsibly in that capacity until 1539 when a young protégé of Viceroy Mendoza, Francisco Vásquez de Coronado, got the nod as new governor. It is another measure of Cristóbal's magnanimity that he handed over the reins of authority with good grace, showing no resentment at being supplanted by a latecomer who had played no part in the winning of the province. Indeed, he and Coronado became fast friends—a fortunate circumstance, since Oñate still occupied the office of lieutenant-governor.

At this juncture, the northern wilderness beyond the limits of Nueva Galicia beckoned the Spaniards. In 1536 four scarecrow figures led by Alvar Nuñez Cabeza de Vaca suddenly appeared at the outpost settlement of Culiacán. Shipwrecked seven years before on the Texas coast, they were the only survivors of a large expedition that had intended to settle Florida. Cabeza de Vaca continued on to Mexico City where he became a guest in the palace of Viceroy Mendoza. He drew a map of his travels and prepared a report in which he recounted stories, really rumors, he had picked up of advanced people living north of his route—people who resided in towns, dressed in cotton clothes, farmed, and traded turquoise and emeralds. Through hindsight we can see that he was describing the Pueblo Indians of New Mexico. But in those excitable times, many Spaniards took his account to mean that another treasure-laden Indian kingdom lay hidden in the interior, awaiting conquest.

There was no shortage of candidates eager to explore the Tierra Nueva, or New Land. They included an aging Fernando Cortés, Pedro de Alvarado (the conqueror of Guatemala), Hernando de Soto, and even, briefly before his downfall, Nuño de Guzmán. However, Viceroy Mendoza decided to lead an expedition himself, so important did he consider the matter. The proposed venture took on a new dimension after Fray Marcos de Niza, sent northward on a reconnaissance mission, returned and told of seeing from a distance the first of seven Indian "cities" on the edge of a rich province the natives called Cíbola. The viceroy shortly concluded that he could not leave his duties in Mexico City, and therefore he turned over leadership of the expedition to his trusted friend, Coronado.

Antonio de Mendoza had been handpicked by the king to become the first viceroy of New Spain in 1535. Of noble lineage, he was resourceful, imaginative, and obedient, just the kind of chief executive the crown felt was needed to preside over the turbulent colony. In February 1540, Mendoza accompanied by a showy entourage of aides and relatives marched overland to Compostela, capital of Nueva Galicia, to give Coronado and his men a proper send-off for their expedition to the north. On February 22, exactly 192 years to the day before George Washington's birth, a gala ceremony unfolded to the flourish of trumpets and the booming of kettledrums. The treasury officer Gonzalo de Salazar was there as an onlooker, having joined the retinue of the viceroy. And his son-in-law-to-be, Cristóbal de Oñate, occupied a conspicuous place near Mendoza during the muster and review of Coronado's 336-man army. Cristóbal, it can be noted, had invested fifty thousand of his own pesos in the venture.

From this occasion we have one of Cristóbal de Oñate's few recorded utterances. He mused that "many of the young gentlemen . . . who were going on the . . . expedition would do more good than harm by departing, for they were all idle and without means of support." Most, in fact, were fortune seekers, recently off the boat from Spain and even the viceroy was relieved they had found something to occupy them far beyond Mexico City. He worried, however, that such persons might abuse the Indians, and he let Coronado know that he wanted his conquest to be "Christian and apostolic and not a butchery." His words illustrate the peculiarly Spanish way of legitimizing military expansion.

For the duration of the expedition, Cristóbal had loaned Coronado a dashing black stallion, valued at a hundred gold pesos. The animal became a favorite of the explorer, who suffered much distress when it died on the return trip. Cristóbal at this time, of course, had no way of knowing that the Tierra Nueva to which he had dispatched his horse would sixty years hence be colonized by his own son. Another curious connection can be noted in the person of Juan de Zaldívar, a young Basque who had served under Nuño de Guzmán and was now enlisted as a junior officer in Coronado's army. Throughout the arduous march that would draw the cavalcade across Arizona and New Mexico and onto the plains of Kansas, Zaldívar was to figure in many of the key events. He was a native of Vitoria and a nephew of Cristóbal de Oñate, being the son of Cristóbal's sister, María. His own nephews, Juan and Vicente de Zaldívar, would ride with Juan de Oñate to New Mexico in 1598 and encounter hazards and disappointments similar to those met by members of Coronado's expedition.

With Coronado away, an absence that would last almost two years, Cristóbal de Oñate was once again acting governor of Nueva Galicia. Hardly were the ceremonies at Compostela concluded than he faced the beginnings of a major crisis. Native medicine men commenced to preach a holy war against the Spaniards, promising supernatural aid and reminding the Indians of their losses during the murderous forays of Nuño de Guzmán. At first the violence was sporadic, but as small victories gave way to larger, the revolt spread and consumed all of Nueva Galicia. The rebels operated from fortified strongholds atop soaring cliffs called *peñoles*. On these they stockpiled food and great numbers of stones to be hurled as missiles in the event of attack. The most imposing of the peñoles was called Mixton. Thus the native rebellion that raged from 1540 to 1542, and presented Cristóbal with the challenge of his life, became known as the Mixton War.

The sixteenth-century chronicler Baltasar de Obregón declares that Oñate, whom he praises as "a deserving and highly qualified caballero," moved out of Guadalajara with a well-armed force of soldiers and settlers to attack the Mixton heights. At this early stage he was unaware of the breadth of the revolt, although he knew it was serious since a Franciscan friar and his ten-soldier escort, sent ahead to plead for peace, had been slain. Like crusaders assaulting the walls of a Moorish castle, Oñate's men charged the ramparts of Mixton and were met with a hail of arrows and stones. Repulsed, they withdrew toward Guadalajara while the jubilant Indians celebrated their triumph with dancing and the music of drums, flutes, and conch shells.

Cristóbal de Oñate played a key role in the bloody Mixton War of 1540–1542, a scene from which is depicted in this sixteenth-century Dutch engraving. (From *Memorias de la Academia Mexicana de la Historia*, Mexico, 1942)

Cristóbal rushed an urgent appeal for military aid to Mexico City, warning that the uprising was so widespread that it could easily spill over to the other provinces of New Spain. While waiting for a response, he received assistance from an unexpected quarter. The conquistador Pedro de Alvarado of Guatemala was sailing up the coast with a proud fleet, bound for the Philippines, when he learned of the Indian war on shore and paused to offer his services. At the head of two hundred men, he marched inland and boldly assailed another native refuge, the peñol of Nochistlán. But he fared no better than had Cristóbal de Oñate, and in a disorderly retreat he fell under a horse and was killed.

This fiasco inspirited the Indians. Fifty thousand of them besieged Guadalajara itself, and only a desperate defense prevented the city from being overrun. In some of the fiercest fighting, Santiago, Saint James, was reputed to have descended on his white steed, backed by an army of angels, and turned the tide in favor of the Spaniards. The natives finally withdrew and gave Guadalajara a breathing spell.

At news of these dire developments, Viceroy Mendoza personally took the field at the head of an army of 180 mounted Spaniards and flocks of friendly Aztec and Tlaxcalan warriors. At his approach Cristóbal de Oñate sallied forth from the devastated Guadalajara and united his force with that of the viceroy. Together, they stormed the peñoles, one after the other, ending with the principal stronghold at Mixton. Thousands of Indians were killed, committed suicide in the final battles, or were seized and enslaved. In the process Santiago supposedly intervened at least one more time, showing the Spaniards a hidden mountain pass and then leading them in a flanking attack.

Mendoza, given the gravity of the rebellion, decided to mete out harsh punishment to serve as both an example and warning. He ordered the most culpable Indian chieftains to be tied to artillery pieces and blown to bits. Reading of that gruesome method of execution moved the anthropologist Eric Wolfe to observe, "It is easier to dismember men with cannons than tame their minds." For the rest, droves of captives were enslaved, branded, and parceled among the victorious Spaniards and their Indian allies from Mexico City. That effectively ended hostilities. The war casualties and a massive epidemic that followed in 1545 reduced Nueva Galicia's native population to twenty-six thousand, from a high of two million when Guzmán first came in 1529. The figures provide some measure of the calamity that had befallen the Indians.

Again, as in earlier historical episodes, Cristóbal de Oñate emerged with his reputation not only intact but greatly enhanced. He had displayed prudence, courage, and dependable leadership during the darkest hours of the war, qualities that did not go unnoticed by Viceroy Mendoza. They were the same qualities he would one day pass on to his son, Juan. In the summer of 1542, Coronado, discouraged and broken in health, returned from his profitless trip north and reclaimed the governor's chair.

Cristóbal, back in his familiar office of lieutenant-governor, awaited a new assignment. And it was not long in coming. Indians in Zacatecas, a remote district 150 miles northeast of Guadalajara, were making warlike noises. Mendoza immediately thought of Oñate. Orders were soon in the hands of a messenger, instructing the lieutenant-governor to go and settle the disturbance, by peaceful means if possible. In the campaign that ensued, Cristóbal's methods were not altogether pacific. But through a combination of negotiation and force, he skillfully restored calm to the area. Before leaving, he even indulged in a little prospecting, a pleasurable activity Spaniards regarded almost as recreation.

Although the fact surely eluded him at the time, Cristóbal de Oñate had now crossed a threshold that opened upon an entirely new phase of his life. Ahead lay honors, staggering riches, and a family at last, all coming to him after the age of forty. And the source of good fortune would be found in the high, wind-blasted, dust-laden, sunlit land called Zacatecas.

CHAPTER 3

Zacatecas

SINCE coming to New Spain in 1524, Cristóbal de Oñate had risen steadily in the hierarchy of colonial society. From the start he was closely associated with persons of power, and by giving loyal and competent service he managed to advance his position, even as the careers of others around him were faltering. Somewhat conservative and methodical in nature, he moved by careful plan. The flamboyance and rashness that typified the actions of men like Cortés, Nuño de Guzmán, Alvarado, and Coronado were foreign to him. This is not to say that Cristóbal was unimaginative or lacking in ambition or boldness, for he was as capable of taking an aggressive stance as the next Spaniard. It was just that he showed little interest in short-term, flashy projects, preferring instead to build for the long term.

That may explain his slow but steady accumulation of wealth during the early part of his life in the colony. It began with his first grants of encomienda. Basically, the encomienda was a tribute system: conquered Indians were required to pay an annual tribute to the crown, as a symbol of vassalage, and in return they received protection and religious instruction. To reward conquistadors in the New World, the king assigned them one or more Indian towns in trusteeship, or encomienda, meaning that the colonist (called an *encomendero*) was allowed to collect and use the tribute that otherwise would have gone into the royal treasury. The encomienda grant was highly coveted, not only because it represented a steady source of income, but also because it conferred upon the holder exalted status, marking him as a select member of the colonial aristocracy.

Over the years Cristóbal de Oñate acquired an assortment of encomiendas, the exact number still a matter for speculation. Royal officials were empowered to make these grants in the name of the king, and thus it appears that Nuño de Guzmán while he was in charge at Mexico City gave Cristóbal his first encomienda, the lucrative Nahuatl town of Culhuacán just five miles from the capital. Later, after

Nuño de Guzmán had despoiled the Tarascan province of Michoacán to the west, Cristóbal received another tributary town there, Tacámbaro, at which place he maintained his residence for a while. The majority of his encomiendas, however, were located in Nueva Galicia, the first ones bestowed, no doubt, by Nuño de Guzmán. But subsequently in the several periods when he was serving as acting governor, Cristóbal de Oñate assigned a number of encomiendas to himself. Since these assignments were an open matter of record, it is evident there was nothing strictly illegal in his action, although it may well have appeared as bad form.

In the matter of personal economics, Cristóbal was quite diversified. In addition to his encomiendas and a salary as lieutenant-governor of Nueva Galicia, he owned stock ranches, farms, and a sugar refinery. Each enterprise was managed by an overseer, or *mayordomo*. Here, though, we see one of his failings—his chronic inability to judge the true character of men—for the mayordomos he placed in charge robbed him unmercifully. Trinidad García, the manager of one property, took him to the tune of six thousand gold pesos. When the mayordomos were exposed in turn, Cristóbal pardoned them all, and afterward offered financial assistance to several who fell on hard times. Such a gesture reflected the grand style most admired by sixteenth-century Spaniards.

Following the Mixton War, Cristóbal took a serious interest in prospecting for precious metals. While he seems to have found nothing, other than promising signs, during his initial foray into Zacatecas, he had better luck in western Nueva Galicia. He discovered valuable ores at two sites near Compostela (the same town from which Coronado had gone north to seek riches), and located mines of lesser importance in the mountains above Guadalajara. These initial successes turned him more in the direction of mining development and provided the capital necessary to undertake this activity on a large scale.

About 1546, Cristóbal formed an association with several other energetic Basques who were headquartered at the frontier Indian settlement and mining town of Nochistlán on the trail leading toward Zacatecas. They were Juan de Tolosa, Miguel de Ibarra, and Miguel's nephew Diego de Ibarra, natives of Guipúzcoa province and veterans of the Mixton War. With the backing of Oñate and the Ibarras, Tolosa engaged in several prospecting expeditions toward the northeast, and in September 1546, he finally struck pay dirt.

With a party of soldiers, Franciscan friars, and Indian allies, he entered a small basin surrounded by a low range of barren hills and pitched camp at the base of a promontory crowned by bare greenish rock, which the Spaniards called La Bufa. From the summit, Zacatecos Indians observed his arrival. They were soon lured off their hilltop by friendly overtures. Given small gifts, they reciprocated by handing the Spaniards lumps of rock threaded with gleaming strands of pure silver. They even showed the location of outcroppings in the vicinity of La Bufa. Tolosa wasted no time in collecting three or four burro loads of ore and returning the ore to Nochistlán for assay. To no one's surprise, the richness of the samples was confirmed.

At once Tolosa entered into a formal agreement with Cristóbal de Oñate and Diego de Ibarra to open the new mines and found a town near them. Later they added another partner, Baltasar Temiño de Bañuelos from Castile. This quartet became the "Big Four" in exploiting one of the largest silver discoveries ever made in North America. Cristóbal's preeminence in the partnership, as dominant voice and chief investor, is underscored by contemporary records that refer to "Cristóbal de Oñate y companía," that is, Oñate and Company.

All four men met at the foot of La Bufa on January 20, 1548, and participated in the formal founding of the city of Zacatecas. Word of the bonanza had gotten out, and shortly the place was booming. Men streamed in from all corners, each with a get-rich-quick gleam in his eye. The silver rush was so great that some other parts of the viceroyalty were practically depopulated. By 1550 Zacatecas emerged as the second-largest municipality in New Spain, outranked only by Mexico City. In that year, it contained fifty reduction works, foundries, and refineries. Cristóbal alone owned thirteen stamp mills and smelters to process ore from the mines, and he built and maintained a large two-story house with a private chapel.

This residence was actually outside the city, at the flourishing mining camp of Pánuco five miles to the north. Here he presided like a benevolent feudal lord. Among the newcomers who poured into the district, many were destitute, and with an openhandedness that became legendary Cristóbal grubstaked them all. There is a persistent story that each day at meal time he rang a bell summoning to his table those who were hungry, acquaintance and stranger alike. A priest, Fray Diego de Vasalanque, praised him for his generosity, nobility, and courage and observed that "his liberality kept pace with his Christian spirit." As further evidence of Cristóbal's benevolence, Fray Diego mentions that he turned the tribute from his encomiendas back to the Indians for development of their communities. In light of the fact that he eventually realized a profit of one and a half million pesos from Zacatecas silver, he could well afford to be generous toward his Indian wards. Still, the magnitude of his charity was remarkable.

At this time documents reveal that Cristóbal maintained another residence in Mexico City where he was listed as a householder (*vecino*). For him, the attractions of the capital were several: not only was it the center of political and social life, but now it served as the main source of supply for the mines in Zacatecas. Therefore, he found it convenient to keep a home at both ends of the 350-mile road that had become the new focus of his activity, and to divide his time between them as business required.

Sometime in late 1549 or early 1550, Cristóbal finally married. He was approximately forty-five years of age. Whether the delay was caused by some previous romantic episode that went awry or whether he was simply being methodical again, awaiting the moment when his financial fortunes were clearly on the upswing, we have no way of knowing. In any case, he found a wife, Doña Catalina de Salazar y de la Cadena, and they were wed in what we have to believe was a ceremony full of pomp and color, since that was the custom among New Spain's upper crust.

Doña Catalina herself was a person of rank, being the daughter of the retired treasury officer Gonzalo de Salazar. His durability had seen him through earlier political reverses, and he was now living with his wife, Doña Catalina's mother, in comfortable circumstances at Mexico City. Just how comfortable is suggested by the nickname his associates gave him. He was called "El Gordo," "The Fat One."

Cristóbal, who first came to the colony in the party that included Gonzalo de Salazar back in 1524, had kept up with the man over the years, for reasons hard to fathom since the two seem to have been poles apart in character. After he acquired his own house in the capital, he must have become a frequent guest at the Salazar home. Perhaps it was there one day that he was introduced to the daughter, Doña Catalina, recently arrived from Spain for a prolonged visit with her parents. In the normal course of things, a betrothal and wedding followed.

About Doña Catalina, only a few details are known. She was born

Armas de Cristóbal de Oñate
(Vínculos No. 261-Archivo Nacional)

Personal coat of arms of Don Cristóbal de Oñate, father of Juan de Oñate. (From José Ignacio Davila Garibi, *La Sociedad de Zacatecas en Los Albores de Regimen Colonial,* Mexico, 1939)

in Granada, native city of the Salazars in Andalusia, at some date before her father's departure for New Spain in 1524. Thus, when she married Cristóbal, a quarter century after that date, she would have had to be a rather mature bride—in her early thirties probably, but still within her childbearing years as she was to give him seven children. This was not her first marriage, however. She had been united originally with Ruy Díaz de Mendoza, of an exalted Granada family, and by him had a daughter, Magdalena de Mendoza y Salazar. The older histories generally state that upon the death of Ruy Díaz, a grieving Doña Catalina took little Magdalena and sailed for the Indies to be with her parents. The story sounds entirely plausible and explains the circumstances that led her to Mexico City to begin a new life and enter a second marriage. The problem is that recent archival research has disclosed that Ruy Díaz de Mendoza did not die, but in reality was deserted by his spouse. He was still living as late as 1572 when, in a public record, he made reference to his wife who had gone to Mexico City a long time ago. Historian Donald Chipman, who has closely studied the Oñate genealogy, risks the assumption that Doña Catalina, upon the day of her nuptials with Cristóbal, became a bigamist!

Their marriage produced in rapid succession five boys and two girls. The eldest was Fernando, who grew up to become the *alcalde mayor* (chief magistrate) of the city of Puebla and inheritor of his father's most valuable encomienda at Tacámbaro in Michoacán. Then followed Juan, Cristóbal, Luís, and Alonso as well as two daughters, Ana and María. The birth dates of none of these children have come to light. Because of Juan's later prominence as colonizer of New Mexico, scholars have made a long but futile search to uncover his birthday. On the basis of often conflicting evidence, they have concluded that it was most likely sometime in the year 1550.

However, an obscure reference would seem to place his birth in 1552. It is found in a letter written from Seville in 1938 by Professor Lansing B. Bloom and published in the *New Mexico Historical Review*. Bloom was collecting copies of documents dealing with the Hispanic Southwest, and he ran onto several that concerned Juan de Oñate. "In a *probanza* [court record] of 1578," he wrote, "a curious idiom caught my eye: one witness testified that he was in Zacatecas at the time when Don Cristóbal and his brother Don Juan were born 'de un solo vientre.' In other words, they were twins! And as Cristóbal was sworn to be twenty-six years old, Juan's birth-year is established

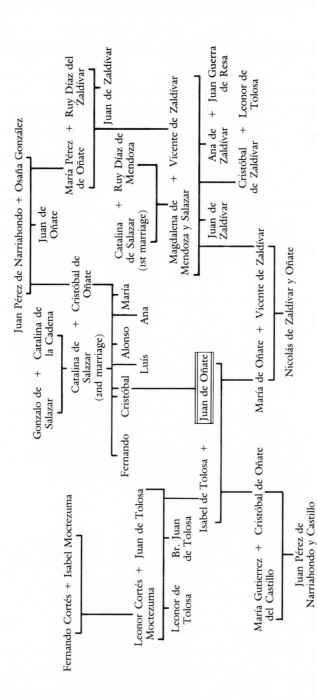

Oñate Genealogy

as 1552." Then Bloom adds: "Fernando was the oldest and head of the family [after] the father's death; Alonso was the last son; and there were two sisters."

Assuming the accuracy of Professor Bloom's revelation—and he was an accomplished researcher and translator—two other significant things are unveiled here beyond the year of Juan's birth. One is that he first saw the light of day in Zacatecas, or more properly at the Oñate mansion located in nearby Pánuco, rather than in Mexico City as has frequently been claimed in the past. But the most startling bit of news is that he and brother Cristóbal (named for their father) were twins.

In no other document currently available is there so much as a hint of that possibility. Juan in all of his New Mexico correspondence makes no mention of it, nor does his friend Gaspar Pérez de Villagrá in his published account of Oñate's first years on the Rio Grande. Indeed, one looks in vain for a sign that Juan regarded Cristóbal in any special way. If they were truly twins, as Bloom was led to believe, then probably they were not identical twins, who tend to show close similarities in behavior throughout life, but rather fraternal twins, who are no more alike than any other siblings of the family. Until more definite information surfaces, the matter will have to be left there.

From the background provided up to this point comes an obvious surmise: that there was a bright side and a dark side to Juan de Oñate's ancestry. The bright side was luminescent, indeed, and fortunately was the one furnishing him the cues that directed his life. But the dark side of his blood-heritage was always ready to make its sinister influence felt in moments of crisis and confusion. His solid and upright Basque father, Cristóbal, represented the best in the family line, while Cristóbal's brother Juan, who fled to Peru to escape crimes committed as an accomplice of Guzmán, represented, if not the worst, at least the negative side. Nor from what is known can much in the way of positive traits be observed on the maternal branch of Juan de Oñate's family tree. His grandfather, Gonzalo de Salazar, "El Gordo," set the tone by his life-long indulgence in crass opportunism. In the end it may have been the environment of his childhood, rather than biological inheritance, that did most to shape the kind of man the young Juan was to become.

As indicated, Cristóbal was in the habit of shuttling back and forth between Zacatecas and Mexico City, and it is clear that on occasion he took his family with him. Juan, therefore, grew up familiar with the sparkle and relative sophistication of urban life in the viceregal capital and with the contrasting mode of living, in all of its rawness and monotony, that was to be found among rough miners on the Zacatecas frontier. At Mexico City, he mastered the social graces and also, we suppose, acquired the polished education that was reflected later in his writing. But the most important part of his boyhood training occurred at his birthplace, the residence in Pánuco.

The bustling mining camp of Pánuco was close enough to Zacatecas that it was considered by people of the day to be not a mere satellite but an actual suburb of the city. It had a plaza, parochial church, the sumptuous homes of the Oñates and the Ibarras, workers' huts, and a great deal in the way of mills and smelters for ore processing. Juan and his brothers in their formative years were literally immersed in the activity and the constant talk of silver mining. The profits from silver fed, dressed, and housed them, and paid for all else that they did.

Silver caused Zacatecas to hum as well. The city, crowded into its narrow basin in the hills, rested at an altitude of eight thousand feet near the southern end of the great central plateau which separated the two chains of the Sierra Madre. At that height, the climate was pleasantly cool in summer, but when autumn waned and winter winds crept over the shoulder of La Bufa, a shuddering cold seeped into the houses, government buildings, churches, and mine works, and there was little one could do to banish it. The extreme temperatures reminded the Basques of their mountainous homeland in northern Spain, but there the similarity ended, for the bleak aridity of Zacatecas that supported only scattered clumps of coarse desert grass, spiny agave, and thorn-bearing mesquite and acacia was a far cry from the emerald lushness of the Basque provinces. In its barrenness, this frontier more closely resembled some of the parched landscapes to be seen in the south of Spain.

The city was oriented along the axis of a central thoroughfare that began at the foot of La Bufa and followed the margin of a sandy arroyo down to an opening in the hills. Situated near the center of this road was the *plaza mayor,* the municipal marketplace, parish church, mercantile establishments, and the city hall, or *cabildo.* The population, occupying homes and huts that straggled up the rocky hillsides, reflected the diversity of ethnic elements to be found in a community experiencing a boom. Mine owners, merchants, ranchers, priests, monks, and royal officials and their relations made up the ruling class of Europeans. Then there were blacks, both slaves and freemen, who labored in the mines, and a large underclass of Indians, mainly Aztecs (or Mexica), Tlaxcalans, and Tarascans from the south. Clinging to the fringes lived a few of the local Zacatecos, dispossessed of their lands and in the process of assimilation.

The Zacatecos were one of many northern tribes, sharing a similar way of life, that the Spaniards lumped together under the collective name of Chichimecas. These peoples pursued a nomadic existence, hunting game and collecting *tunas,* the crimson fruit of the prickly pear cactus. Some built rude shelters, but the majority simply scooped holes in the earth for living quarters. They went naked, or virtually so, covering the bare skin with exotic body paint. But most remarkable was their fierce attachment to warfare.

The Chichimecas had long waged unremitting war upon one another, using bow and arrow, sling, club, and lance. But as soon as Spaniards had gained a toehold at Zacatecas, they focused their bloodthirsty attention upon the newcomers. Those attentions, in truth, were so horrible that they filled their Spanish enemies with revulsion. For the Chichimecas habitually tortured and scalped victims alive, then beheaded them and paraded the grisly trophies on wooden pikes. Captive children were forced to drink the blood and brains of their murdered parents. And the tribesmen themselves were cannibals, for as one contemporary Spaniard testified, "Those whom they carry away alive are sacrificed. They are roasted on spits and eaten as one would do with cows."

By the early 1550s the unpacified Zacatecos and neighboring tribes began to launch full-scale attacks upon outlying mining camps and ranches, and especially upon travelers and freight caravans plying the Camino Real between Zacatecas and the viceregal capital. One of their earliest assaults was directed against a mule train belonging to Cristóbal de Oñate and Diego de Ibarra, just three leagues below Zacatecas itself. The Spaniards quickly learned to band together in convoys for protection, and they placed fortified strongholds at strategic points along the silver highway. But these measures were only partially effective. In 1550, for instance, a caravan of sixty wagons was wiped out by a Chichimeca horde. Such attacks greatly impeded the flow of supplies to the mines and left the inhabitants of Zacatecas feeling cut off from the outside world. Spanish reprisals failed to stop the raids, with the result that the Chichimeca War stretched on and on, lasting almost half a century.

This war and these Indians had a powerful influence on the early years of Juan de Oñate. Stories of massacres and gruesome tales of torture were common topics of conversation in Zacatecas and could not have failed to make a lasting impression upon all the youth of the city. Juan must have been personally acquainted with some of the casualties, and when he traveled to and from Mexico City with the family, in one of his father's heavily guarded caravans, doubtless his attention was called to spots where others had earlier given up their lives in Chichimeca ambushes. It would have been surprising if this formative experience had not colored his attitude toward Indians in some deep and permanent way. That, plus the realities of a hard and brutal frontier life may have contributed to the air of melancholy that seemed to mark his adult years. Certainly, there exists nothing in the written record to suggest that humor softened his speech or lightened his mood. But in this grim time and place, most men had an element of seriousness about them, so that Juan's apparent gravity was probably not all that unusual.

By order of the viceroy every citizen of Zacatecas was obligated to arm himself with harquebus or crossbow and go on forays against the fearsome Chichimecas whenever he received a summons to duty. As in the days of the Moorish crusades, it was a case of every Spaniard a soldier. Cristóbal de Oñate and Juan de Tolosa often assumed command of these punitive expeditions. In later years Juan de Oñate would claim that he accompanied his father on such occasions, "from the time he was able to bear arms." So, precisely how old was he when he first faced the Chichimecas? His friend Pérez de Villagrá with a flowery pen wrote that Juan was a mere boy of ten, undoubtedly an exaggeration. But Spanish youths were in the habit of going to war at a tender age, not uncommonly in their beginning teens, hence it is safe to conclude that Juan got a very early start as an apprentice fighter. There is no proof, however, that any of his brothers followed his example, which, if actually the case, leads one to believe that he was the one son to inherit the adventuresome and resolute spirit of their father, Cristóbal. Subsequent events confirm that Juan, of the five Oñate brothers, was the natural leader and a born soldier.

Sometime in his early twenties, Juan himself took command of campaigns against the Indians, not only directing the operations but, as was customary among colonial aristocrats, paying all the expenses out of his own pocket. As he proudly explained, he was merely following in the footsteps of his ancestors who, as knights and caballeros, had always given devoted service to the crown. More particularly he was trying to emulate his father, who had conquered, pacified, and settled a great portion of Nueva Galicia. Juan obviously considered himself the family standard-bearer and with eagerness accepted the challenge of adding fresh luster to the Oñate name. According to his statement, for two decades he fought the Chichimecas, an achievement that must have been attended by innumerable skirmishes and battles (mentioned as "bloody encounters" in early chronicles). Yet, since he makes no mention of them in later writings, the details have to be left to our imagination.

In warring against the Indians, Juan ranged over wide stretches of country, mainly lying north and east of his Zacatecas home. Nor, of course, was he the only one so engaged. His father's old business partner, Juan de Tolosa, nicknamed "Barbalonga" or "Long Beard," was often in the field. Sometimes he was accompanied by Francisco de Ibarra, the precocious young nephew of another Zacatecas founder, Diego de Ibarra. Francisco at age ten had been sent from his native Vizcaya in Spain to live with his uncle on the silver frontier, and at sixteen he commanded his first expedition. Afterward, he explored much of the north-central reaches of New Spain, hewing out of the wilderness another province, Nueva Vizcaya (the modern states of Durango and Chihuahua), and founding the capital city of Durango, in 1563, and later the farming center at Nombre de Dios—all this before his premature death from tuberculosis at thirty-six.

Both Juan de Tolosa and Francisco de Ibarra pursued and gave fight to the Chichimecas over a period of years. But they were spurred on by motives other than just punishing the Indians—the desire to explore, and to add new realms to the empire, and especially the hope of finding silver mines. Indeed, they and Spaniards like them made important strikes over an ever-widening arc above Zacatecas. In 1623 the aging Juan de Oñate would testify that Tolosa had discovered the significant mines of Sombrerete, San Martín, and Aviño. These had produced a huge return to the treasury through payment of the *quinto,* a kind of tax or royalty representing the king's portion of all silver production. Oñate further noted that Tolosa had developed the famous salt deposit of Santa María, which produced thirty thousand bushels a year. That was important since salt was a chief ingredient in the process of extracting silver from its ore.

The same motives that animated Tolosa and the young Ibarra also drove Juan de Oñate. As he marched through the mountain ranges that rose above the central plateau rooting out small bands of elusive Chichimecas, he kept a sharp eye peeled for rocks and outcroppings with a tell-tale glitter. Contemporary documents attest that he made some rich finds, and following the example of his father and his father's partners, he quickly brought in miners and missionaries to create new and productive Spanish outposts. Again, not much is known about this activity, and we have the names of only a few of the mining centers he is believed to have opened.

One of them was Charcas, located in a mountainous zone less than one hundred miles northeast of Zacatecas. The early history of this silver camp is murky, but the best evidence points to its founding about 1574. Juan de Oñate then would have been twenty-two years old. He brought in workers and Franciscan friars from Zacatecas and probably directed preparation of defenses to repel attacks by the Guachichiles, a particularly ferocious tribe of Chichimecas who claimed the area. Twice over the next several years, the Spaniards were forced to retreat from Charcas because of the Indian threat, but it was reoccupied for good in 1582. Its troubled on-again, off-again history was perhaps typical of the kinds of situations Juan de Oñate was involved with during his early adult life. Everything he did in the way of marching, fighting, prospecting, and building provided further experience and training that would prove useful down the trail when the grandest opportunity of all opened before him.

In the conduct of his life and the goals he set for himself, Oñate in these years epitomized the spirit of the colonial nobility. He and men like him felt Spain's strong sense of mission and believed themselves part of destiny's tide. The modern writer Américo Castro goes so far as to declare that Spaniards of that era considered themselves people chosen by god, just as Israel had been. That curious notion, really a towering conceit, evoked the popular myth of a New Spain united in an ongoing Christian crusade for king and faith. The idea, an outgrowth of the Moorish wars, was reinforced when the monarchy made the defense and propagation of Hispanic Catholicism the supreme aim of the state. The explorers, prospectors, and Indian fighters of Oñate's generation took that goal to heart. Wherever their expeditions penetrated, no matter how difficult the circumstances, there were always priests along to minister to the men and to initiate missionary work should the chance appear. Spaniards saw nothing unusual about entire armies kneeling out-of-doors and praying in unison for remission of sins and success in battle. They did that many times in conquering Nueva Galicia and Nueva Vizcaya, and later in pacifying New Mexico.

Cortés's devoted soldier, the historian Bernal Díaz del Castillo, stated matter-of-factly: "We came here to serve God and the King, and also to get rich." His words truthfully became the credo of all those who followed in the footsteps of Cortés, although some, like Nuño de Guzmán, twisted the meaning of service to advance their own purposes. Nevertheless, church and crown did actually have first claim on the attentions of the majority of Spaniards, so that whatever was left to them in time and energy, after the performance of duty, could be turned toward the agreeable pastime of getting rich.

They did not, however, consider wealth to be an end in itself and a means to acquire creature comforts. The austere Spaniard set little store upon the pleasures of life—he had it in his head that to endure regular hardship was a supreme virtue—and correspondingly he placed small value upon the acquisition of things. More than one soldier who risked his neck in the conquest of Mexico or Peru lost a fortune in gold, his share of the booty, in a single evening of gambling with his comrades and did so with no expression of regret. The Oñates, Ibarras, and other members of the frontier gentry, while not addicted to gambling, spent literally millions of pesos, the fruit of their hard-won silver mines, to underwrite military enterprises that benefited the king, and to sponsor construction of churches, missions, and monasteries, and other religious establishments. Nearly all of them in their declining years claimed that this openhanded generosity had badly depleted their estates and threatened to reduce their families to poverty. Such statements show up in their petitions to the crown, asking for pensions.

In the years that Juan de Oñate was pushing back the frontier, fighting Indians, and creating settlements, he was also laying the foundation of his own personal fortune. A portion of his new wealth must have come from the silver strikes at places like Charcas. But much of it derived from the family mines in Zacatecas. Juan took a special interest in both the mining and smelting of ore at the Pánuco works, and his brothers, for the most part, seem to have been content to let him gradually assume management of that part of the Oñate properties. Only one of them, Alonso the youngest, shared with Juan an attachment to mining; he went on to become the solicitor-general for New Spain's association of mine owners.

On October 6, 1567, the old warhorse and family patriarch Cristóbal de Oñate died. Historians have alleged that at the end he was in severe financial straits and unable to provide any solid security for his heirs. They evidently based that belief upon claims of one of Cristóbal's grandsons, who declared that his grandfather had entirely consumed the profits from his mining investments, a million and a half pesos, in outfitting expeditions against hostile Indians. It has also been said that Cristóbal mismanaged his estate, so that what should have been a valuable legacy to his children was in reality nearly worthless.

Such a picture, however, wanders considerably from the truth. While Cristóbal may, indeed, have spent enormous sums in financing Indian campaigns and lost more in careless attention to paperwork, his far-flung business interests were so vast and varied that it is hard to imagine him reduced to penury. His Pánuco mines alone were still healthy producers and would continue to provide yields for years to come. In the settlement of Cristóbal's estate, title to those mines passed to Juan's mother, Doña Catalina, and then upon her death a few years later to Juan himself. From that fact probably arose the common assertion that the settlement of New Mexico in 1598 was financed largely by Zacatecas silver. Of course, the statement would not hold water if Cristóbal had really died bankrupt.

It is a reasonable assumption that Juan de Oñate by his thirtieth birthday had become a man of means in his own right. He had accumulated wealth, not to retire at ease in Mexico City, but to turn it to some great enterprise to benefit the twin majesties, the church and crown, and to acquire for himself honor and glory. All signs point to his being a visionary, but one endowed with a streak of tough practicality that enabled him to move decisively toward the realization of dreams. He also had a touch of romanticism in his nature and a good measure of idealism, which in Spaniards manifested itself in a lofty pride and an exaggerated sense of honor. And he was ambitious. But Juan's ambition was not the soaring type—say, of a Cortés who had made grandiose and rash plays—but rather it was an ambition measured and cool after the manner of his father. He seemed to know at mid-career that destiny held something uncommon in store for him, but he did not succumb to impatience and was content to wait.

An unwillingness to rush things also governed his personal life. Like his father he married late. The exact date is lost, but it was sometime toward the end of the 1580s, which would have placed him in his late thirties. His wife was Isabel de Tolosa Cortés Moctezuma, daughter of Juan de Tolosa and Leonor Cortés Moctezuma. The soldier Villagrá, who knew her, described Doña Isabel as "a lady of surpassing beauty, highest virtues, and most estimable qualities." It proved an extraordinary match, comingling some remarkably distinguished bloodlines.

Isabel was the granddaughter of the conqueror Fernando Cortés and his native mistress Isabel Moctezuma, who was the offspring of the late Aztec emperor. The two had an illegitimate daughter, Doña Leonor, who at age twenty-one was packed off to Zacatecas (this was in the early 1550s) to become the bride of the newly prosperous Juan de Tolosa. By all accounts, the wedding, in what was still a raw mining settlement, turned out to be a splendid social event. No stigma appears to have adhered to Leonor's reputation owing to her birth out of wedlock.

Since Cortés was a marquis, Doña Leonor came from nobility on her father's side, and on her mother's she was descended from native royalty, a pedigree illustrious enough to overshadow the matter of illegitimacy. Nor did the fact of her mixed blood—half Spanish, half Indian—prove to be a social impediment. In Spain intermarriage between Christians and Moors had long been practiced during intervals of peace, so that when Spaniards came to America it felt perfectly natural for them to seek wives, or openly take mistresses, among the native Indian population. Obviously, the process was greatly facilitated, given the Spanish affinity for noble status, when the woman could trace her lineage to the preconquest aristocracy.

The Tolosas had three children. One was Isabel, the future wife of Juan de Oñate. Another, the only son, Juan, entered a monastic order and became vicar of Zacatecas in 1595. And then there was Leonor (named after her mother), bride-to-be of Cristóbal de Zaldívar. Juan de Oñate and his brother-in-law, Cristóbal de Zaldívar, were to work closely in development of the New Mexico project, and Cristóbal's two brothers Juan and Vicente were to play a key role in that undertaking. Thus, some reference to the background of the Zaldívars is in order.

Coat of arms of the family of Oñate's wife, Isabel de Tolosa Cortés Moctezuma. (From Jóse Ignacio Davila Garibi, *La Sociedad de Zacatecas en Los Albores de Regimen Colonial, Mexico,* 1939)

Like the Oñates, the Zaldívars were Basques. Ruy Díaz de Zaldívar, listed as a native and citizen of Vitoria, married María de Oñate, perhaps about the time her brother Cristóbal left for New Spain in 1524 to fill his new job in the treasury office. This couple produced two sons: the elder, Juan de Zaldívar Oñate, went to Nueva Galicia first where he participated in its conquest with his uncle, Cristóbal de Oñate, and Nuño de Guzmán, and then later in 1540 marched with Coronado in search of the golden cities of Cíbola. Juan was followed to the New World years later by his younger brother Vicente, who settled at Zacatecas, prospered in mining, distinguished himself as a soldier, and received the rank of lieutenant captain-general by viceregal appointment. This Vicente made a marriage that further tangled the relationships between the Zaldívars and Oñates, for he took as wife Magdalena de Mendoza y Salazar. She was the little girl, now grown, who had come from Granada with her mother, Doña Catalina de Salazar, to Mexico City where her mother committed bigamy, we suppose, when she married Cristóbal de Oñate. Thus, Vicente de Zaldívar Oñate's wife, Magdalena, was his uncle's stepdaughter.

Later, Vicente and Magdalena's sons became involved in the settlement of New Mexico. It would have simplified matters considerably for historians if they had named two of them something besides Juan and Vicente, but they didn't. The third was given the name Cristóbal, quite probably in honor of Cristóbal de Oñate. These three brothers were nephews of Juan de Oñate, and normally he referred to them in that way. But a scanning of the family tree shows that they were likewise his second cousins, and one of them, Cristóbal, became also his sister-in-law's husband.

Such a tortured mixing of family lines must have confused and perplexed even those who were directly involved. The Oñates, Tolosas, and Zaldívars, together with the Cortés-Moctezumas, were interlinked by a complicated web of marital alliances, creating an influential and cohesive bloc in the ranks of frontier bluebloods. French author François Chevalier speaks of the peculiar strength of the blood tie, the family relationship, and common ancestry among peoples of the Mediterranean countries, particularly those of Spain. The Basques, as pointed out earlier, placed the highest value on familial bonds, so that their houses were customarily filled with numerous cousins and other persons more distantly connected. When a man of daring commenced some large undertaking, he was able to fall back on this extended family for resources, both financial and physical. That is what Juan de Oñate would do in 1595.

After his wedding, Juan brought Isabel de Tolosa to live at his residence outside Zacatecas at Las Minas de Pánuco. Following the example of his father, he also may have kept a second home in Mexico City as an aid in preserving social and political bridges in the metropolis. We infer this from the fact that about 1590 the couple's first child was born, not at Pánuco, but in the viceregal capital. It was a son, christened with a mouth-filling name that reflected the spectacular diversity of his lineage: Cristóbal de Naharriondo Pérez Oñate y Cortés Moctezuma. But for simplicity's sake he was known to his family, and to history, as just plain Cristóbal de Oñate.

A brother, cousins, nephews, the father, and the great-grandfather of Juan de Oñate all bore the name Cristóbal, so in bestowing it upon this infant son he merely followed family tradition. However, the name doubtless seemed even more appropriate because of the most celebrated man to have it, Cristóbal Colon (Christopher Columbus). In the light of his own career and aspirations, Juan naturally hoped that the newly born Cristóbal would himself become a great discoverer and leave a mark on history's page. Surely that was in his mind eight years later when he took this "niño de tierna edad," as he referred to him then, this "child of tender age," on the perilous and painful expedition to New Mexico. Juan commissioned him with the rank of lieutenant—yes, an eight-year-old lieutenant—and placed him under the tutelage of his kinsman Sargento Mayor Vicente de Zaldívar.

Juan de Oñate and Isabel de Tolosa had only one other child, an unusually small family by the standards of the sixteenth century. Their daughter, María de Oñate y Cortés Moctezuma, was born in late 1598 or early 1599 at the family home in Pánuco. A pregnant Isabel had remained there while her husband and young son marched northward to beget a new kingdom for church and crown on the faraway Rio Grande. More than a year later (on March 2, 1599), Oñate wrote to the viceroy asking permission to bring his new daughter, whom he affectionately called Mariquita, and other relatives to New Mexico. Among "other relatives" he must have included his wife Isabel, but his failure to mention her specifically is curious. Whether they actually made the trip to join him is uncertain.

One other brief episode in Oñate's career during this period, about which we have a few details, serves as something of a prelude to what followed. It concerns his part in the founding of a new silver boomtown, San Luís Potosí, located in some gray hills on the far side of a cactus-studded plain, a hundred or so miles southeast of Zacatecas. There in March 1592, an able frontiersman and soldier, Miguel Caldera, discovered a new bonanza, which he optimistically named Potosí, after the phenomenally rich silver mine in the Peruvian Andes. Born at Zacatecas in 1548, Caldera was son of a Spanish miner and a Chichimeca mother. This parentage made him an extraordinarily effective soldier for the crown over four decades of warfare with the Chichimecas, and it also furnished him the opportunity to play a leading role in the achievement of peace by 1590. Viceroy Luís de Velasco held him in high regard and warmly welcomed news of his discovery at San Luís Potosí.

Miguel Caldera, however, possessed no social standing. Hence, when it came time to establish formally a new Spanish municipality at San Luís Potosí, Velasco tapped Juan de Oñate to carry out that prestigious function. But he tactfully instructed him to allow Caldera a major role in presiding over the official founding. On August 27, 1592, the viceroy designated Oñate as alcalde mayor of the community with responsibility for demarking plazas, blocks, and streets and distributing land for government buildings, churches, residences, and ore mills. Juan reached San Luís Potosí and with Caldera conducted formal ceremonies on November 3. He also drew a plat giving the layout of the proposed city and initiated assignment of lots to eager fortune hunters already pouring in from Zacatecas and other points along the rim of the viceroyalty. In approved Spanish fashion, he registered valuable tracts near the plaza in the names of two of his brothers, his infant son, and two members of the Zaldívar clan. A great and powerful man was expected to look after his family in this manner.

During the year that Oñate remained in charge of San Luís Potosí, he was kept busy organizing a municipal council, enforcing royal mining ordinances, adjudicating claims, and looking after the welfare of Indians who had settled on the fringes of town. His efficiency and skill in civil administration impressed the viceroy, and according to some writers this helps explain the favoritism Velasco afterward showed toward Oñate in the early stages of the New Mexico project. Because of his good performance here, Mexican historians have generally credited Oñate as the true founder of San Luís Potosí and the moving force in shaping its early character.

On the other hand, Philip Wayne Powell, biographer of Miguel Caldera, takes serious issue with that view. "As far as San Luís Potosí and its history are concerned, Juan de Oñate was merely an accidental bird of passage, made famous by later events," he declares. The true genesis of the city traces to Miguel Caldera, and Don Juan was no more than official cofounder of what was really a Caldera creation. And he contends that for Oñate, "the post of alcalde mayor was simply a viceregal recognition of the importance of his family, a passing moment on the way to greater things." Nor does Powell leave us in doubt as to where "greater things" were to be found. "The honors of San Luís Potosí belong to Miguel Caldera; Juan de Oñate belongs to New Mexico." With the completion of his work at San Luís Potosí, Don Juan was ready to direct his attention northward where he hoped the stars would reward him.

CHAPTER 4

New Mexico

JUST when the name of that distant land New Mexico first caught Juan de Oñate's attention is anyone's guess. George P. Hammond, the scholar who burrowed the deepest into Spanish archives in search of Oñate documents, suggested that he may have become interested in it as early in 1592, if not before. In fact, it could have been as early as 1583 when Philip II issued a decree calling upon New Spain's viceroy to find a wealthy and able colonist willing to undertake the settlement of New Mexico. Oñate assuredly learned of this, because it was talked up all along the frontier, but as of 1583 other matters engaged him, and there is no evidence that he gave serious consideration to becoming a candidate for the job at that point. The seed may have been planted, however, since in late 1595 Oñate declared that for many years he had been receiving reports on New Mexico, studying them, and learning everything he could about conditions there. Clearly, that early seed, over time, germinated in Oñate's thoughts, took root, and flowered.

The king's directive of 1583 reflected a sudden revival of Spanish interest in New Mexico. For many years following Coronado's fruitless expedition northward, the country bracketing the upper Rio Grande attracted neither explorers nor missionaries. But as a new generation came to the fore, memory of earlier disappointments with New Mexico waned, and frontiersmen began to cast curious glances in that direction once more. By now the line of settlement, buttressed by mines, missions, and ranches, had pushed far inside Nueva Vizcaya, establishing a forward base for the launching of new expeditions to the interior.

The northernmost outpost during the last third of the sixteenth century was Santa Bárbara, a small mining community of thirty Spanish families and a few Indians founded in 1567 by one of Ibarra's men, Rodrigo del Río de Losa. It was located in central Nueva Vizcaya (now southern Chihuahua) on the San Gregorio River, a tributary of the Conchos that flowed east a short distance, then turned north to join the Rio Grande above its big bend. The town contained a mission and was surrounded by bountiful fields of wheat and corn, but its silver mines produced poorly owing to the shortage of native labor. That prompted certain residents, in violation of the law, to conduct slave-hunting raids down the Conchos Valley and into modern Texas.

Santa Bárbara, while utterly nondescript and seemingly out-of-the-way, nevertheless assumed a vital role in frontier expansion after 1580 because its geographical position allowed it to become the gateway to New Mexico. It lay on the central plateau at the far end of the thousand-mile-long Camino Real, or King's Highway, which wound north from Mexico City through Querétaro, Zacatecas, Nombre de Dios, and Durango. Oñate himself would extend the famous road another seven hundred miles beyond Santa Bárbara when he came later with his New Mexico–bound company of settlers. This represented an entirely new route to the country of the Pueblo Indians, for when Coronado had made his entry, he used a corridor running between the Sierra Madre and the Pacific coast and trails that led through Arizona to the Zuni pueblos in western New Mexico.

About 1579 an Indian captive or slave, held in Santa Bárbara, told of a remote province hidden beyond the Chihuahuan desert that was bisected by a great river and inhabited by native peoples dwelling in large towns, who farmed, and produced cotton clothing. It was not immediately apparent to the residents of Santa Bábara that this report referred to the land seen by Coronado. In point of fact, their notions of geography and knowledge of recent history were so limited that many assumed the captive's tale had reference to some undiscovered Indian realm locked away in the arid fastness of the north. What excited their interest was mention of an advanced people—later identified as the Pueblos of New Mexico—who had houses, practiced agriculture, and wore clothes. That was in marked contrast to the backward Chichimecas living around Santa Bárbara, and for that matter all across Nueva Vizcaya, who were described by a soldier of the period as "naked barbarians, very poor and having nothing to eat except roots and prickly pears."

This news reached the ears of Fray Agustín Rodríguez, a Franciscan lay brother stationed at the nearby mining camp of San Bartolomé. At once it stirred his missionary impulse. Fray Agustín, a native of Niebla in Spain, hastened down the Camino Real to Mexico City, gained an audience with the viceroy, and won permission to explore the newly revealed region on the great river, or Rio Grande. Under the Colonization Laws of 1573 no military expeditions or new discoveries were allowed without the express review and approval of the king. However, these ordinances, which later governed the activities of Oñate, contained a provision that permitted the viceroy to grant churchmen license to go in search of potential missionary fields and to take with them a small number of soldiers for protection. The viceroy in this case went even further in demonstrating his support: he furnished the Franciscan brother ninety saddle horses and pack animals for the proposed expedition. Here is another instance, albeit a small one, of the mutually supportive relationship between Spanish church and state, extending to the outermost rim of the empire.

At Santa Bárbara, Fray Agustín assembled his party—a pitifully small one for the work ahead. Two Franciscan priests were enlisted: an Andalusian, Francisco López, and a young Catalán, Juan de Santa María, remembered for his knowledge of astronomy. Nine soldiers volunteered as an escort. Their number included an elderly officer, Francisco Sánchez Chamuscado, nicknamed "The Singed," who was elected commander shortly into the journey, and the ambitious Hernando Gallegos, a Spaniard with eight years of frontier experience, who was designated as the official diarist for the expedition. Added to this were nineteen Indian servants, and a herd of six hundred cattle plus sheep, goats, and hogs that served as a walking commissary for the men.

The little company departed June 5, 1581, descended the Conchos to the Rio Grande, then climbed that stream to the first of the Pueblo districts in the heart of New Mexico. The Franciscans were elated by what they found. On both sides of the river appeared a scattering of Indian towns whose adobe dwellings resembled the half of a multi-layered wedding cake, rising to five and six stories with upper terraces reached by pine log ladders. Chronicler Gallegos was impressed that these townspeople—that is, the Pueblo Indians—made artful pottery, wove cotton blankets, wore shoes, and kept turkeys and shaggy dogs. Clearly, in the matter of culture, they were degrees above the uncouth Chichimecas with whom he was familiar. "They are the most domestic and industrious people, and the best craftsmen found in New Spain," he wrote with pardonable exaggeration. And he added that if interpreters had been available, the Franciscans could have converted them to Christianity right away, "because they are very intelligent people and willing to serve."

As the Spaniards continued their ascent of the valley through clusters of towns speaking different languages, they got a mixed reception. Some of the natives were fearful and fled to the mountains at their approach, as they would do later when Oñate encountered them. Others were won over by friendly overtures and gifts, showering the party with foodstuffs in return. But in several places, the residents proved sullen and made hostile gestures, convincing Commander Chamuscado that "they planned to seize us by force and kill us." To strike terror in Indian hearts and forestall a united attack, the soldiers burned several small Tano Pueblo towns in the Galisteo Basin, a few miles south of the future site of Santa Fe.

At one point Father Santa María concluded to return alone with a report for his superiors, describing what had been discovered thus far and asking that additional missionaries be dispatched at once to take up the challenge in this rich new field. After he left, a Tano war party followed his trail, overtook him on the third day, and crushed his skull with a rock. The Indians must have guessed the priest intended to bring back more Spaniards, and they had no wish to be imposed upon further. Archaeologist Adolph Bandelier, nevertheless, offers another explanation for the slaying. He judges that because Santa María was an astronomer, always star-gazing, the Pueblos interpreted his conduct to mean he practiced witchcraft, and as a matter of course they killed sorcerers. In any case, the Spanish party soon learned of his death, a bit of startling news that underscored the danger of their position.

At the end of January 1582, Chamuscado and his men resolved to return to Nueva Vizcaya. By then they had visited most of the Pueblos, missing only the Taos in the far north and the Hopis in today's Arizona. In addition they had ventured onto the eastern plains as far as the Canadian River and had collected ore samples from throughout the province to carry home for assaying. Rodríguez and López elected to remain behind with several of their Mexican Indian servants and begin conversion of the Pueblos—a decision, Gallegos tells us, that went against the wishes of the soldiers who feared for their safety. On the long trip home, Chamuscado fell ill. The medical kit and lancet had been left with the friars, so one of his companions opened a vein with a horseshoe nail to bleed him. Not surprisingly Commander

Chamuscado died and was buried in a desolate place at trailside not far from Santa Bárbara.

This small-scale and scarcely remembered venture in exploration offers some interesting parallels and contrasts to the Coronado expedition. When Francisco Vásquez de Coronado marched forth in 1540, Spaniards confidently expected a glittering Indian kingdom to turn up in the mysterious northern wilderness. The prospect of instant wealth had drawn volunteers by the hundreds, attracted investors, and led to the tumultuous fanfare at the send-off (which was attended, recall, by Juan de Oñate's father and maternal grandfather). Coronado, although he scoured a prodigious sweep of country from Arizona to the plains of central Kansas, discovered nothing in the way of an Aztec-like bonanza. After assaulting and burning several rebellious Pueblo towns on the middle Rio Grande, he ended his quest and hurried homeward to try and explain away his failure. Although he accomplished next to nothing, historians and popular writers ever since have made much of Coronado and his lengthy ramble, owing, it would seem, to the magnitude of the expedition and the high drama and Quixotesque adventures associated with it.

In stark contrast, humble Fray Agustín and his small party left Santa Bárbara forty years later, unheralded and virtually unnoticed. They covered much of the same country as Coronado and, like him, burned a few pueblos (towns) to prove Spaniards were not to be trifled with. But there, any similarity ends. Agustín Rodríguez's purpose was strictly religious, that is, humanitarian in his view, and he looked at the Pueblo Indians in terms of their potential for evangelization. Chamuscado and the other soldiers had something else in mind, for they had come along to watch for signs of mineral veins. The vision of treasure-rich native empires had long since dissolved, but they knew of the fabulous silver strikes beginning at Zacatecas, which by now studded New Spain's frontier zone. The geography of New Mexico, resembling that of the central plateau to the south, suggested to these prospectors that lodes of precious metal were just waiting to be discovered. At any rate, the importance of the Rodríguez-Chamuscado expedition rests in the fact that, unlike Coronado's, it spurred further exploration, and indeed set off a chain of events that brought about, in the course of time, Oñate's settling of New Mexico.

When Hernando Gallegos and the remaining men drew near to Santa Bárbara at the end of their perilous adventure, they fired harquebuses in the air and told residents who came out in response to the noise that they had discovered a wondrous new kingdom. Certain persons, loyal to Nueva Vizcaya's Governor Diego de Ibarra, then plotted to arrest Gallegos and the others, and seize their papers and maps to prevent them from asserting first rights to return and follow up this auspicious discovery. Gallegos and another, Pedro de Bustamante, managed to escape and rode at breakneck speed down the Camino Real, reaching Mexico City on May 8, 1582.

There they presented their story to the viceroy, the count of Coruña, and set the capital buzzing. The first concern of His Excellency was the welfare of the two Franciscans who had remained behind on the Rio Grande, Rodríguez and López. Unfortunately, word soon arrived that one of Chamuscado's Indian servants, left with the friars, had shown up in Santa Bárbara bearing tidings of their deaths at the hands of the Pueblos. In light of that, the viceroy consulted with a high-ranking soldier then in Mexico City, Rodrigo del Río de Losa, who, it will be remembered, had founded Santa Bárbara. He advised sending an armed invasion force of three hundred men to confirm the fate of the friars and "seek information about the whole region." The viceroy dutifully passed his recommendation on to the king, and at the same time, strangely, downplayed optimistic reports of Gallegos about New Mexico's silver prospects. In a cover letter, he said, "Your Majesty will give orders for study of the whole [New Mexico] question, . . . and adoption of such measures as may seem best for the royal service." The measure settled upon by the crown in 1583, as already mentioned, was the decree instructing the viceroy to begin a search for someone trustworthy and prestigious to occupy and pacify the land of the Pueblos.

"Truly the journey of Agustín Rodríguez had stirred up large ideas," comments Spanish Borderlands scholar Herbert E. Bolton. What it did in the short term was fan the ambitious and arouse the cupidity of a flock of opportunists who foresaw in all of this a splendid chance for personal gain. One of the earliest contenders for the honor of pacifying New Mexico was Hernando Gallegos himself, who sailed for Spain not long after delivering his report to the viceroy. There he submitted lengthy petitions to the king and his advisers, now claiming that he had been the leader of the recent expedition, spending eight thousand pesos to outfit it, and asking His Majesty for aid and permission to return. Adventuresome men in Madrid and Seville, he noted, were clamoring to join him.

On the one hand Gallegos claimed that he had impoverished him-

self in the service of the crown, and then on the other he proposed
to enlist and supply an army of five hundred men for his next New
Mexico excursion. Such inconsistencies did not help his cause. The
king ultimately directed officials in New Spain to give him some
suitable government job when he should return, but the chance to
harvest the New Mexico plum was denied him. In fact Gallegos stayed
on in Spain and as late as 1589 was still arguing his qualifications.

The pattern established in this instance was repeated with all of
the other petitioners who came forward during the 1580s and early
1590s, that is, before Oñate himself became a candidate. The king
listened, vacillated, and after excruciating delays rejected each one,
either because his wealth was considered insufficient to underwrite a
major colonization project, or because he lacked the social standing
to command respect as the governor of a new province, or because
he demanded too many concessions and rewards from the royal
government. Such temporizing by King Philip II derived in part
from his sincere desire to find the right man to settle New Mexico.
But some of it can be attributed to his chronic indecisiveness, as Juan
de Oñate would discover to his sorrow.

While matters were entangled in red tape at Mexico City and
Madrid, interest in New Mexico remained high all along New Spain's
upper border. Shortly after survivors of the Rodríguez-Chamuscado
party returned, the Franciscan Order decided to send north a rescue
expedition, on the faint chance that the reported death of the two
friars was in error. Fray Bernardino Beltrán, then serving in the city
of Durango, was assigned to carry out the mission. A prosperous
frontier rancher, Antonio de Espejo, stepped forward and offered to
accompany him with fourteen soldiers and to pay all the expenses.
While the three-hundred-man expedition proposed by Río de Losa
to the viceroy required approval from Spain—which meant nothing
further was heard of it—the more modest relief party suggested by
Espejo could be launched solely on the authority of local officials in
Nueva Vizcaya. Espejo couched his proposition in pious and patriotic
terms, but from what happened afterward it is clear that prospecting
for silver and gold was his true motive.

The Espejo company set forth on November 10, 1582, on a journey
that would consume almost a year. Traveling north they reached
the pueblo of Puaray above Albuquerque, where Fray Bernardino
established that his brethren, Rodríguez and López, had indeed perished. Although the announced purpose of the expedition was now

achieved, Espejo with assent of the friar commenced a far-ranging exploration. His probings carried them from the edge of the eastern plains to the western villages of the Hopis and beyond. Before returning to Nueva Vizcaya he searched for a rumored lake of gold and collected rich ore samples from the distant mountains of Arizona. His findings would lure Oñate two decades later to retrace much of Espejo's trail in the west.

Back in Santa Bárbara, Antonio de Espejo composed a lengthy narrative of his excursion and, at the end of October 1583, sent the document to King Philip. In it, he begged to be entrusted with "the exploration and settlement of these lands and others which I may discover, for I shall not be satisfied until I reach the coasts of the North and South seas." In an accompanying letter, he promised to serve the crown "with greater advantage than any others who are attempting to make a contract with you regarding this enterprise." His words demonstrate that by then the competition to win New Mexico was already in full swing. Apparently, Espejo wrote the king before he had seen the royal decree conveying power of selection to the viceroy. All later applicants submitted their proposals to Mexico City for review. For him, though, it made no difference; he was weeded from the list of candidates early in the game.

Among the men rich and powerful who became rivals for the New Mexico contract, two soon emerged as leading contenders. One or the other might well have gained the title that finally went to Oñate. The first was an overbearing Andalusian, Juan Lomas y Colmenares, who had built up a feudal barony encompassing the entire basin of Nieves in central Nueva Vizcaya. His properties took in whole villages, mines, vast wheat fields, vineyards, and livestock innumerable. Many persons claimed he was the wealthiest man in western New Spain. As emblematic of his exalted status, he traveled everywhere with a huge escort, made up principally of Castilians and Andalusians and including relatives, in-laws, friends, dependents, and their servants.

In 1589 Lomas y Colmenares submitted to the viceroy, the marquis of Villamanrique, his set of proposals for the settlement of New Mexico. They were broadly drawn, even audacious in scope, demanding concessions far in excess of what was allowed by the Colonization Laws of 1573. Indeed, they convey the impression that the man aimed at nothing less than creation of a semiautonomous principality on the Rio Grande. He sought, for instance, supreme civil and military authority, power to expand the northern boundaries of New Mexico to both oceans, overlordship of forty thousand Indian vassals in perpetuity, a personal grant of twenty-four square leagues of land (that is, more than sixty square miles), the rank of count or marquis, and the title of adelantado for his family in perpetuity. No one since Columbus had dared ask for so much.

Such a proposition could have only been framed by a person of medieval mind, and one seriously out of touch with current trends in royal thinking. The crown was bent on harnessing the ambitions of petty empire builders, as the Colonization Laws made plain, and thus Lomas y Colmenares's proposal appeared outlandish. Viceroy Villamanrique, although empowered to make a final decision, wisely referred the matter to Spain where the king sat on it for five years before rejecting it utterly.

While the star of Lomas y Colmenares was sinking that of the second individual, Francisco de Urdiñola, began its assent. Like his fellow Basques, Urdiñola had come to New Spain's frontier to fight in the Chichimeca wars, discover mines, and acquire estates. Chevalier says that he truly had land fever, and in eastern Nueva Vizcaya he hewed out a half dozen enormous haciendas embracing several million acres. By 1591 he was lieutenant-governor of Nueva Vizcaya and regarded as one of the most talented and vigorous of frontier leaders. Three years later, in 1594, he got a summons from the then viceroy, Don Luís de Velasco II, who wanted him to negotiate a contract to head the New Mexico project. Velasco had recently been advised by Spain that Lomas de Colmenares's bid was at long last rejected and speedy measures should be taken to find someone else. Eleven years had now gone by since the king first ordered the pacification of the Pueblos, and the able Velasco felt some urgency in bringing the matter to a conclusion. Urdiñola, he believed, possessed the proper qualifications for the job.

Scarcely were the negotiations opened, however, when the High Court, or Audiencia, of Nueva Galicia indicted Urdiñola on charges of poisoning his wife and murdering several servants. The original accuser seems to have been none other than Lomas y Colmenares, an unscrupulous and vindictive sort who was not yet willing to surrender his New Mexico dream to another. Urdiñola's biographer, Vito Alessio Robles, affirms that Lomas y Colmenares resorted to intrigue through agents in Madrid to win approval for his New Mexico proposal, and when it was turned down, he persisted in trying to

Don Francisco de Urdiñola. His legal difficulties gave Oñate an opportunity to win the contract for the settlement of New Mexico. (From Vito Alessio Robles, *Francisco de Urdiñola y el Norte de La Nueva España*, Mexico, 1931)

have the decision reversed. At the same time he became the bitter foe of Urdiñola, and used his influence to have him arrested for murder. In fact a nephew of Lomas y Colmenares was a judge on the Audiencia. Once the judicial process had been set in motion, Urdiñola became enmeshed in the legal details of his defense and thus was unable to pursue talks with the viceroy about New Mexico. Ultimately, Urdiñola was absolved, in part through testimony of his mother-in-law who declared that her daughter had died of a fever and not poisoning. But by then, 1598, the moment had passed, and another man, Juan de Oñate, was already on the road to New Mexico.

Soon after Urdiñola's arrest, Viceroy Velasco abandoned him as a candidate and turned to Oñate as his next choice. He was thoroughly familiar with the past contributions of the pioneering Oñates, and knew of Don Juan's success in the founding of San Luís Potosí. Moreover, he seems to have personally done some military campaigning in the Chichimeca country in the company of Juan de Oñate, so he probably had firsthand knowledge of his soldiering skills and leadership qualities. And it is possible that by now Don Juan had expressed an interest in New Mexico to the viceroy, so that when Urdiñola made his forced withdrawal, he stood ready as a logical replacement. At any rate, what followed was Oñate's signing of a formal contract with the viceroy on September 21, 1595, as described earlier.

Juan de Oñate wasted no time in launching preparations for his New Mexico *entrada*, a term Spaniards used to mean the formal entry into a new land. To aid in the endeavor he enlisted his kin and a wide circle of influential friends, some as direct participants and others as investors. His four brothers were made official agents of the enterprise, their duty to remain behind and to use Juan's power of attorney to raise money, dispatch supplies, and represent him in business matters at the viceregal court. The nephew Cristóbal de Zaldívar was assigned special tasks in the formation and provisioning of the expedition, but he too was to be left home as an agent. His two brothers, on the other hand, were selected to accompany Oñate: Juan de Zaldívar, later picked as second in command with the rank of *maese de campo* (field marshal), and the younger brother Vicente de Zaldívar, named *sargento mayor* (lieutenant marshal).

Recruitment of soldier-settlers was one of the first orders of business, and to that end Oñate promptly "raised his standard." A silken standard decorated with religious figures and coats-of-arms and blessed by a priest served as a visible symbol of authority for all great undertakings and was the personal emblem of the man in charge. The old butcher Nuño de Guzmán had marched up the Pacific coast under a banner of silver cloth emblazoned with a gold image of the Virgin Mary. And before beginning his conquest of Nueva Vizcaya, young Francisco de Ibarra received as a gift from his uncle Diego a gorgeous standard of blue damask embroidered in gold and silver with the images of Christ and the Virgin upon it.

Doubtless as a mark of affection and respect, Viceroy Luís de Velasco himself provided Oñate with a suitable standard. The foundation was of Castilian figured white silk stamped on one side with the pictures of Our Lady and St. John the Baptist (San Juan Bautista), Oñate's patron saint, both images surrounded by a rosary and with the Oñate coat of arms below. The reverse held a picture of Santiago on horseback with Viceroy Velasco's arms below. It was this standard that Don Juan raised aloft to symbolize inauguration of the recruiting process, and it was the one he would carry with him to New Mexico.

Overnight Zacatecas became a center of feverish activity. To it came rough men of the border who had heard a new entrada was in the offing and to it flowed supplies of every description from remote corners of the viceroyalty. Vicente de Zaldívar rode to Mexico City, kissed the hand of the viceroy, and in the great plaza drew crowds with fife and drum. His speeches, extolling the marvels to be found in New Mexico, attracted enlistments and, as soldiers in Europe used to say, "they followed the recruiter's drum," in this case back to Zacatecas. With an equal measure of flair and flamboyance, Juan de Oñate made his own recruiting swing through the towns and farmlands of Nueva Galicia, attracting volunteers to his dazzling standard. At this moment fortune shone brightly upon him, and the fates seemed to have granted him his fondest wish—a secure place in the sun.

But what the fates give, they can also take away, or at least diminish, just as suddenly. On September 18, 1595, three days before Oñate met with Velasco to arrange his contract, Don Gaspar de Zúñiga y Acevedo, the count of Monterrey, had landed at the port of Vera Cruz bearing his appointment as the new viceroy and displaying royal documents that transferred Luís de Velasco to the post of viceroy of Peru. The change came as a surprise to Velasco, and, as events would soon demonstrate, it was to prove an extraordinarily bad piece of luck for Oñate. With his cumbersome retinue and the necessity of ceremony at places along the way, it took the count of Monterrey several weeks to move inland and approach the capital. Sometime after October 14, Velasco went forth with much pomp and met him six leagues from Mexico City at the town of Acolman. Amid formalities, the two held a conference at which the count learned of the problems and issues he would be facing.

Velasco took special pains to inform his successor of the contract just concluded with Oñate and of the need, after so many years of delay, to get the New Mexico project off the ground. He realized that the count had it within his power, once he took office, to alter or disapprove the contract, and thus Velasco dwelled upon the reputation and wealth of Oñate and praised him as the best man available for the work in New Mexico. The count of Monterrey agreed to extend conditional approval, so that Oñate could continue his preparations for the expedition, but at the same time he expressed his intention of examining the contract at his leisure and making any changes deemed advisable. Upon reading this in a letter from the new viceroy, Oñate took it to mean that everything was still on track, so he confidently went on recruiting and gathering supplies. What he could not know was that unflattering appraisals of his fitness were reaching the ears of the count and giving him pause. At the back of this sinister development lurked the shadowy figure of Juan Lomas y Colmenares.

In late October, before relinquishing his office, Viceroy Velasco issued two documents on behalf of Oñate. One appointed him governor and captain-general of New Mexico, and the other was a set of instructions to guide his conduct as a colonizer. In these he reminded Don Juan to pay strict observance to the Colonization Laws of 1573, since they reflected the king's determination to protect the Indians.

A pair of episodes in recent years, both involving illegal entries into New Mexico, had underlined the crown's resolve to assert control over the frontier through those laws. In 1590, Gaspar Castaño de Sosa, lieutenant-governor of Nuevo León (the province east of Nueva Vizcaya) had led an unauthorized party of 170 men, women, and children into New Mexico for purposes of settlement. The next year fifty soldiers sent by the viceroy arrested Castaño and escorted all of his people out of the area. Then, in 1593, Captain Francisco Leyva de Bonilla, while heading a small force in pursuit of renegade Indians along the upper border of Nueva Vizcaya, seized the opportunity to invade New Mexico. It was just the kind of self-serving, conquistador-

like behavior that the king had been trying to curb with his Colonization Laws, and Leyva de Bonilla's foolish rush after glory and gold
infuriated him. Therefore, the viceroy instructed Oñate to pursue
and apprehend the captain and his accomplices, a task that would not
prove easy since they had disappeared into the northern plains.

The primary desire of the crown, as embodied in the instructions
given to Oñate, was to initiate conversion of the "many large settlements of heathen Indians who live in ignorance of God and our holy
Catholic faith . . . so that they might have an orderly and decent
Christian life." This was no smoke screen to conceal other, baser
motives of territorial expansion or mineral prospecting. The royal
government took seriously its obligation to provide energetic support
for the missionary program. And that support was vigorously encouraged by the missionaries themselves, whose interests were sometimes
as much material as they were spiritual.

The Basque friar Gerónimo de Mendieta, a sixteenth-century Franciscan chronicler, proclaimed that God had not given the Indies to
Spain for the reaping of gold and silver, but for the harvesting of
Indian souls. Antonio de la Ascensión, priest and map maker, saw the
shrewd hand of the Almighty in the placement of rare and scattered
mineral deposits along the frontier. They were heavenly lures, he
wrote, drawing Spanish expeditions into the wilderness so that friars
and ministers could use them as vehicles to reach the heathen in need
of conversion.

The importance of the missionary program, and its function as an
arm of the empire, meant that priests enjoyed enormous influence.
Indeed, because of their power Spanish colonial policy in this era is
often interpreted as being guided by religious motives, sacrificing
practical interests of the state to crusading zeal. Fray Alonso de
Benavides, recording his observations of New Mexico in 1630, implied
that the original founding expedition had been put together mainly
as a convenience for the missionaries, and that Oñate and his colonists
merely came along for the ride. Father Juan de Escalona, one of the
friars of the Oñate expedition, knew that in fact most of the settlers
had joined with the hope of making a spectacular mineral strike. But
as he explained to the viceroy in a letter of 1601, he believed God had
ordained no silver should be found in Mexico, lest it impede the progress of conversion. In sum, it can be said that when the viceroy instructed Juan de Oñate to give first attention to affairs of the church,
he meant it.

Contained in the instructions is reference to another matter, seemingly small, but in actual fact looming large in a list of motives behind Spanish occupation of New Mexico. The viceroy spoke of the search Oñate would be making to discover the coast and navigable ports, and when these were found he ordered him to send news of it speedily to Mexico City. He was not interested in just any coast, but the one that was supposed to front on the hard-to-find Strait of Anián.

Worry over possession of that elusive waterway was plaguing Viceroy Velasco when he gave Oñate his instructions. Now with New Mexico about to be established as a forward bastion in the interior of the continent, he felt Spaniards would be in an excellent position to discover and claim the strait. That hope was probably also present in the viceroy's mind when he signed a contract, in that same year of 1595, with the Basque merchant-sailor Sebastian Vizcaíno to explore coastal California, ostensibly in search of pearl beds. Later when Vizcaíno was in the vicinity of Cape Mendocino, his diarist specifically mentioned scanning the shoreline in search of the strait. Historian John Walton Caughey reminds us that in Viceroy Velasco's eyes Oñate and Vizcaíno were part of the same cooperative enterprise in the extension and strengthening of the northern frontier.

While Juan de Oñate firmly subscribed to the purposes of his sovereign in the occupation of New Mexico as laid down in the viceroy's instructions, he had his own vision as well of what he hoped to accomplish. That vision was grounded in a wish to continue where his father Cristóbal had left off, expanding the family's wealth and adding new laurels to the Oñate name. He was now a royal governor, admittedly only of a province-to-be, and as soon as New Mexico was settled he would receive the much-desired title of adelantado. But that was just a start, for like Lomas y Colmenares, Oñate early on asked for a title of nobility, count or marquis, which he could expect to receive only if New Mexico proved a spectacular success. Likewise, his new government had to thrive for him to realize that other desire he may have secretly nursed—to be made a viceroy.

The titles that Oñate longed for had to be earned and also won through a bit of luck, but they represented distant goals, to be reached by completion of more immediate ones. In the latter category was the assembling of his expedition. Everything that he sought depended upon the enlistment of a willing and solid body of colonists—hence, the importance he attached to the recruitment process. Secondarily, success in New Mexico would rest upon finding silver—Oñate's own area of specialty—to furnish a viable economic foundation for the new realm. To that end, he carefully selected a full stock of mining tools and smelting equipment to be packed tightly into carts for the long journey north.

We must consider too, in enumerating Oñate's personal motives, that religion and furtherance of the missionary program played a fundamental role. He did not just give lip-service to the viceroy's command that he support and encourage the Franciscans; he was wholly committed to it. Father Benavides reckoned him "a goodly Christian gentleman," and there are a number of incidents in his New Mexico period that show Oñate to have been unusually faithful, pious, and strict in his religious observance.

In this connection, the influence of a curious priest, Fray Diego Márquez, upon Oñate bears consideration. Unlike many of the clergymen then serving in the colony, he had been born in New Spain rather than in the mother country, a circumstance that gave him an American rather than a European perspective. In 1587, Márquez sailed for Spain, but his ship was captured by English sea dogs and he was taken as a prisoner to London. Conducted to the court of Queen Elizabeth, he underwent a lengthy interview by Her Highness, who was keenly interested in what he had to tell about New Spain, and especially about New Mexico. This was just a few years after the Rodríguez-Chamuscado and Espejo expeditions, and New Spain, when Márquez left, was still full of excited talk of the Pueblo country. The queen and her advisers knew practically nothing concerning the geography and people of Spain's overseas empire, so what this knowledgeable Franciscan had to say was eagerly received.

And Father Márquez said plenty. He evidently held nothing back with regard to the potential wealth and strategic value of New Mexico. Subsequently, he attempted to justify the divulging of state secrets by claiming that the queen had imposed upon him a religious oath to speak truthfully, so he was morally bound to answer all questions. His cooperation won him a quick release, and he was allowed to proceed to Spain. There he recounted to Philip II all that had occurred, emphasizing that the English showed an uncommon interest in New Mexico. That information shook the king, just as Father Márquez calculated it would. And Villagrá states that a royal order quickly went to New Spain's viceroy, in that year of 1589, urging that the search be accelerated to find an adelantado and governor for New Mexico. What followed shortly was the application of Lomas y

Colmenares, which was allowed to languish on the king's desk, in part, because the English threat Father Márquez had warned of failed to materialize.

The Franciscan Order, ever since Fray Agustín Rodríguez and his two companions were martyred on the Rio Grande, had been pushing for the conversion of the Pueblos. The order was a powerful force in New Spain and the pressure it could exert, formidable. Nevertheless, it had to wait until the king chose the leader for a colonizing expedition, and as delays followed one another Franciscan impatience grew. It seems clear, therefore, that what Father Márquez did was engage in a small piece of international intrigue, playing upon the Spanish king's fears in an effort to get him moving on the New Mexico project.

The same priest reappears in New Spain a few years later, working closely with Juan de Oñate in the formation of his expedition. According to Villagrá, Márquez was in on the planning from the very beginning, contributing direct help, and was soon a figure beloved by all those associated with the enterprise. Other sources refer to him as an intimate friend of Don Juan. Precisely when Father Márquez attached himself to Oñate has not been determined. But the question arises, could he have been responsible, upon returning from Spain, for persuading Oñate to submit a contract for the New Mexico venture? If so, it would suggest that in Don Juan the Franciscans saw their best hope for an early beginning to their long-sought missionary field among the Pueblos. What befell Márquez, which prevented him from going to New Mexico and deprived Oñate of a trusted adviser, will be related shortly.

The king, the church, and Oñate, then, each had distinct objectives in mind committing them to the occupation and development of New Mexico. But fortunately their purposes overlapped sufficiently to permit mutual support and to bring about a truly cooperative undertaking. There was still another element in the equation, however, that produced a separate set of goals. The men now rallying to Oñate's standard and to the seductive sound of his recruiter's drum created their own agenda and list of rewards they counted upon New Mexico to deliver.

At bottom, they were motivated, as Cristóbal de Oñate had been when he left his Basque home for the Indies, by the eternal Spanish quest for fame and riches. The prospect of striking silver or gold in the rock-ribbed and wrinkled mountains of New Mexico served as an irresistible magnet. Attractive, too, was the knowledge that Governor Oñate would be parceling out grants of encomienda, blocs of Pueblo Indians who would render yearly assessments of valuable tribute. Some of the men enlisted out of a spirit of adventure, or from personal loyalty and friendship to Oñate, or through a hankering to assist in the king's and the church's work. But even these motivations drew upon the assumption that the individual would reap personal profit. In the last analysis, probably the most seductive reason behind the rush to join this colonizing scheme was the promise of the privilege of *hidalguía*, something all commoners craved with unquenchable passion. Every head-of-household risking the hazards of settling New Mexico became eligible, at the end of five years of residency, to receive a patent of hidalgo, the lowest rank in the hierarchy of Spanish nobility. With it went the designation of caballero, or knight, together with the same rights, honors, and privileges enjoyed by hidalgos and caballeros of Castile. Among these was the right to use the title *Don* before one's name (an acronym formed from the first letters of the phrase, *de origen noble*), exemption from taxes, and freedom from arrest for debt.

The concept of hidalguía was essentially aristocratic and medieval. In exchange for his privileges, the hidalgo rendered military service to his king whenever called upon, from whence arose the Spanish respect for the profession of arms and corresponding distaste for the sweat of manual labor. To work with one's hands came to be viewed as undignified, since it reduced a man to the level of a Moor or peasant. Juan de Oñate would find a reluctance on the part of his own colonists to put shoulders to the wheel or hands to the plow because of their pending admission to hidalgo status. But it was precisely that "hidalgo-mania," as historian Jaime Vicens Vives has labeled it, that baited Oñate's colonists into volunteering in the first place.

The recruiting process was swept along by the exuberance of the hour and the heady speech making in the plazas, so that within a matter of weeks fife and drum had lured some five hundred men to enlist under Oñate's colors. That was well beyond the two hundred he had committed himself to in his capitulaciones, and had he tried to arm and supply them all, his finances would have been severely strained. As it was, the bulk of the men, in Villagrá's words, "sold all their worldly goods that they might outfit themselves properly." Here at the outset, the magic of the name of New Mexico was pulling in

Sections of the original Oñate contract, granting his men lands and the titles of hidalgo and knight of Castile. (From Lansing B. Bloom and Thomas C. Donnelly, *New Mexico History and Civics*, Alburquerque: University of New Mexico Press, 1933) all sorts of individuals, but probably a disproportionate number who were not good colonist material. Shortly afterward, members of the Council of the Indies told the king that New Spain was full of idle, lazy, and undisciplined people and that if they went to New Mexico, the viceroy would be well rid of them. But that would mean, of course, that Oñate inherited the problem.

Meanwhile, the new viceroy, the count of Monterrey, was reviewing the contract Oñate had signed with Viceroy Velasco. However, he took his time about it, not because he thought the matter unimportant, but rather owing to the avalanche of official business suddenly thrust upon him. Oñate found the uncertainty more than just exasperating as he informed the king in a plaintive letter of December 16, 1595. "This delay has been very harmful," he wrote, "not only for me and the progress of the expedition, but for the many people I recruited to undertake it, because some lost interest and became discouraged and because the rainy season is near at hand, which will hinder the entrada." And he added that failure to get under way had already caused him financial loss.

At length, the viceroy used part of his Christmas holidays to study Oñate's capitulaciones. A number of small points and a large one he found not to his liking, so he modified them, as his authority allowed. The small matters, having to do with such things as recruitment procedures and handling of finances, were mere irritants for Oñate. Not so the main change imposed by Monterrey. That one took away Oñate's privilege of answering only to Spain's Council of the Indies. Now he was to be directly responsible to the viceroy at Mexico City, a significant procedural point that undercut his independence and prestige and might well cripple any efforts in the future to make New Mexico a separate viceroyalty, if that in fact was what Oñate had in mind.

Unlike former Viceroy Velasco, the count of Monterrey was not a personal friend of Oñate, so he had no reservations about clipping his wings. As the new man in office, he likely wanted to assert his power in some forceful way, so he called in Oñate's representatives in Mexico City, his brothers Cristóbal and Luís, and informed them of the modifications. They protested, of course, but to no effect, and they then accepted the viceroy's changes, knowing full well that Juan would immediately appeal over Monterrey's head, directly to the crown. Oñate did make such an appeal to Philip II, but without avail. The new conditions imposed by Monterrey were allowed to stand.

The good news was that as soon as Cristóbal and Luís agreed, however reluctantly, to the viceroy's terms, he issued a decree granting permission for the occupation of New Mexico to proceed at once. And the word came none too soon. Many of Oñate's recruits, who had been cooling their heels in camp since the previous October, were more than just discouraged. They were becoming rebellious and threatening desertion. Men gathered in groups to complain about the food and the interminable delays, as soldiers have always done. But the chief source of their discontent was the persistent rumor that the expedition might be abandoned. The encampment increasingly became disorderly and could have dissolved altogether, each man going his own way, had not Oñate periodically delivered conciliatory speeches. His remarks are described as being "kind and spirited," and his eloquence received credit for calming the restless troops and holding them in place until arrival of the viceregal decree that cleared the way for departure.

To what degree Oñate attributed his difficulties, including the inordinate delay, to the intrigues of his enemies is difficult to say. But that he was aware of forces working against him seems fairly clear. In all likelihood, he discussed the threat in meetings with his officers and from that, or maybe just from camp scuttlebutt, Captain Villagrá learned that the cautious new viceroy had been led to question Oñate's qualifications and resources. These reservations, he states, were based on false rumors circulated by deceitful and envious persons who wanted to wreck the expedition. Monterrey himself reported that while he considered Don Juan to be an honorable man, others had advised him that he was unfit to head a colonizing effort, and that his wealth was insufficient and his estate overburdened with debt.

Villagrá doesn't identify the "instigators of these falsehoods," as he puts the matter, but he openly declares that they hid their scurrilous motives under a cloak of fake concern for the welfare of the empire. At the root lay simple envy and jealousy, Villagrá believed, and that might not have been far from the truth. He implies that the envy was on the part of those resentful of Juan de Oñate's success at securing the New Mexico contract. As mentioned earlier, suspicion focuses on Juan Lomas y Colmenares. Certainly he had both motive and means to hurt Oñate, but the exact manner in which he proceeded is, of course, not recorded in any remaining written document.

In the end, Viceroy Velasco's firm recommendation, united with the advanced state of Oñate's preparations, outweighed any passing consideration the count of Monterrey may have given to cancelling the whole project. So he granted his nod of approval. Oñate sighed with relief while the spirits of his men soared. The bureaucratic bottleneck was at last uncorked, and the beckoning trail to New Mexico had opened wide before them. Or so it seemed.

CHAPTER 5

Moratorium

IN the spring of 1596, Oñate began preparations to move his body of colonists from Zacatecas northward some four hundred miles to Santa Bárbara, the frontier outpost designated as the final rendezvous and departure point for New Mexico. Recruits were still coming in, small parties arriving almost daily and many with entire families. Word that the viceroy had extended his blessing greatly enhanced Oñate's reputation and lent a new air of respectability to all that was in progress.

In a dispatch to the king, dated April 17, Viceroy Monterrey noted that many of those persons from Mexico City going with Oñate had already left for the north, and he was hurrying along the remaining ones so they could catch up and complete the expedition's roster. He mentioned, in addition, his trouble in learning precisely how many men had volunteered and what was the quantity of supplies assembled to date. To secure this information, the viceroy said he was searching for a competent individual who could go and hold a muster of troops and inspection of provisions. The aim would be to determine whether Oñate was fulfilling the terms of his contract, because if he failed to come up with all of the supplies promised, his colonists would be the ones to suffer.

Shortly afterward, Monterrey selected as inspector of the expedition his own captain of the viceregal guard, Lope de Ulloa, an individual who enjoyed his complete trust. He ordered him to proceed to Zacatecas and from there accompany the colonists to Santa Bárbara, which would give him a chance to become familiar with the people and their circumstances. Thus, when he conducted the final inspection, or *visita,* at Santa Bárbara, he would be in a better position to gauge whether Don Juan had actually met all the requirements of his contract.

Ulloa was also given broad police powers. Reports had reached the viceroy's ears that parties of volunteers on their way to Zacatecas were disturbing the countryside, some simply by their roistering, but others by committing thefts and vandalism. Therefore, he empowered Inspector Ulloa to intervene to protect the inhabitants and to punish those guilty of crimes. Upon his arrival, however, he was to defer to Oñate's authority. Spaniards joining expeditions of discovery and settlement in the sixteenth century were, by custom, subject to military discipline. Consequently, the commander of what was, in essence, a private army could impose the severest penalties—even capital punishment—for serious breaches of conduct. Later in New Mexico, Oñate would use that prerogative in meting out stern punishment to mutineers.

When Ulloa appeared in the encampment with his assistant, Francisco de Esquivel, and an assortment of other staff, Oñate was wary, fearing that further obstructions lay in store for him. But to his surprise, the inspector went out of his way to be both courteous and accommodating. Promptly, he handed over letters from Monterrey that displayed a new friendliness toward Oñate and his endeavor. Now that all issues seemed to have been resolved, the viceroy was willing to offer his complete support, and he expressed the wish that the expedition reach New Mexico by August of that year, 1596.

Perhaps anticipating that Don Juan might be apprehensive over the forthcoming inspection, Monterrey took pains in the letters to provide reassurance. Ulloa's review of troops, arms, and supplies, he explained, was a mere formality, ordered as a matter of course and not because of any suspicion that Oñate would fail to fulfill the letter of his contract. Ulloa had instructions to detain the expedition should deficiencies be found, but he also had full authority to send it on its way when everything was in readiness. In closing, the viceroy wished the new governor and all his volunteers "a prosperous journey and Godspeed." Oñate chose to interpret the inspector's arrival and Monterrey's communications in the best possible light, doubtless because he needed a boost and knew that the impatient men of his camp did as well. When he shared the viceroy's encouraging phrases with his assembled soldiers, there were shouts of joy followed by tournaments and unbridled partying.

It was about this time that the missionaries promised to Oñate by the government walked in, sandal-footed, from Mexico City and presented themselves for duty. Head of the party of five Franciscan priests and a lay brother was Father Rodrigo Durán, characterized by Villagrá as "a prudent and saintly man." Among his companions were Oñate's cousin, Fray Cristóbal de Salazar, mentioned as "a priest distinguished in letters," and the well-traveled Fray Diego Márquez, recognized as a special friend and confidant of the expedition's leader. Fray Diego inspired awe among the men, as one who had talked his way out of the clutches of English Protestants at Queen Elizabeth's court. But he was also possessed of a common touch, and maybe even a jovial streak, for within the space of a few days he became the most popular individual in camp. One and all, Don Juan was delighted to see them, for these men of the cloth, by their mere presence, added the final and most exalted sanction to his undertaking.

Sometime in early summer, the vanguard of Oñate's force began moving slowly up the Camino Real toward Santa Bárbara. Don Juan remained in Zacatecas for a while longer, then followed with the main body of the expedition. Along the route he paused to buy cattle and additional supplies, mindful that Ulloa, who was riding at his side, would demand a strict accounting, once they gained the frontier. All of this consumed more weeks than Oñate would have liked, and by late August, when the viceroy had wished him in New Mexico, he was still plodding up the road in central Nueva Vizcaya.

Near the beginning of the second week of September, Oñate encamped on the Rio Nazas, seventy miles south of Santa Bárbara, where he announced that the party would rest for several days. The site was surrounded by barren hills and plains presenting a dismal, even depressing viewscape. It was now almost a year since Oñate had met with Viceroy Velasco to sign his original contract, and the past twelve months had been burdened with frustrations, not to mention expenses. He had every reason to believe, nevertheless, that once he cleared the mournful valley of the Rio Nazas and ascended to Santa Bárbara, his misfortunes would come to an end.

Then on September 9, a courier, who had come all the way from Mexico City, dashed into camp. In his letter pouch were dispatches for Inspector Ulloa, and before an excited throng that quickly gathered he claimed *albricias*, rewards that by ancient tradition were owed to messengers bearing good news. Oñate, his colonists, and the courier himself assumed that among the dispatches was one from Spain, giving Philip II's confirmation of the viceroy's marching orders. Don Juan, however, was anything but uncautious, and wisely he invited Ulloa to his field tent where the flap could be secured and the sealed documents opened and read in private.

The news they carried was quite the opposite of joyous. It was

The Franciscan scholar Fray Juan de Torquemada, author of *Monarquía Indiana* (1615), the first general history of the colonies to include an account of Oñate's settlement of New Mexico. Torquemada may have resembled some of the Oñate friars in appearance. (From Lucas Alamán, *La Historia de la Republica Mexicana*, Mexico, 1860)

catastrophic, hitting Oñate with the force of a thunderbolt. On top
was a royal *cédula,* a decree of the king, suspending Oñate's agreement
and commanding the viceroy to prevent the expedition from setting
forth or, if it had already started, to stop it where it was until further
notice. The only reason His Majesty gave was that he had decided to
review the offer of a Spanish nobleman, Don Pedro Ponce de León,
who was eager to embark for America and carry out the discovery of
New Mexico.

A second document bore the title, in large script, "Orders of the
Viceroy." Addressed to Ulloa, it directed him to show Oñate the
king's cédula, reiterated the command to halt, and issued dire threats,
including permanent revoking of the original contract, should there
be any disobedience. The orders also instructed Ulloa to announce
in camp the details of the suspension and to warn every member of
the expedition that failure to comply would be judged as disloyalty
to the king, which carried a sentence of death and forfeiture of all
property. They were also to be told "neither to heed nor obey Don
Juan."

It is difficult to imagine a more callous or damaging pair of dispatches. In an instant Oñate's authority was completely undercut and
his project reduced to shambles. Yet he did then what all Spaniards
were required to do in similar circumstances: he respectfully kissed
the royal documents and placed them over his head in token of
submission, a ceremonial gesture that reached far back into the Middle Ages. Next, he went to work persuading Ulloa to delay announcement of his suspension, lest it produce immediate disintegration of
the expedition. From what followed, we have to infer that the inspector recognized the seriousness of the situation and agreed to go along
at least for the time being.

According to Captain Villagrá's eyewitness account, Don Juan
emerged from his tent, and "he cried in a loud and happy voice,
'Forward, comrades, forward to the conquest! The order has been
given!' " On hearing that, the soldiers cheered and applauded, gathering around Oñate and congratulating one another. Some men leaped
on their horses and raced about the camp. Quickly a sham battle was
organized, like a tournament of knights, with one side led by Juan
de Zaldívar and the other by his brother Vicente. The celebrating
continued for hours, and during one pause Oñate summoned the
courier, thanked him for his welcome news, and repaid him with the
traditional gift. Out of loyalty to his commander, Villagrá describes

this as cleverness rather than duplicity, and compares it to the "maneuverings of the wily Greeks who enticed the warlike Trojans into taking the wooden horse within their walls." The play-acting on Oñate's part, he contends, was necessary to keep the colonists from learning the dire condition of things.

What had occurred in the lofty precincts of government to bring about this sudden and unexpected renunciation of Oñate? The tortuous course of events, in fact, had its origin in a letter Viceroy Monterrey wrote to the king on December 20, 1595, right after taking office in Mexico City. In it, he noted that he was just starting to review Oñate's contract and indicated he might want to make some modifications (which he later did, as we've seen). Therefore, he asked Philip II to withhold final confirmation of the project until this was done. By now attacks upon Oñate's reputation by his enemies and rivals had come to the attention of the viceroy, prompting him to tell the king that he entertained certain doubts, but nothing as yet substantial enough to write about.

This brief letter took a number of weeks to cross the Atlantic, reaching the desks of the king and the Council of the Indies, just as an unidentified individual from New Spain, referred to in the records only as "a creditable person," appeared at court and began to vilify Juan de Oñate. According to his testimony, Don Juan had little wealth and was deeply in debt. Few men had been willing to follow his drum and enlist for New Mexico, and those who did join were mostly half-breeds and mulattos. Furthermore, the recruits were thoroughly undisciplined and committed outrages against Spanish citizens and friendly Indians alike. In short, these "facts" confirmed that Oñate was incompetent, ill prepared, and too poor to launch a conquest of such magnitude.

At almost the same time, that is in early 1596, Don Pedro Ponce de León, count of Bailén, stepped forward with a petition asking that he be allowed to replace Oñate as governor and adelantado of New Mexico. The King's councilors appeared delighted with his papers and with his rather grandiose plans for enlisting volunteers in New Spain. On April 7 they recommended that a new contract be arranged with Ponce de León, picturing him as "an intelligent and well-qualified gentleman," who was far wealthier than Oñate and would do a much better job. They justified annulling Oñate's contract on the basis that neither Viceroy Velasco nor Monterrey had given it final approval. They also suggested that if Don Juan had already expended sums in preparation for his expedition, he could be given some government job by way of compensation.

Later that same month members of the council issued another report to the king, again extolling the virtues of Ponce de León and sparing no effort to discredit Juan de Oñate. The latter they characterized as being weighted down with thirty thousand pesos in bad debts, and as resorting to deceit to fend off a horde of creditors. Further, they reported that soldiers who had served under him previously thought poorly of his leadership abilities and refused to obey him. And finally, the councilors said that "reliable parties" claimed it would be impossible for Oñate to head any expedition because no one of importance would want to follow him or be under his government. Thus, he would only be able to recruit outcasts and vagabonds— persons given to "disgraceful disturbances and riots." It is clear these accusations were not founded simply on misinformation. They went too far beyond that. The trumped-up charges were part of a campaign to destroy Oñate and his carefully laid plans.

Don Juan's detractors, recently off the boat from New Spain, were obviously men of influence who had access to the most powerful of the king's officials. Many of their complaints against Oñate were almost identical to those delivered earlier to Viceroy Monterrey, which supports the conclusion that an organized plot was afoot. As already observed, the most likely candidate for chief conspirator is Juan Lomas y Colmenares, the rejected applicant for the New Mexico contract. He was fully capable of sending agents to Spain in a bid to scuttle Oñate's project, as in fact he had done with the earlier rival, Urdiñola.

And what about Don Pedro Ponce de León? How did he fit into this picture of intrigue? Why did he become interested in New Mexico? Again, the answers are not easily discovered. He was from a titled Andalusian family, long resident in the Villa of Bailén, whose surname had been made famous back in 1513 by another Ponce de León who discovered and named Florida. In 1580, Pedro Ponce de León accepted an invitation to accompany the count of Coruña to New Spain where he was taking over as viceroy. Two years later the count died in office and, with his patron gone, Ponce returned home. Thus the sum of his New World experience was extremely small, and all of it restricted to the viceregal court. That glaring deficiency in no way dissuaded the Council of the Indies from throwing its firm support to him. Indeed, on the strength of its recommendation,

Philip II on May 8, issued the cédula suspending the contract made earlier with Oñate. That was the decree Don Juan received from the viceroy's messenger the following September.

During the summer of 1596, following the king's instructions, the council negotiated with Ponce for a new set of capitulaciones. Ironically, Oñate's contract, earlier forwarded by Velasco, served as the model, Ponce using it to determine what he ought to offer in the way of men and supplies—and cunningly pledging something more than Oñate had in all categories, from helmets to horseshoes. In total, his expedition promised to be far larger and grander, and as a result he asked for greater concessions, such as a governor's salary of twelve thousand ducats, twice the amount granted Oñate. In September of that year, the king accepted Ponce's terms and declared that he wanted him, "and no other person whosoever [to] undertake the said pacification, settlement, and exploration [of New Mexico]." At that moment, Ponce's victory and Oñate's eclipse seemed complete. So confident was Ponce that he wasted no time in setting plans in motion, sending his brother to Seville to establish a receiving point for men and equipment.

In the succeeding winter months, however, several things occurred. First, Ponce suffered a major illness, and although he recovered, his health remained precarious. His age at this time is not known, but indications are that he was well along in years, something the council had chosen to overlook. Second, Ponce's wealth turned out to be less than represented. The king must have been dismayed to learn that he was trying to mortgage his estate to raise money, and not only that, he had the temerity to ask the royal government for a loan. This news cast serious doubt upon Ponce's capacity to deliver even a portion of what he had promised. Notwithstanding, the Council of the Indies doggedly persisted in arguing his case.

For once Philip rejected its advice. Instead he reviewed Viceroy Monterrey's most recent letters and reports, which had suddenly turned very favorable toward Oñate, and in so doing concluded what should have been obvious long before—that Don Juan was the most qualified and deserving person for the job at hand. In light of that, he flip-flopped once more, ordering the suspension of Ponce's contract and secretly instructing Monterrey to find out whether Oñate's expedition at this late date was still intact and able to proceed. If so, permission to march should be given immediately.

This action abruptly ended Don Pedro Ponce de León's involvement in the whole affair. What brought him into the game in the first place remains a mystery. His manifest lack of experience, physical fitness, and resources for such an enormous task ought to have been readily discernible. The fact that these deficits were papered over at the same time that Oñate's assets were belittled and his character slandered adds weight to a conspiracy theory. It is not beyond possibility that Juan Lomas y Colmenares, acting through his agents, persuaded Ponce to advance his New Mexico proposals as a means to check Oñate, and had this long shot succeeded, he might have continued to use Ponce out front while pulling the strings of the New Mexico expedition in secret.

This is purest conjecture, of course, and must remain so in the absence of documentation. Nonetheless, it is known that Lomas y Colmenares had a nephew in New Spain named Diego Ponce, raising the suspicion that he may have actually been related also to Don Pedro Ponce de León. If there was a family connection, then Ponce de León's effort to supplant Juan de Oñate begins to make sense.

Before matters in Spain were finally resolved in his favor, Oñate went through a time so stressful that it would have crippled a lesser man. From that September day in 1596 when he received notice at the Rio Nazas of his suspension by the king down to his belated leave-taking for New Mexico sixteen months later, he lived under a heavy cloud of anxiety and uncertainty. That he weathered the period of crisis says something about his qualities as a leader and furnishes as well a convenient yardstick for measuring the depth of his character and his capacity for survival.

Still, it is a wonder that he did not quit, withdrawing in disgust after the king suspended him. Can his determination to hang on be traced to plain Basque persistence? A stubborn belief in destiny? The image of his father who pursued the eternal Spanish call of *Plus Ultra*? Blind faith in the rightness of his cause? Or a conviction that the king sooner or later must recognize his merits and the justice of his complaints? Perhaps it was a combination of all of these that led Juan de Oñate to persevere in hopes that simple endurance would be enough to see him over this latest obstacle and get him moving toward New Mexico once more.

As we have seen, when the messenger first brought notice of his suspension, Oñate attempted to conceal the fact from his men. Indeed, he deliberately misled them by saying the king had authorized the expedition's departure. But as Villagrá sagely observed: "There is no secret so well hidden that it is not revealed to someone." And before long, he tells us, "The truth was noised abroad."

One person Don Juan did initially confide in was his strongest financial backer and in-law, Juan Guerra de Resa, who was married to Ana, sister of the Zaldívar brothers. He owned a large estate and productive mines at Aviño, located on the Camino Real, midway between Zacatecas and Santa Bárbara. From the outset, his devotion to Oñate and the project had been unstinting, with the result that Don Juan had named him lieutenant-governor of New Mexico and second in command of the soldiers.

When Guerra de Resa got a look at the king's order, he recognized the gravity of the situation immediately. Appeals would have to be made, all the way to Spain, and while awaiting the outcome, the expedition must be preserved and maintained. To that end, he offered the entire annual income of his properties, amounting to one hundred thousand pesos, for Oñate's use, a magnanimous gesture that Don Juan accepted with profuse declarations of gratitude.

A few days after arrival of the king's decree, Oñate composed a letter of distress to the count of Monterrey. In it he reported that the crown's action had hurt him deeply and he was beside himself with grief. Moreover, the viceroy's threat of harsh penalties should he fail to heed the royal command had offended him greatly, for never before had his obedience or loyalty been in question. "I will carry out faithfully whatever is ordered," he solemnly told the count. And then he added, probably with more hope than conviction: "I am satisfied that His Majesty will not permit me to suffer such a great injustice as I would if the expedition was taken away from me."

After that Oñate got down to cases, explaining his present circumstances and the prospects for the whole enterprise should Pedro Ponce de León actually come from Spain and at this late hour try to fill his shoes. The officers of the expedition were all his relatives who had brought with them their own families and friends. And then the main body of soldiers was made up of men who had fought earlier with Don Juan in the Chichimeca wars and had joined this colonizing effort out of respect for their old commander. "The moment they learn that a change has been made and that the expedition is being taken from me and given to another, not more than twenty persons will remain," Oñate informed the viceroy. "What has most strongly moved these people to accompany me on this journey," he continued, "was my long association and acquaintance with them, which would not be true of a newcomer." There is no reason to doubt the accuracy of this claim because colonial Spaniards of the period bound themselves not to individual projects or expeditions, but to strong leaders. When leaders were removed or failed, they felt no hesitancy, therefore, in dissolving their allegiance to the whole undertaking.

Oñate went out of his way to praise Inspector Lope de Ulloa, saying that without his prudent help the expedition might have fallen apart. Even so, disintegration remained a real possibility because everyone was eating at Don Juan's expense, meat and bread cost dear on the frontier, and supplies were being consumed that had been intended for the march. Furthermore, pasturage around the encampment had grown scarce, and horses and mules were escaping the herders and joining bands of wild mustangs. If departure was delayed through the winter, Oñate advised the viceroy, he likely would run out of money, food, and livestock. Equally troubling, he said, was the loss of prestige and reputation he would suffer as a consequence of the king's order to halt.

Specifically, Oñate asked the count of Monterrey for several things in his letter. First, he wanted permission to move his entire company ahead to Santa Bárbara, a more hospitable and better supplied location. "I promise your lordship on my word as a gentleman that I will not go any farther," he wrote. Second, he requested that Lope de Ulloa be authorized to proceed with his inspection and inventory to demonstrate, as Oñate put it, that he had fulfilled all the obligations under his contract. That should influence the king in his favor, he believed, and the mere conducting of the inspection would persuade his restive followers that progress was still being made toward departure. Third, he had heard that rumors from Spain were already circulating in Mexico City to the effect that Oñate was being replaced. That had caused some two hundred late volunteers, recently recruited in the viceregal capital, to abandon plans to join the expedition on the frontier. Don Juan urged they be arrested as a public demonstration that the count still supported him. And finally and most significantly, he pleaded with the viceroy to intervene on his behalf with the king in an effort to restore to Oñate his rights and titles.

This letter, along with the pressure that Oñate's partisans soon brought to bear, placed the viceroy in something of a quandary. His earlier reservations about Don Juan had long since dissolved, and he plainly saw that a replacement from Spain, whether Pedro Ponce de

León or someone else, would stand little chance of success. In fact, he boldly stated that, in a lengthy report to the king, wherein he also warned that if previous commitments made to Oñate were not honored then others in the future would be unwilling to invest private funds in such expeditions. But while the viceroy was prepared to become an advocate for Oñate's cause, he was quite unable to go against crown orders. He explained that to Don Juan in a new letter that was filled with sympathy and encouragement, and not much else.

Meanwhile, in the north Don Juan with permission of Inspector Ulloa had moved the main part of his force a short distance forward to the mines of Caxco, which they reached on November 1. By now not a person in camp remained unaware of the true state of affairs. In consequence discipline began to erode, and the expedition threatened to crumble. Soldiers who had joined late and had the fewest ties to Oñate deserted, taking with them valuable provisions. Children of the colonists, according to one description, wandered aimlessly "like loose cattle" through the gloomy camp. Even some of the clergy lost heart and spoke of abandonment. At this point, Doña Eufemia, wife of one of the officers, stepped forward and delivered a ringing speech of the kind so often found in the ancient sagas of Iberia.

"For shame!" cried the brave lady. "These are not the actions of Spaniards. Where is your courage?" And she exhorted them to stand fast until such time as the king would allow them to go north to the great river and raise a mighty city that would immortalize their names. It was just the sort of appeal a Spanish soldier admired, one that challenged his manhood and patriotism while reminding him of the national credo, *Plus Ultra*. Although the little episode sounds melodramatic to modern ears, it nevertheless had the effect of slowing down defections.

In the meantime, Oñate's resources continued to drain away. In mid-October, two weeks before the army advanced to Caxco, Captain Gregorio César left camp with a party of men, riding southeast in the direction of Nieves and the hacienda of Juan Lomas y Colmenares. Early in the morning of October 14 he led a raid on one of the estate's outlying settlements, running off a large number of oxen and mules and seizing several people, among them two native women and a boy. Lomas y Colmenares promptly went before the local judge and charged his old rival with theft and kidnapping. In the proceedings that ensued, a witness to the incident stated that he had heard one of Oñate's men say that they had been sent out to search for deserters.

If those were indeed their original orders, then they could have turned to banditry on their own initiative. However, it seems too much of a coincidence that the estate pounced upon by Captain César, and which lay well off the normal route of travel on the Camino Real, should just happen to belong to Don Juan's leading foe, Lomas y Colmenares, the probable cause of his current difficulties.

Lomas y Colmenares, of course, believed that the raid had been instigated by Oñate who, he said condescendingly, was "claiming to be governor of the provinces of New Mexico." It further came out in the judicial record that Lomas y Colmenares had learned from a man in Oñate's camp, perhaps his own spy, that Don Juan wished to ride to Nieves and assassinate him. That particular charge may have been a pure fabrication, but it is indicative of the bitter enmity that existed between the two men. The episode gives plausibility to the thesis that Lomas y Colmenares was actively trying to thwart Oñate, and that Oñate knew it. In the end, the criminal case involving the raid was referred to the Audiencia of Nueva Galicia and then to the viceroy, who simply allowed the matter to die quietly. Still, the ugly incident tainted Don Juan's name, leaving him with the reputation of a marauder.

Oñate lived on the border of despair throughout the winter of 1596–97. One morsel of relief came on December 9, when, after repeated urging, Ulloa finally agreed to conduct the review of troops and inspection of supplies. He emphasized, nevertheless, that his action in no way affected the royal order placing the New Mexico entrada on hold. Since the work of inspecting all the provisions, item by item, dragged on for nearly two months, Don Juan was kept occupied and had his attention diverted from his woes. As the examination approached completion, it became apparent that Oñate showed a surplus in practically every category of supplies to which he was committed by his contract. That in itself offered eloquent testimony to his ability to manage and equip an expedition under the most trying conditions.

As Ulloa was making preparations to muster and count the troops, he received an official dispatch from Mexico City appointing him commander of that year's Pacific fleet, soon to leave for the Philippines. Before starting for the capital and his new assignment, he hurriedly reviewed the main portion of the army at Caxco, but he was unwilling to take time to conduct reviews of detached units located at Santa Bárbara and an encampment called La Puana. That task he left to his assistant Esquivel. Accompanied by Don Juan, Esquivel completed the count, determining that the expedition totaled 205 men, that is 5 more than the minimum required by the contract.

In both soldiers and supplies, Oñate had met his obligations and under ordinary circumstances would have had abundant reason to feel proud and to engage in self-congratulation. But given the suffering inflicted upon him to this point, much of it needless, he felt inclined to do neither. Only at immense cost had he and his backers, most notably Juan Guerra de Resa, been able to fulfill the commitments for provisions, while continuing to feed the idle army, and surely they were aware that sums wasted now through delays were sums that would not be available at a later date to support the newly won colony of New Mexico.

As to the membership of that colony, Oñate lamented bitterly in a letter that at one point it had numbered a thousand volunteers. But owing to his assortment of troubles, culminating with the order of suspension, many of his recruits had melted away, leaving him close to the minimum originally stipulated by the viceroy. He might have viewed that as a culling process in which those who were faint of heart or lacking in dedication were weeded out. However, the losses were so great that the deserters must have included some individuals with talents and skills that would have been highly useful in New Mexico. More than a few of them quit because Oñate's obstacles looked insurmountable. It is not unreasonable to suggest that the prolonged delay in getting the enterprise off the ground was a prime factor in Oñate's later failure in colonization. But the best evidence indicates that even had Don Juan been allowed to start a year or two earlier, before his finances and ranks of soldier-settlers were depleted, success would still have eluded him.

Once the inspection was finished, Oñate rushed word to his brothers Fernándo, Cristóbal, and Luís, who immediately began to lobby at the viceregal court. They argued that Don Juan had fully complied with the terms of his agreement and ought to be allowed to set forth. Yet the count of Monterrey, while favorably disposed to their appeal, was helpless, at least until the next convoy of galleons arrived from Spain bringing new instructions from King Philip. Pending that, he continued to address messages to Oñate brimming with expressions of reassurance. With nothing else to be done, Don Juan waited and waited, watching a bleak winter turn into an equally cheerless spring.

Two incidents during this period illustrate how much Oñate's prestige and authority had slipped. The first involved a band of his soldiers who conspired to break away and strike out for New Mexico as independent adventurers. Since the camp was under strict military regimen, this amounted to a mutiny. When details of the plot reached Oñate's ears, he ordered Vicente de Zaldívar to take swift and forceful action. Without hesitation his nephew seized the ringleader and beheaded him. That effectively cooled the spirit of revolt but created a legacy of resentment that would surface farther up the trail.

The second unnerving episode involved the expedition's squad of missionaries. Unexpectedly, their leader Father Durán served notice that he was withdrawing from the project and returning to Mexico City where he would give his reasons to his superiors in the Franciscan Order. His leave-taking, in the company of several other friars who joined him, reflected badly upon Oñate even though no public criticism of the commander had been voiced. Don Juan could only grind his teeth at this additional setback and hope that replacements might soon be forthcoming. The priests remaining with him included his cousin Father Salazar and the genial and ever-supportive Father Márquez.

Unfortunately, the latter was shortly lost to him as well. In addition to his role as a Franciscan missionary, Márquez had received appointment by the Holy Office of the Inquisition to be its agent, or representative, in New Mexico. Viceroy Monterrey challenged the Holy Office's right to extend its jurisdiction over the new province without his permission, which he was unwilling to give in any case, so Father Márquez was recalled. Captain Villagrá attributed this latest disappointment to "the evil influence of our enemies," who he thought would have been pleased to see Oñate separated from one of his fittest advisers. Indeed, it was a telling blow. When Don Juan realized that he could not prevent Father Márquez from going, he bid him a tearful farewell and presented him with parting gifts, a rosary and a religious statute.

The royal cédula that finally released Oñate from the ban of suspension and authorized him to proceed on his way was issued by the king on April 2, 1597. But owing to the slowness of the mails carried to New Spain by the annual fleet, the order did not reach Mexico City and the hands of the viceroy until well into summer. Monterrey promptly put a courier on the road to bring Oñate the welcome news. At the same time he asked him for an honest assessment of his current situation. Was he fully prepared to carry the project forward, and did he still have the necessary supplies and the requisite number of men under his colors? The viceroy frankly had his doubts that the answers would be in the affirmative. Therefore, he was pleasantly surprised weeks later to receive Don Juan's positive response.

In a report to the king, Monterrey declared: "He [Oñate] replied with much assurance and confidence in his ability to make the expedition at once, and quickly. He spoke with such extreme earnestness that I found myself obliged to send a person there to conduct the review, inspection, and inventory, even though he claimed that he was under no obligation to submit to one for a second time." That reference to a second inspection must have curbed some of the elation Don Juan would have experienced upon learning of his restoration by the king. Nonetheless, given the hurdles he had already cleared, this latest impediment probably seemed no more than a minor annoyance.

As matters developed, it turned out to be a bit more than that. Oñate dutifully assembled his colonists and informed them that another inspector would be sent within two months according to the viceroy. Until then they could only maintain what was by now a well-practiced habit: they must wait. When the inspector failed to arrive at the promised time, the soldiers loudly upbraided their commander and shouted that they had heard enough of his lies. A new wave of desertions speedily followed this outburst.

The inspector at last put in an appearance during the second week of November, an occasion that produced a welcoming salvo of harquebus shots. Oñate went forth to greet him, and the two men embraced in the Spanish style. Then they retired to Don Juan's tent to confer. The new arrival was Juan de Frías Salazar, an aging soldier who had fought with the king's armies in Flanders and afterwards came to New Spain where he made a fortune in mining. Oñate had every reason to expect that Salazar would prove as accommodating as his predecessor, Lope de Ulloa, but unhappily he was in for another jolt.

At their first meeting Salazar displayed his true character. He was arrogant, pompous, willful, and petty, the sort of man to let power go his head and assume dictatorial authority. Brusquely, Salazar informed Don Juan that all of his commands must be executed promptly and without challenge. His initial terse order astonished Oñate. The entire expedition, the inspector declared, must start north at once, and several days up the trail he would halt it at his pleasure and conduct the *visita*.

He said dourly that that was the best way to hold a proper inspection, since only on the march could the men and supplies destined for New Mexico be counted accurately. In Santa Bárbara, where the viceroy had indicated the review ought to take place, Oñate had plenty of opportunity to borrow goods to make up any shortfalls, and then secretly return them after the inspection was done. And similarly, he could draft local residents to pass themselves off as New Mexico–bound colonists to meet his manpower quota, releasing them after completion of the muster. Those temptations, announced Salazar, must be removed. But in the removal lay the implication that Oñate was untrustworthy, ready to commit fraud should the inspector relax his vigilance.

Actually, an immediate departure was not so easily accomplished. Don Juan had anticipated a leisurely inspection in Santa Bárbara. His tons of provisions and equipment were still locked in warehouses where they had been stored for the winter. Wagons and carts, left standing idle for months, needed repairs and their wheels required tightening. And his multitudes of livestock were grazing in distant pastures where it was impossible to collect them on short notice. He explained these problems carefully to Salazar in hopes of getting the order to set forth rescinded. But the inspector remained unmoved: the expedition must leave Santa Bárbara without delay.

While Oñate made an honest effort to comply, an immediate advance was simply beyond the question. In fact almost a month elapsed before the motley train of colonists lumbered into motion and began its ascent of the northern trail. During that time Salazar had fumed and issued repeated orders to march, brushing aside all of Oñate's appeals for consideration. And because it had all started so slowly, his imperious orders to hurry having little effect, he rode beside the cavalcade in a black mood.

Two days out of Santa Bárbara they reached the San Gerónimo River, where Salazar loftily announced that this was to be the inspection site. On December 22, 1597, he administered an oath to Oñate, under the sign of the cross, and commenced a meticulous examination of everything and everybody associated with the entrada. In spite of the magnitude of the task, work progressed so rapidly that it was finished by January 8. But by that date every man of the company cordially detested Juan de Frías Salazar. Inflexible and mercurial, he had found fault with all, from leader to soldier to servant. At one point a young recruit had passed by his tent and inadvertently neglected to doff his cap. Incensed at this slight, the inspector ordered him flogged. Oñate was enraged but helpless, and he angrily warned his men that not a word of protest should be raised, lest Salazar use it against the entire expedition.

In the final count Don Juan came up short in both men and supplies, not unexpectedly perhaps, given the ruinous vexations that had been heaped upon him. In goods he was deficient by 2,300 pesos' worth. The head count showed a total of 129, or 71 soldiers less than the contract required. The viceroy had instructed Salazar to allow Oñate to provide bond that would cover deficiencies. So Don Juan put Captain Villagrá on a fast horse and sent him south to Aviño and the residence of Juan Guerra de Resa with another plea for aid. Wrote the Captain: "No sooner had Juan Guerra and his wife Ana been informed . . . than they cheerfully agreed to sacrifice their entire fortune if need be." On the night of January 21 they signed a formal document bonding themselves to make up the deficits revealed in Salazar's inspection. Once that paper was in hand, Oñate asked permission to continue the journey.

Inspector Salazar, however, had not quite finished turning the screws. Now he forced Don Juan to certify that he would enlist, equip, and pay all expenses for eighty soldiers, a number that was nine more than the actual shortage. These new men could be recruited later and sent on to New Mexico to join the colony. Considering that at one stage of his long preparation Oñate claimed to have had one thousand men, the sparse ranks he turned out for Salazar's final muster demonstrate just how deeply he had been harmed by the protracted delays. In the end, the inspector released the expedition upon condition that should Oñate fail to meet any of his contractual obligations he must forfeit all his rights, privileges, and titles. Villagrá says that with resignation Don Juan turned his eyes toward heaven and agreed to everything. And he adds: "This army once so proud to see, now marched forth, a mere shadow of its former self."

The calendar read January 26, 1598, when Don Juan de Oñate guided his people out of San Gerónimo and pointed the lead wagon toward New Mexico. Inspector Salazar remained in attendance, for he planned to hold a parting ceremony at the Conchos River, which was reached four days later. The colonists were much dismayed to find this stream flowing swift and noisy between wide banks.

Soundings taken from the edge showed such depth that a crossing appeared impossible. Oñate, nevertheless, refused either to halt or to turn back. If the observant Captain Villagrá can be fully credited, Oñate delivered a weighty sermon that included this admonition: "Come, noble soldiers, knights of Christ, here is presented the first opportunity for you to show your mettle and courage to prove that you are deserving of the glories in store for you." It was a typically Spanish call to action, probably a near duplicate of the kind that had been uttered countless times on far-flung Moorish battlefields.

Oñate ordered up one of his stoutest horses, and with hardly a pause he plunged into the foaming torrent on its back. Pushed by the current's rush, man and beast struck for the far shore at a diagonal, finally reaching it in safety. Turning rein, Don Juan once more braved the angry waters and returned to the column, his glistening mount snorting and trembling. Of this display, one of his officers would later say: "How well a good example serves us. It demonstrates how easily we can accomplish those things which we would not dare attempt without being shown." The incident sounds like storybook heroics, the pure invention of a fiction writer, but it truly may have happened just the way it was recorded. At least no substantial reason exists to disbelieve it. Spaniards set great store by individual performance, and Oñate could have concluded that here at the inception of the journey was a good time to show his people he was fit to lead them.

What followed was scarcely less dramatic. Oñate shouted encouragement to his men, then seized a goad and himself prodded the first yoke of oxen into the dangerous stream. Seeing this, every soldier leaped into action, and the air was suddenly filled with cries and the pop of whips. Vehicles rolled down the steep banks and into the swirling river where, according to one witness, "they were tossed about like ships in a heavy sea." Younger men stripped off their clothes and swam out to the struggling oxen to urge them onward. Others, mounted on their swiftest horses, drove the loose stock with shouts and shrill whistles. It was a scene of the wildest confusion, underlain by an element of terror. Yet the whole bawling, seething effort retained direction and purpose because of the forceful presence of the man at its head.

Soon the caravan was across the Conchos with only the sheep in a large flock left behind on the south bank. They were unable to swim because the weight of their wool when soaked with water would pull

them under. Don Juan declared that a special bridge must be built
for the animals. His companions expressed their doubts that the
menacing river could be spanned with a substantial bridge, given
their limited resources. But they had not reckoned with the ingenuity
or determination of their commander. He had the solid, wooden
wheels removed from the carts. These were anchored in pairs to rafts
and strung in line over the water. Upon this foundation, the colonists
working ant-like spread a layer of branches and bark capped by a
surface of earth. Dry-shod the bleating sheep crossed the Conchos
on their way to New Mexico. By nightfall the fording of the river
was done, and the men gratefully took to their beds, aching in every
limb.

At dawn the camp was astir, for this was the day the despised
Inspector Salazar was to turn over the final paper of certification and

Signature and rubric of Don Juan de Oñate. (From an original document, in the Archive of the Indies, Seville, Spain)

make his exit. All assembled for an open-air Mass, then afterward officers of the expedition took their places for what was expected to be a ceremony and speech by the departing official. Instead, Salazar stepped forward and curtly informed Don Juan that the march could proceed. Nothing else: no speech, no certification, no parting well-wishes. Turning on his heel, he signaled his staff members to mount, and they rode out of camp headed south.

Oñate was perplexed beyond measure, and his men were left anxious because they had been denied the last document that would have sealed authorization for the expedition. Such documents meant so much to Spaniards! In an act of frustration, Don Juan summoned thirty horsemen and went to overtake Salazar, hoping perhaps that he might relent. He offered him an escort—his excuse for coming—but the inspector coldly refused it, and Oñate had no choice but to return and tell his people that, for good or ill, they were now on their own. "Hardships and misfortunes are the common lot of brave, adventurous men," he reminded them. "And, who knows but what these present trials and tribulations are sent for the express purpose of preparing us for the glorious future which awaits our expedition?" That was a lame explanation for all the misfortune they had endured at the hands of Salazar, but it was all Don Juan had to offer.

Retiring to his quarters, Oñate sat alone at his camp desk and composed a long and caustic letter to the viceroy summarizing the affronts and obstructions he had experienced over the past two years and pointing out how they had sapped his resources and diffused his energies. There was nothing that he poured onto paper that the count of Monterrey had not heard before, but still he wrote on, the scratch of his quill audible to any soldier who chanced to pass his tent. Now that Salazar was out of the way and at long last the northern trail opened wide before him, he deposited his accumulated frustrations in this letter. It was an act of unburdening, a purging of dark emotions that served to cleanse his thoughts, refresh his spirit, and put him in the confident frame of mind he would need to confront the physical challenges of days to come. When Juan de Oñate folded and sealed the stiff writing sheets, it is a fair assumption that he realized he was closing a disagreeable chapter in his life and opening what he earnestly hoped would be a far more promising one.

CHAPTER 6

The Trail

FROM the camp north of the Río Conchos, a newly inspirited Juan de Oñate guided his followers onward thirty miles to the San Pedro River, whose crystalline waters flashed in the winter sun. Here he called a halt once more to take care of two remaining pieces of business. The first involved a new band of Franciscan missionaries, sent as replacements for those who had earlier abandoned the expedition. Don Juan received word that they were making their way up the Camino Real, but at the same time he learned that Tepehuan Indians had gone to war along the road and he feared for the safety of the clergymen. To escort them through the danger zone and guide them to the new encampment on the San Pedro, Oñate dispatched a troop under Captain Marcos Farfán de los Godos. This forty-year-old native of Seville was a seasoned campaigner who would return, more than three weeks later, with the missionaries securely in tow.

The enforced intermission allowed Oñate to address the second item of business on his agenda, the sending ahead of a scouting party to blaze a new trail due northward through two hundred miles of Chihuahuan desert. The Rodríguez-Chamuscado and Espejo expeditions of the previous decade had avoided that forbidding obstacle by skirting it on the east, that is, descending the Conchos to its junction with the Rio Grande and then climbing the curve of the great river into New Mexico. But that was too far out of the way, Oñate reckoned. He wanted a shorter, more direct route. Besides, word had it that the Indians dwelling along the lower Conchos had grown hostile of late, probably as a result of one too many slaving expeditions raiding their villages. Therefore, as Oñate saw it, the desert was the way to go.

Now, he called upon the younger of the Zaldívar brothers, Vicente, to assume charge of a sixteen-man detachment that would search out a trail suitable for wagons and one offering some promise of water.

The youthful Vicente—he was in his twenty-fifth year—had been born and raised in Zacatecas where the frontier environment had conditioned him for precisely the kind of job his Uncle Juan now asked him to perform. Taking three guides who professed to have knowledge of the country, Sargento Mayor Vicente de Zaldívar and his party galloped out of camp and soon disappeared into the wide and empty land.

Finding a trail proved far more difficult than either he or Oñate could have imagined. The party chose to follow a broad desert plain that trended south to north and was marked at its distant edges by hazy mountain ranges. In this flat country, the guides quickly proved their incompetence and became hopelessly lost. Disoriented, the Spaniards wandered in circles for days, three of which were passed without finding water. Some of the men suggested turning back, but Zaldívar reproached them and pushed on. Finally, columns of smoke appeared on the horizon and a scout sent forward reported the presence of Indians.

The advancing soldiers managed to seize four native men, who were promised their liberty if they would guide the Spaniards to the Rio Grande. When the march resumed, it was toward the northeast because Zaldívar understood from his new Indian guides that in that direction lay the shortest trail to the river. Again, the party experienced severe water shortages and now hunger, since supplies had been exhausted. At one point the Sargento Mayor divided his party, sending half of the men back to Oñate while warning them not to speak to the colonists of the hardships they had endured. Zaldívar pressed on, reaching the river on February 28. After a brief rest, he turned back to bring his report to Don Juan.

In the meanwhile, Oñate had grown anxious because of the extended absence of his nephew, so he sent out a relief squad whose number included the redoubtable Captain Villagrá. According to that officer's statement, they encountered young Zaldívar after a ride of ten days, and he and his companions were in dire straits. They had been without water for some time and one of the men, Juan Rodríguez, was folded over the back of a horse, more dead than alive. Commented Villagrá, "We gave the party all the assistance we could, and, in truth, it was very badly needed." Then the rescuers, following Zaldívar's suggestion, made a rapid scout toward the mountains. The broken country at their base, they perceived, was more difficult to travel than the open plains explored by the Sargento Mayor, but that was offset by an abundance of pasturage and springs. The officers, therefore, decided to urge Don Juan to take this higher route.

Back at the San Pedro River, Oñate welcomed on March 3 the return of Captain Farfán, escorting the new contingent of friars. He saw them coming in the distance and hastily formed his army into six columns that marched forth briskly to extend a ceremonial greeting. Fray Alonso Martínez presented himself as the head, or commissary, of this band of ten Franciscan priests and lay brothers. Oñate conducted the new arrivals to a leafy bower raised near the river and in its shade seated them at a sumptuous banquet. That finished, the robed missionaries retired to tents to rest from their journey and to prepare for what lay ahead. For the first time, Oñate had all the manpower of the expedition under his direct control.

A week later, on March 10, Vicente de Zaldívar and party reappeared and delivered a full account of their experiences. So impatient was Oñate to be under way that he ordered an immediate departure. Within minutes, men were striking the tents, driving in the livestock, and unfurling the banners. After a wait of two and a half years, Juan de Oñate was of no mind to delay an hour longer. Just beyond sprawled his unformed kingdom of New Mexico. Although by now his head was gray and his beard threaded with silver, in his eagerness to go he must have resembled more an expectant schoolboy.

When Coronado had taken his leave for New Mexico exactly fifty-eight years before, Viceroy Mendoza and a host of other luminaries, like Cristóbal de Oñate, had traveled to the launching town of Compostela, lending their presence to the pageantry. But now on the lonely banks of the San Pedro not a single well-wisher, of either high or low degree, was on hand to bid Don Juan and his army farewell. So, without benefit of fanfare, the New Mexico caravan surged and heaved into motion, and that was that.

The column, when completely lined out, stretched more than two miles, its length studded with fluttering pennants and spiked with polearms, such as lances, hatchet-like halberds, and wicked half-moon blades, or *media lunas*. In the vanguard, like a pair of colorful sails, rose the crimson and gold standard of the king and the richly ornamented standard of Oñate, the one given him seemingly so long ago by Viceroy Velasco. From a distance, the train must have resembled a giant caterpillar crawling slowly under its canopy of dust.

Upon closer examination, separate elements could be distinguished: eighty wagons and ox carts rumbling on their heavy wheels,

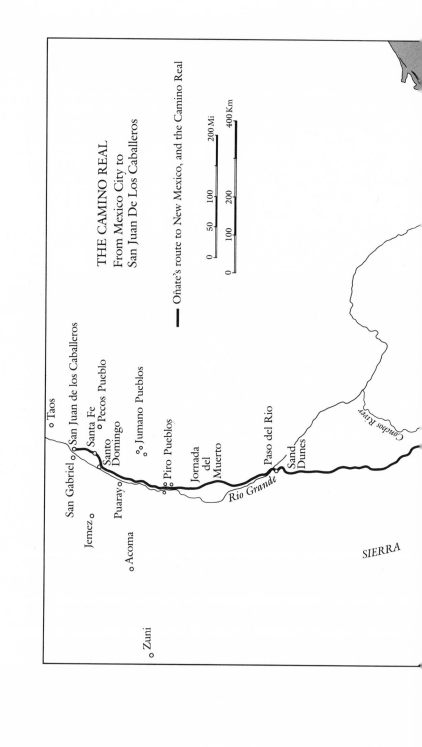

THE CAMINO REAL
From Mexico City to
San Juan De Los Caballeros

—— Oñate's route to New Mexico, and the Camino Real

0   50   100   200 Mi

0   100   200   400 Km

Taos

San Juan de los Caballeros

San Gabriel

Santa Fe

Pecos Pueblo

Santo
Domingo

Jemez

Puaray

Jumano Pueblos

Acoma

Piro Pueblos

Jornada
del
Muerto

Paso del Rio

Sand
Dunes

Rio Grande

Conchos River

Zuni

SIERRA

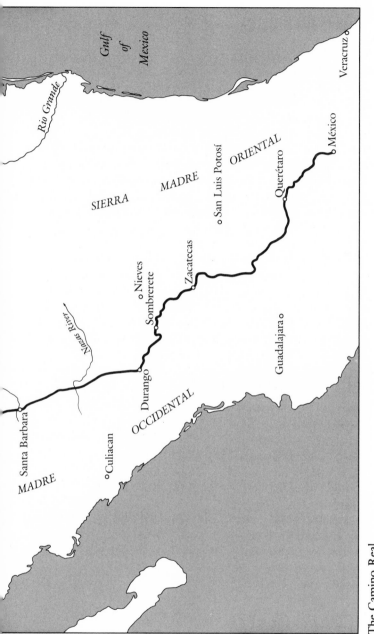

The Camino Real

the loads covered with stout white canvas. Two luxury coaches drawn by mules and owned by Juan de Oñate. Three small pieces of artillery (no mention of gun carriages, so they were probably transported on muleback). Seven thousand head of livestock—beef cattle, spare oxen, horses, pack mules, donkeys, sheep, and goats. And finally, the people—Oñate's colonists.

The best estimates put their number somewhere above 500 for the total, but we have no way of knowing with certainty since Inspector Salazar in the muster roll made earlier at the Conchos saw fit to list only the men of fighting age, 129 of them by his count. Even that figure, however, cannot be considered accurate. On arriving back in Mexico City, he told the viceroy he believed some soldiers had not appeared before him for formal enrollment and inspection because they were guilty of offenses and would have faced rejection. He was certain, Salazar explained, that the majority of such individuals had ridden on and would quietly rejoin the expedition along its way. But exactly how many men he was talking about, he could not say.

The ages of Oñate's warriors ranged from the mid-teens into the sixties with a preponderance in the twenties. Pioneering in colonial New Spain was decidedly a young man's activity. The sixty-year-old officer Pedro Robledo, gone entirely gray, was a conspicuous exception. When the frailties of age prevented him from carrying his own weight on the march, he had four stalwart, red-headed sons, the eldest twenty-seven and the youngest eighteen, who amply compensated.

Nearly all of the adult males in the expedition wore facial hair, their chin-beards either trimmed to a point or cropped straight across to form a wide brush. A number showed battle scars on their faces or had cheeks pitted by smallpox. None, so far as can be told, appeared overfed. The impression given by Salazar's scanty physical description of each man entered in the muster roll is of an army honed and fit. The profusion of armor and weapons, meticulously itemized by the inspector, heightens the image of men who were vigorous and battle-ready.

While use of armor was on the wane in Europe by this date, it remained in vogue among colonial soldiers who appreciated the protection it afforded them in Indian warfare. Juan de Oñate and his officers bore a surprising amount of full armor plate and partial body armor to New Mexico, including helmets in various styles, beavers (a plate guarding the face and throat), cuirasses to protect the upper body, steel gauntlets for the arms, and cuisses and greaves for the legs. Quite a few of the stallions—for that is what Spaniards habitually rode—were also clad in partial or full armor. For weapons, the men in the main carried harquebuses, a term that could apply to firearms generally, but commonly specified a heavy matchlock whose barrel had to be supported by an iron fork rest. Pole arms, swords, and daggers completed the inventory of personal armaments. All in all the men who followed Oñate up the northern trail had very much a medieval look about them.

The wives, children, and other relations of the soldiers comprised a significant, if uncertain, number of the expedition's colonists. The *alférez* (or ensign) Juan Pérez de Bustillo was accompanied by his wife, seven daughters, and two grown sons, for example—none of the females being identified by name. The women were generally ignored throughout, so we have very little notion of the role they played in the caravan or later in the settling of the new land. Their story, however fascinating it may have been, seems irretrievably lost to the historian. And the same is true for the army of hirelings who went in support of the Oñate expedition—the herders, drivers, packers, and personal servants whose ranks were made up of assorted shades of mestizos, mulattos, and Indians, plus even a few Chichimeca slaves held by Don Juan.

Not in question is the fact that this great concourse of people— half a thousand of them—offers a vivid contrast to the English colonists who made their first settlement at Jamestown, Virginia, just nine years later. The Englishmen, who of course came by ship rather than ox cart, totaled only 104 upon landing, and they had no women with them. In thinking, in temperament, in religion, and in attitudes toward government, they differed markedly from Oñate and his settlers struggling amid the desert two thousand miles toward the southwest. But we can guess that in time the two groups came to share at least a common appreciation for the privations and grief associated with carving homes out of the raw wilderness. In that sense, all European colonists were brothers in misery.

At the time Oñate set off on this last leg of his journey to New Mexico, March 10, 1598, the country remained largely a dismal winter brown: last season's dried grass, bare patches of sandy soil, the flat silhouettes of far-off mountains—all brown. Now the Spaniards were moving through what is today northern Chihuahua, a sprawling, arid landscape bathed in brilliant sunlight and with horizons that seemed always to be backing away from the traveler. To discover the infrequent waterholes and springs, Don Juan angled toward the higher ground, passing a succession of sierras, one of which he named Oñate.

Ten days of steady travel brought the column to a small stream course, which they named the Rio Sacramento because it was encountered on Holy Thursday, the feast of the Blessed Sacrament. To celebrate the sacred day, Don Juan ordered a halt and the construction of a temporary chapel. There at eveningtide the priests, officers, and men assembled to pray on their knees, weep for their sins, and beg forgiveness of the Almighty. Villagrá maintains that the prayers were directed to "He who led the children of Israel through the trackless deserts," and that He was asked to lead the colonists "through the parched plains over which they wandered." His allusion to the biblical exodus from Egypt was not inappropriate, for the Spaniards, like the ancient Israelites, were bound for a Promised Land, which if not across the River Jordan did at least require the crossing of another fabled river, the Rio Grande.

Later, the women and children came barefoot to join the men at the shrine and pass the night in prayer and penance. Soon the soldiers began to whip their backs with scourges "until the camp ran crimson with their blood," or so claims our chronicler. Penitential discipline, self-administered in atonement for sin, was a common practice among the Spanish faithful during Holy Week. Even Juan de Oñate left the chanting crowd in the chapel and went to a secluded spot where he lashed his back unmercifully, opening many wounds. The simultaneous spilling of tears and blood evoked a profound religious emotion in these God-fearing Spaniards.

One other incident of note that occurred in negotiating the Chihuahuan desert reveals the nature of their faith. Beyond the Sacramento, water grew scarcer, and Don Juan again sent Vicente de Zaldívar ranging ahead with seven companions to pick the best route for the expedition. Although they located some springs, still several of the marches were long and waterless. After a particularly dry and grueling stretch of trail, on April 1, Don Juan made this recording in the official log: "God succored us with a downpour so heavy that very large pools were formed. Then we unyoked the cattle . . . and [they] drank. Therefore we named this place Socorro del Cielo [Aid from Heaven]." For ordinary troubles, the Spaniards willingly relied on their own powers of endurance and strength of will, but in real emergencies, they were quick to seek divine assistance.

A week after the rain from heaven, Oñate and his followers reached the edge of Los Médanos, a Sahara-like expanse of sand dunes extending toward the Rio Grande. Today the main asphalt highway from El Paso and Ciudad Juárez leading south toward Chihuahua City cuts through the heart of these dunes, which although bleak in appearance present no particular obstacle to motorists. In the sixteenth century, however, the sand posed a severe hindrance to weighty carts and wagons drawn by oxen. By following Zaldívar's tracks, which pointed off to the northeast, Don Juan was able to skirt the worst of the dunes for several days. But then, on April 19, he arrived at a point where they could no longer be avoided.

Dividing the train, he ordered draft animals from wagons in the rear brought up and double-hitched to the vehicles in front. With the extra motive power, Oñate guided half of his fractured caravan into the loose, yellow sands that sprawled in a wide arc before him. A day later he brought his colonists safely through to the Rio Grande, joining it at a point about twenty-five miles below the future city of El Paso. Zaldívar and his men were awaiting them, having arrived earlier and in desperate need of water. Indeed, two of their thirst-crazed horses had plunged into the river and drunk until their sides burst. After allowing his oxen to recuperate, Don Juan sent them back with some of his officers to the stranded half of the train so that it too could be dragged forward through the dunes.

Shortly, the entire expedition was reunited, and Oñate, seeing the fatigue etched in the faces of the people and the gauntness of the livestock, proclaimed a week's rest there on the south bank of the river. The campsite was a congenial and restful one. Dense willow thickets grew at water's edge and were interspersed with stately cottonwoods that cast a welcome shade, now that the weather was turning warm. The abundance of wood allowed large bonfires to be kindled at night, and around them the entire colony gathered to hear Vicente de Zaldívar recount his recent adventures in the scouting of the desert and to listen to their commander Don Juan praise their zeal and stamina during the rough experiences of the days just past.

Food was suddenly plentiful and fresh, for men cast hook and line into the waters and pulled in abundant fish, and hunters crept forth and bagged braces of ducks and geese. So the Spaniards took their ease, the horses and cattle grazed contentedly in the grassy bottoms, and Oñate drew a breath of relief, knowing that the journey's first trials had been met and overcome. Remembering this brief and pleasant interlude long afterward, one of the men would write: "It seemed these were the Elysian fields of happiness where we could forget our misfortunes . . . and enjoy those comforts so long denied us."

In the last days of April, the expedition began moving at a leisurely pace toward the upper end of the narrow valley. Oñate was looking for a convenient ford and, selecting half a dozen men from the ranks who were excellent swimmers, he sent them at various points plunging into the murky, slow-moving current to test for a shallow bottom. About April 30 they reported the discovery of a suitable crossing up ahead. Thereupon, Don Juan called another halt and proclaimed that the day had arrived for conducting a formal ceremony to take possession of the new land and government. Now at the threshold of New Mexico, custom and law required that the occasion be marked by proper ritual, both secular and religious.

To accommodate the latter, Oñate directed the construction of a spacious bower to serve as a chapel. Here, with all in attendance, the Franciscans celebrated a solemn high Mass, and Father Martínez delivered a lengthy sermon. Later in the morning the entire company adjourned to a natural park in a grove of giant trees where Don Juan, assisted by the royal notary Juan Pérez de Donís, read in a firm voice the official act of possession. It was a long-winded document that, among other things, asserted Philip II's claim to New Mexico; summarized Oñate's assorted rights, privileges, and titles; and finally called attention to the numerous benefits that would accrue to the Almighty and His church as a result of the forthcoming settlement.

The army was drawn up in formation on horseback, each man having polished and donned his armor for the ceremonies. As soon as their commander and governor finished speaking, they fired shots in the air while trumpets blew and families and servants shouted in a demonstration of approval. Oñate with a great flourish signed and sealed the official act at the same time the royal ensign lifted Philip's regal banner and waved it aloft. With that, the kingdom of New Mexico came into being, at midday on April 30, 1598. It may well have been Don Juan de Oñate's proudest moment.

The afternoon was given over to celebrating, "with great joy and mirth," as one participant described it. The landmark day closed with enactment of an original drama written by Captain Farfán de los Godos, he who had escorted the Franciscans through Indian country to join the army at the San Pedro River. No written copy of this play survives, at least none has been found, but we know something of its theme from reference by the chroniclers. Not surprisingly, center stage went to the missionaries who were shown entering the Pueblo field, to be kindly received by actors portraying humble Indians. The natives approached on bended knee, asked to be received into the faith, and were promptly baptized in large numbers. Quite possibly that represented a mental projection of the Spaniards: what they hoped and fully expected to occur once they were firmly ensconced in their New Mexican kingdom.

Early next morning, Oñate got his expedition rolling again, slowly up the valley toward the ford located by the swimmers. He soon began to meet bands of shy and amiable Indians, dwelling along this section of the river. To the delight of his whole party, they attempted to make the sign of the cross by raising their thumbs. These Indians cut their hair and plastered it to the skull with blood or red paint in such a way as to remind the Spaniards of Milan caps. They greeted the newcomers with the words *manxo, manxo,* which, as Oñate explains, meant "peaceful ones" in their language. As that sounded very close to the Spanish term *manso,* signifying "mild" or "meek," they were promptly dubbed Manso Indians, and by that name they remained known to history.

On May 4, Oñate encamped at what he called "the pass of the river and the ford." He was now in the extreme upper end of the valley, just above the downtown area of the modern El Paso. The Rio Grande, flowing from the north, cut through a narrow wall of mountains here to form its pass and then turned in a southeasterly direction through the pleasant valley that the Spaniards had been ascending the previous week. In this vicinity lay the river crossing, marked by a heavily used Indian trail. Oñate commented that the trail offered the only acceptable passage northward for his carts for many leagues in either direction. Assisted by some forty of the friendly Mansos, the Spaniards got themselves across the ford and began climbing the east side of the Rio Grande into their new and luminous Canaan.

Almost at once they beheld evidence that others of their countrymen had used this same trail before them. Deeply scored in the sandy soil were Gaspar Castaño de Sosa's wheel tracks, left seven years earlier when he and the members of his illegal colony were taken out of New Mexico, following their arrest by Viceroy Luís de Velasco's soldiers. In fact, one of Oñate's own officers, Captain Juan de Vitoria, had participated in that ill-starred entrada and he was able to confirm that the ruts seen now were those of Castaño de Sosa's ten carts. Although no mention of it appears in the surviving record, we ought to assume that the captain, owing to his previous experience in this country, frequently consulted with Oñate and furnished valuable information on both geography and the native people.

Day by day the caravan crawled onward, its progress impeded by the usual mishaps and small tragedies commonly associated with trail life: carts broke down, oxen wandered away from an overnight grazing ground, two horses drowned in the river, and an unnamed child died. At this stage, the expedition was moving up the long trough of the Mesilla Valley whose eastern perimeter was steeply walled by the fluted ramparts of the Organ Mountains. It perhaps occurred to some of the onlookers that from this distance the granite formations bore a striking resemblance to the bastions and towers lining the walls of the medieval Spanish city of Avila.

Don Juan summoned another of his captains on May 12, Pablo de Aguilar, who had been scouting for him since they first touched the Rio Grande. A Spanish-born officer in his middle thirties, Aguilar now received instructions to explore the road up ahead, advancing as far as the first Indian pueblo, or village, in central New Mexico. He was to spy it out, Oñate carefully informed him, neither entering it nor even letting his presence be known. So crucial was the matter of secrecy that Oñate freely stated he would impose a penalty of death for violation of his orders. He had a fear, and a legitimate one, that the Indians upon learning of the Spanish presence might flee to the mountains and take their foodstuffs with them. And his own dwindling supply of provisions required that he purchase grain from the Pueblo people as quickly as possible.

Eight days later as the train neared the head of the valley, Captain Aguilar returned from his errand. Don Juan listened in dismay and then in cold fury as he learned that the reconnoitering party, in complete disregard of orders, had approached the first pueblo and entered it. So angered was he that he determined to have Aguilar executed by strangulation for gross disobedience. He came very near to carrying out the sentence, too, but at the last moment the men intervened, pleading for leniency. In consequence, the insubordinate officer was given his life and a stern rebuke by the captain-general. Oñate retired to his tent that night, exceedingly troubled and apprehensive.

Unhappily, the dawning of the next day produced a still more solemn distraction. Pedro Robledo, one of the senior figures in the colony, died. The official log notes only that he succumbed and was buried on the twenty-first, the day of the Most Holy Sacrament. Cause of death is left unmentioned, but we can readily conclude that the hardships endured on the march thus far were a contributing factor. The sudden loss must have weighted heavily upon his four sons and cast a pall of gloom over the entire company. To the end of the colonial period, Spaniards would refer to this place as the *Paraje de Robledo,* the Robledo Campsite. And a solitary eminence, bleak and darkly gray, that looks down on the spot from the west side of the Rio Grande is known to this day as Robledo Mountain.

Given that the Pueblos now had warning of his entrance, Oñate resolved to leave the slow-moving caravan and hurry forward with an escort of about sixty persons. His intention was to calm the fears of the Indians, acquire grain, and then go on to find an appropriate site for his first settlement. With him went the Zaldívars, the head Franciscan Fray Alonso Martínez, Oñate's cousin Fray Cristóbal de Salazar, soldiers (including the Robledo brothers), a few of their wives, and probably his eight-year-old son Cristóbal, who had his own set of armor and weapons. Don Juan left the main expedition in charge of Francisco de Sosa Peñalosa, the man granted the office of interim lieutenant-governor after Juan Guerra de Resa, who held it first, had been obliged to stay behind.

The parting of the governor from his wagon and cart train occurred on the morning after the funeral of Pedro Robledo. A short distance beyond that last camp, the Rio Grande began angling toward the left, marking the start of a broad, flat U-shaped bend to the west. Continuing to follow the river on that out-of-the-way course was impractical, not only because it added extra leagues of travel, but also because the country became broken and difficult to traverse.

Therefore, Oñate and his mounted party abandoned the Rio Grande at the onset of its curve and struck out across an elongated and level plain that stretched due north ninety miles where it rejoined the river at completion of its westward arc. This plain, seared and gravelly, was later named the *Jornada del Muerto,* that is to say, Dead Man's March, because the scarcity of water could prove fatal to the unprepared. The weather held fair but hot. Overhead the sky shimmered like a bowl of molten brass, the cracked earth seemed to smoke, and Oñate lamented, "We all fared badly from thirst."

Several times at camp he was forced to send a detail of his weary men on an hours-long side trip, driving the loose horses into the closest mountain range in search of water. Once a pet dog wandered away from the party and later returned with muddy paws. Captain Villagrá and Father Salazar did some skillful backtracking and found two small but welcome waterholes. Another day some deep grinding stones, used by wandering Indians to crush wild seeds, yielded a few cupfuls of stagnant rainwater. It was also on this crossing of the Jornada that Father Martínez was stricken by a severe attack of gout.

On the fifth day Don Juan led his followers out of the dry plain and brought them once more to the Rio Grande, which now obligingly resumed its northward direction. A restful overnight stay at riverside allowed man and beast to recuperate. At sunup the priests said Mass and gave communion, as the record said, in hopes of improving their luck when later that day they encountered the first Pueblos. Oñate set an unhurried pace, partly because the wheels of several supply carts he had brought along dug into the valley's loose sand halfway to their hubs, but also because Father Martínez's gouty condition had worsened and he traveled in great pain. Therefore, it took most of the day to advance four leagues to where camp was made on the Rio Grande's east bank, directly opposite Qualacu, southernmost of the Piro-speaking Pueblo settlements. Oñate had reached central New Mexico and the portal to a vast territory inhabited by sedentary agriculturalists whom he intended to make coparticipants in his freshly minted kingdom.

The Piros of Qualacu, however, were not certain they wanted anything to do with these bearded newcomers bristling with weapons. The entire population abandoned the pueblo, withdrawing a short distance and appearing to the Spaniards to be highly agitated and suspicious. To calm and reassure them, Don Juan sent gifts of trinkets and that, together with the thoroughly domestic and unhostile picture of his people setting up tents, had the desired effect. The Indians returned to their village and commenced the process of adjusting to life alongside the new occupiers of their land.

The pause at Qualacu turned into a stay of many days. The state of Father Martínez's health made it impossible for him to continue, and in addition Oñate had received word by courier of troubles plaguing the main wagon train that was creeping at snail's pace up the Jornada. The water shortage and dissension among the officers lay at the source of the problems and nothing would do but that Don

Juan return and handle things. Taking a skeleton bodyguard and probably some of the corn his supply-master Diego de Zubía had acquired from the Piros, he hastened back down the trail in the last days of May to rejoin his caravan.

Lieutenant-governor Sosa Peñalosa, he soon discovered, had been unable to keep his prideful, self-assertive, and uncooperative hidalgos-to-be under control. A truism that had emerged during the early years of conquest in the New World plainly still applied: individualistic Spaniards could only be held together by a strong and confident leader, one who knew how to speak with a firm voice and impose discipline. But any slight faltering or misstep and the leader's authority might crumble beyond repair. We don't know specifically what the governor did to put matters right, for the documents state only that "he smoothed everything by his tact." It is not unwarranted to say, nevertheless, that this seemingly inconsequential episode foreshadowed later developments, when disruptive and even disloyal factions within Oñate's colonization household would cause him profound grief.

By the twelfth of June, Don Juan, now apparently satisfied that Sosa Peñalosa could manage the wagons, arrived back at Qualacu bringing extra provisions with him. Two days later, he gave the signal to march, for Martínez was vastly improved, and he himself was impatient to make up for lost time and reach the upper river. As the Spaniards forged their way up the valley at a brisk clip, the landscape took on a depth, a clarity, and a patina of colors not evident earlier in Nueva Vizcaya. The air had grown clearer as they gained in altitude. The folded mountain ranges, east and west of the Rio Grande, looked as if they had been created from an artist's palette, their sides mottled in every shade of purple and blue. Small cotton puffs of cloud drifted across a cobalt sky and at night a starry roof arched overhead. Don Juan may well have smiled in satisfaction, with the growing realization that this New Mexico was after all a place of splendid beauty.

One afternoon lightning flared in the distance. Low thunder rumbled along the horizon. And within minutes heavy black clouds overtook the party. In eloquent terms, Villagrá recalled what happened: "The elements clashed in terrible combat . . . [as] the entire earth shook and trembled [beneath] a veritable downpour of rain, accompanied by such mighty claps of thunder that we were terrified." Spaniards frightened by weather? It must have been a raging tempest, indeed. In its midst, the priests appealed to heaven, chanting litanies and prayers, and sure enough, if Villagrá's word can be believed, "God took compassion on us, . . . for the skies emptied as suddenly as they had become clouded and the sun shone forth bright and clear." After the storm, the clean, ozone-scented air proved downright exhilarating and helped restore spirits.

As Oñate progressed on his way, he was disturbed to find one Piro pueblo after another deserted and the storerooms stripped bare of grain. Then he came to a large village looming across the river whose inhabitants did not flee but instead crowded the flat rooftops to stare at the strangers on horseback. Their leader, or *cacique,* came forward boldly and made Oñate and his men understand that his name was Letoc and he wished to be friends. He furnished proof of his good intentions by offering them a huge gift of corn, and in gratitude Oñate called the pueblo Socorro (meaning Assistance), a name retained by a modern New Mexico town on the site. Of almost equal importance, Letoc through elaborate signs informed his visitors about the country and the people that lay ahead. Afterward, the Spaniards' experience confirmed the accuracy of what he had told them.

Above Socorro, they came to a small pueblo, which they named Nueva Sevilla, New Seville, because its location reminded them of that city in Spain. Here Oñate tarried a week awaiting return of his two nephews who had been sent eastward through a pass called Abó to examine a cluster of pueblos said to exist on the edge of a great plain. For the first time he and his soldiers forsook their tents, lodging themselves in the kivas (or religious chambers) and in the tiny, dark rooms of Nueva Sevilla. The reason given in the official log was that the Spaniards decided the pueblo would afford protection "in case of attack by Indians of the country." Plainly, they were uneasy, seeing themselves so few and the surrounding native people so numerous.

Upon return of the Zaldívars, Don Juan pushed on another fourteen miles to a pueblo he titled San Juan Bautista, because he halted there on June 24 to celebrate the feast of Saint John the Baptist, from whom he took his Christian name. We deduce that the men were again quartered in kivas, for they spoke of seeing wall murals of "the demons they worship as gods." To mark the day, the Spaniards staged a sham battle, an exercise that allowed them to display their proficiency in arms. Numerous Indians from other pueblos came to witness the spectacle and must have been duly impressed.

One native man approached Oñate and his companions at the end of the celebration and astounded them by uttering the Spanish words for "Thursday, Friday, Saturday, and Sunday." The only other intelligible thing he could say was "Tomás and Cristóbal," which the Spaniards thought must be the names of Mexican Indian servants, left by some earlier expedition, who were now living in a pueblo farther along. Don Juan regarded that as a promising bit of news. Thus far he had been severely hampered by his inability to speak with the Pueblo people. The mysterious Tomás and Cristóbal, assuming they could be located, might have potential as interpreters.

From San Juan Bautista, Oñate pressed forward at an accelerated pace, passing dozens of the blocky Indian apartment buildings, varying in height from two to six stories, and scores of bright green fields. Seldom did he see a resident or a farmer since all had fled in fear. That development was more than just exasperating. It was positively dangerous. The main caravan, when it reached this stretch of the river, would need safe passage, and that required the goodwill of the inhabitants. And it would be on the lookout to buy corn, and that presupposed that the native sellers had not decamped with their stores. At this stage, Don Juan's company was threading its way through the thickly settled province of the Tiwa-speaking Pueblos, which extended through the valley above and below the site used by a later governor to establish the Spanish municipality of Albuquerque. It was, in fact, a district that had been devastated by the Coronado expedition almost sixty years before, the recollection of that calamity perhaps explaining the scarcity of faces now.

At the large pueblo called Puaray near today's Bernalillo, the Spaniards finally found somebody at home. The Indians greeted them enthusiastically and ushered the priests into a chamber whose walls had been newly whitewashed and were still wet. The next day, however, when the whitewash had dried, the clerics observed the shadow of paintings underneath that turned their blood cold. They depicted the martyrdom of their fellow Franciscans, Agustín Rodríguez and Francisco López, who had been stoned to death at this very village back in 1582. Wisely, it would appear, Oñate admonished his angry followers to keep silent about their grisly discovery, and with considerable celerity they departed the gloomy tenements of Puaray.

Proceeding upriver, Don Juan reached another populous and still-occupied pueblo, Santo Domingo, which he approached in the dark hours before dawn. Reports indicated that the Christian Indians from New Spain, Tomás and Cristóbal, dwelled here, and he intended to make a lightning entry into the village to prevent their flight. Members of his bodyguard, searching the pueblo, found them in bed still asleep. Brought before Oñate, the pair spoke in good Spanish, saying that they had come with Castaño de Sosa, remained behind by choice, and were now married in the pueblo and contented with their life there. Villagrá judged their seizure as an extraordinary piece of good fortune, because thereafter the governor could communicate with the natives of this land, since Tomás and Cristóbal were conversant in their languages.

Santo Domingo proved a significant stop for another reason. Oñate determined to hold a ceremony bringing the central section of New Mexico under his authority. A call went out, therefore, to native leaders living in the four directions, summoning them to a grand council. Whether through a healthy respect for Spanish commands or out of simple curiosity, they responded, crowding into Santo Domingo's huge central kiva on July 7. With Tomás and Cristóbal acting as interpreters, Don Juan explained that the reason for his coming was the salvation of their souls, and that it was the wish of King Philip of Spain and the Holy Father at Rome that they become good Christians and go to heaven to enjoy eternal bliss.

It is difficult to know what the Pueblo elders made of these and similar remarks, but when Oñate demanded that they kneel, kiss the hand of Father Martínez, and render obedience and vassalage to himself and Philip II, they did so willingly and of one accord. All of this was faithfully recorded by the secretary and royal notary, Juan Pérez de Donís, who with much expenditure of precious paper drew up sworn statements and certified, endorsed, and stamped with the great seal of the governor's office the required documentation. How the Indian leaders described the proceedings to their people upon returning home must be left to the imagination.

In all, the Spaniards spent six days at Santo Domingo. While there, Oñate grew concerned about the progress of his wagon train, which in the absence of recent news he supposed was somewhere in the Piro country. It had been moving without his direction for more than a month, and so he detached some of his men under Juan de Zaldívar with instructions to descend the trail and guide the colonists forward to the valley of San Juan, the expedition's ultimate destination, located about thirty-five miles upriver from Santo Domingo.

How Oñate settled upon that particular valley as the site for his first settlement and the capital of his kingdom is not altogether clear. Fray Gerónimo de Zárate Salmerón, who served in New Mexico twenty years later, claims that since Don Juan was intent upon making expeditions and exploring the land, he could not have found a more convenient situation than this place (the valley of San Juan) "because of its being in the center of the realm." While strategic placement may have been a consideration, other factors must have entered into Oñate's decision. For example, he knew from the experience of earlier expeditions that many of the Pueblos, particularly the Tiwas in the area of Puaray, had learned to shun the Spaniards. By contrast, the Tewas who held the valley of San Juan and surrounding country (that is, the region north of Santa Fe), having had less contact with Europeans, remained relatively friendly and receptive.

Furthermore, Castaño de Sosa had observed that the Tewas produced large crop surpluses that kept the inner storerooms of their pueblos bulging, a fact Captain Juan de Vitoria, who had accompanied his expedition, surely passed on to Juan de Oñate. And then there were persistent rumors that the towering green-robed mountains encircling the Tewa province showed traces of silver and other valuable minerals, supplying still another drawing card for the Spaniards. Whether for these reasons, or perhaps some other known only to himself, Oñate chose the valley of San Juan as his seat of government, even before seeing the place. So he told his nephew to bring the people and the wagons there.

Traveling above Santo Domingo, the governor soon quit the Rio Grande, because it flowed through a virtually impassable canyon. After crossing a short plain, he surmounted a nine-hundred-foot basaltic escarpment whose upper rim marked the edge of a plateau that swept gently northward twenty miles to the foot of blue-tinged mountains. This range, far loftier than anything Oñate had encountered thus far, was the one first called by colonial Spaniards the Sierra Madre (the Mother Range) and known later as the Sangre de Cristos, the southernmost extension of the Rocky Mountains. Riding a course that paralleled the river in its canyon several miles to the west, the Spaniards made their way over the plateau, crossed some low, sandy hills studded with piñon and juniper, and finally dropped into the lower end of the valley of San Juan (today known as the Española Valley).

On July 11, Oñate at last reached San Juan pueblo on the left bank of the Rio Grande, one of the largest of the Tewa group. This site, chosen for his capital, commanded vistas of haunting beauty. Facing east, one beheld the soaring ridgeline of the Sierra Madre whose

Pueblo of San Juan de los Caballeros, 1881, where Oñate established his headquarters in 1598. (Courtesy Museum of New Mexico)

heroic peaks, come winter, would be capped with heavy bonnets of snow. West, across the river, the pueblo faced the yawning mouth of the Chama Valley, its northern perimeter marked by a succession of black and red mesas and its southern by humpy foothills that graded into a parent range, the Jemez Mountains. The highest summit in that chain, Tsicomo at more than 11,500 feet, could be plainly seen from the pueblo on clear days, which were the rule most of the year. The Indians cast frequent glances toward its massive crown because some of the most sacred shrines of the Tewas lay there. To this mountain Indian religion assigned a trove of stories tinctured with the marvelous.

San Juan, called in the native tongue *Okhe,* was companion to a smaller pueblo, Yunge, directly across the river. Excellent farmlands surrounded Yunge, extending south of the village for a distance of three harquebus shots to the Chama River, a secondary stream from the northwest which here emptied into the Rio Grande. When Don Juan drew rein on July 11 and surveyed the twin villages, the rivers and the awesome backdrop of mountains, we can presume he was swept by a feeling of elation, similar to the one he felt at El Paso upon claiming possession of this new land. It had taken him nearly six months to get here from Santa Bárbara, and it was going on three years since he had signed his original contract with Viceroy Velasco on that bright September day in Mexico City. But eventually, he had reached the point, at this brown adobe pueblo of San Juan, where he could begin his chosen work.

At least one important goal had already been accomplished, by the mere completion of Oñate's journey. In making his way from Santa Bárbara to San Juan, he had blazed a new trial, lengthening the Camino Real by more than six hundred miles, and designating the official campsites (*parajes*) that would be used by overlanders for the next three hundred years. This Royal Highway, running a little less than two thousand miles from Mexico City to upper New Mexico, would remain for several centuries the longest road in North America. But Juan de Oñate on July 11, 1598, was not thinking of his achievement, for his attention was squarely focused upon the need to raise quickly the edifice of a colony. In this, no one knew better than he the importance of haste.

CHAPTER 7

San Juan

BY all accounts, the Indians of San Juan pueblo were as receptive to the Spaniards as Juan de Oñate had been led to expect. Upon his approach, they came out and met him with hospitable gestures, and by signs indicated they were willing to share their homes with the newcomers. Anyway, that was how the Spaniards interpreted things. One of the friars remarked that these were "the best infidel people" he had ever seen.

Don Juan generally was impressed with the Pueblo Indians, whose total population, he estimated later in a letter to the viceroy, numbered around sixty thousand. He compared their terraced residences of stone and adobe favorably to Spanish houses and noted that the dusky brown apartment blocks occasionally reached to the seventh story. He called their clothing, woven of cotton or agave fibers "good quality and well decorated." For warmth they wrapped themselves in buffalo robes, and to demonstrate the beauty of the wool on those articles, Oñate clipped several tufts for enclosure in his letter to Mexico City. On the whole, he thought the Pueblos to be persons of good disposition, an opinion he first formed at San Juan and one he refused to abandon afterward, even when outlying villages rose in revolt.

Although Don Juan had reached his destination, little could be accomplished there until arrival of the caravan with his colonists and their equipment. Filled with grand hopes and unwilling to remain idle, he cut out a small escort of horsemen and taking his cousin Fray Cristóbal, he headed northward on the first of a series of lightning tours. These excursions had the dual purpose of introducing him to the other Pueblo towns and of providing the first opportunity to engage in a bit of prospecting in the intervening country.

On this occasion, he visited Picurís pueblo, situated in a fertile valley on the west flank of the Sierra Madre, about six leagues above San Juan, and then continued over a spur of mountains to Taos, northernmost of the Pueblo settlements. At that point Oñate had ridden the entire length of Puebloland, beginning at Piro Qualacu in the south and extending almost two hundred and fifty miles to Taos— in other words, the heartland of the future American state of New Mexico. During this northern swing he found "a quantity of ore which had accumulated in the riffles of an arroyo," and while that was encouraging it fell far short of the spectacular strike he needed to give his colony economic stability.

By July 19, Oñate was back in San Juan, but only for an overnight stay, since on the following morning he set forth again, this time to push his survey toward the east. In that direction he visited the huge and splendid pueblo of Pecos, a native town that stood at the entrance to the buffalo plains. From there, he moved southwest through the Tano villages of the Galisteo Basin, a district fully explored by the Rodríguez-Chamuscado and Espejo expeditions in the previous decade. Near San Marcos pueblo on the northern edge of the basin, the Spanish party took heart at finding extensive turquoise and lead mines, long worked by the Indians, and abundant sign of other minerals in the vicinity. Oñate eagerly collected samples of ore for assaying.

A swift march on July 27 took Don Juan westward from San Marcos down the thinly flowing Galisteo River to its mouth on the Rio Grande at Santo Domingo, where three weeks earlier he had accepted the allegiance of native leaders. Coincidentally, at the hour of his arrival the Maese de Campo Juan de Zaldívar reached the same pueblo at the head of the wagon-cart caravan. It must have been an exhilarating, even joyous occasion, this reunion of leader and followers, but characteristically the Spanish chronicles accord it only perfunctory mention.

For five days the train remained camped beside the river and pueblo, presumably to allow the women and children a good rest before the final leg of the trip to San Juan. When travel was resumed on August 1, Oñate enjoined his nephew to guide the settlers and vehicles up the Galisteo to San Marcos, a roundabout detour but one that avoided the barrier of the volcanic escarpment due north of Santo Domingo. Don Juan himself with his escort went on to explore some of the pueblos in the mountainous country to the west, the one region that so far had escaped his examination.

On this tour, which lasted more than a week, Oñate veered around the southern end of the Jemez Mountains and entered a wide red-walled canyon containing a scatter of Towa-speaking pueblos. Eight were visited, their inhabitants appearing amiable and cooperative. The Spaniards discovered one of the petty chieftains wearing a silver paten, the plate used to hold the sacred wafer during Mass. A hole had been punched through the center, and it was suspended from the neck by a leather thong. The assumption was that it had belonged to either Father Rodríguez or López, martyred at Puaray. The Spaniards obtained the object by trading hawk bells for it, and they carried it to San Juan to become a sacred relic when an altar should be erected there.

Oñate was back at his San Juan headquarters by August 10, the feast of San Lorenzo. Zaldívar and the wagons, still grinding up the new Camino Real, were not expected for several more days, so Don Juan used the time profitably. He issued a call for volunteer laborers, and fifteen hundred Indians, including many from adjacent villages, responded. They were put to work under Spanish overseers digging irrigation ditches for a proposed city and capital to be called Saint Francis (San Francisco), a name surely suggested by the company of Franciscan missionaries.

Just where was the site of this future municipality and the irrigated fields that were intended to provide it food? That is a question that continues to plague scholars, since historical documents neglect to give the answer. The logical assumption is that the townsite was very close to San Juan pueblo and on the same side of the river. If that was the case, then the newly irrigated farms would have been separated from it by the Rio Grande because the San Juan Indians insist, even today, that most of their agriculture has always been west of the river. That raises the possibility, of course, that St. Francis too may have been set across the Rio Grande, either above or below the existing San Gabriel pueblo (as the Spaniards called the village of Yunge). The significant point in all of this is to be found less in the location than in the fact that Governor Oñate initially laid ambitious plans for the building of a true city to shine like a lodestar over his New Mexican realm. However, misfortune, which had dogged his steps since 1595, would soon render that scheme unfeasible.

When Juan de Zaldívar brought the wagons and the wearied colonists into San Juan on August 18, Oñate began, as he said, "to prepare the people of the army for the rigorous winter of which the Indians and the nature of the land warned us." Those preparations seem to have included the assignment of apartments within the pueblo to individual Spanish families, the collecting of native blankets and robes for redistribution to the settlers, and levies made upon the Indians' foodstores, particularly dried buffalo and deer meat and corn. As one of the priests so aptly phrased it, "Here corn is God!"—by which he meant that supplies of the grain, during the long, dark months of cold, spelled the difference between survival and extinction. Hence, corn was worshiped.

Before he could give much attention to the requirements of food and shelter, however, Oñate was confronted by a full-blown mutiny. Coming only a day or two after arrival of the caravan, its occurrence so early in the game appears all the more puzzling. Involved were forty-five officers and soldiers, more than a third of the expedition's total manpower. They plotted to desert and return to New Spain, taking with them slaves and plunder seized from the pueblos, or so Oñate claimed. In his summary report of the affair, he stated that the men were angry at not immediately finding bars of silver lying on the ground. And because he had prevented them from abusing the Indians, they had become sullen and resentful and were now dissatisfied both with the prospects of the country and Oñate's leadership.

Their complaints sound surprisingly similar to those the chroniclers tell us were articulated by members of the Coronado expedition, who also expected to stumble over silver and gold bars and who, when New Mexico proved lacking in such instant riches, "cursed the barren land and cried out bitterly against those who had led them into a [worthless] wilderness." Evidently, the discontent among Oñate's men had been simmering for some time, aggravated by the length and hardships of the overland journey as well as by a breakdown of discipline in the caravan after Don Juan had left it to go on ahead. Upon gaining San Juan and perhaps hearing from the soldiers who had served in Oñate's escort that the first attempts at prospecting had not miraculously produced a bonanza, those in the ranks qualifying primarily as fortune-hunters, rather than sincere colonists, banded together and plotted to betray the oath they had sworn when originally enlisting under the governor's standard.

It is quite possible too that the majority of the mutineers actually never believed New Mexico would yield any silver and had signed on fully intending to resort to slaving. As mentioned, illegal slaving expeditions were not uncommon along the northern border at this period, defying attempts by the king and viceroy to stop them. In the last months before departure for the Rio Grande, when Oñate was scrambling to meet his quota of men, he appears to have been forced to enroll all comers, whether desirable candidates or not. One wonders how many of them were in reality professional slavers, taking advantage of Oñate's colonizing entrada to get a free ride to the populous land of the docile Pueblos.

Moreover, the possibility has to be considered that among the conspirators were men planted by enemies of the project, like Lomas y Colmenares, or other shadowy foes Don Juan alludes to frequently. Agents bent on undermining the expedition's mission could scarcely have found a better means than organizing a large-scale desertion. But in trying to grasp the motives of the persons involved in this incident, we are once again hampered by the scantiness of the written sources.

Now, acting under the code of military discipline, Oñate arrested two captains and a soldier, identified as ringleaders, and condemned them to death by strangulation. One of the guilty officers appears to have been the troublesome Captain Aguilar, who had narrowly missed execution once before when he entered the first pueblo against orders. Again, he was to escape with his life, owing to the intervention of the friars and virtually the entire army, all of whom pleaded with Oñate to grant the offenders mercy. But in relenting and extending them a pardon, the governor was being more practical than merciful. He could ill afford the loss of three fighting men, and even less could he risk sowing deeper discontent among his colonists. However, while he bowed to pressure, Oñate knew only too well that his leniency was insufficient to heal entirely the wide fissure opened by the conspiracy. As he expressed it metaphorically: "A spark of this great fire remained hidden in the ashes."

Notwithstanding, the whole episode was publicly resolved on August 21 with what the official record refers to as "the famous sermon of tears and of universal peace." That would suggest Oñate orchestrated a ceremony of atonement to serve as a catharsis and relief from tension. As a follow-up, he ordered work to begin two days later on the first church in New Mexico—a missionary chapel for the San Juan Indians, which could also serve the Spaniards until construction of their own church in the projected city of St. Francis.

This first building must have been rather simply formed since it was ready for dedication within two weeks. In size, however, it was spacious enough "to accommodate all the people of the camp." Either

Oñate or Father Martínez named the church San Juan Bautista, a logical choice given the name of the pueblo it served.

According to Villagrá, when Oñate first arrived he called the pueblo San Juan de los Caballeros, honoring not only his own patron, Saint John the Baptist, but also the explorer-knights (*caballeros*) who had preceded him in bringing the cross to the upper Rio Grande Valley. That may or may not be true, for there certainly exist other possible explanations for use of the title *Caballeros* by Oñate.

One theory is that it had some link in his mind with the medieval Caballeros de San Juan (Knights of Saint John), also known as the Knights Hospitalers, or Knights of Jerusalem. The Caballeros de San Juan, together with five other crusading military orders, fought in Spain against the Moors and became leaders in expanding and resettling the Christian frontier. From that activity doubtless arose the custom of adding *Caballeros* to the names of numerous towns and churches (the town of Jérez de los Caballeros, and the church of San Juan de los Caballeros at Segovia, for example).

No direct connection can be found tying Oñate to the still-existing Order of San Juan, although his father Cristóbal had been associated with several men who were members. On the other hand, by drawing a parallel between the experiences of knights in Spanish orders and his own experiences, and those of his men, on this cutting edge of a new Christian frontier, he could have been inspired to dignify the pueblo of San Juan with the designation *de los Caballeros*. Knights by definition were noblemen, and since Oñate's soldiers were potential hidalgos (their titles to be conveyed upon fulfilling residency requirements in New Mexico), it might have seemed fitting to him to honor their place of first residence by embellishing its name with the *Caballeros* title. Still, all of this is guesswork and will probably remain so.

The dawning of the eighth day of September brought the dedication of the new church of San Juan Bautista and the opening of a week-long celebration. Father Martínez blessed the church and consecrated the altar and chalices. Father Salazar, as personal chaplain and cousin of the governor, delivered an appropriate sermon. That very afternoon the secular festivities began with staging of a sham battle between Moors and Christians, which was followed, asserts Villagrá, by many Moorish and Christian games. The rousing history of the Spanish crusades had been transformed into a ritualized and

stylized body of popular spectacle and entertainment that was dissem-
inated throughout Hispanic America, and now reached even to this
remotest outpost on the northern frontier.

And there was more: tilting matches, bullfights, and a drama composed just for the occasion. The author is left unmentioned, but we
fancy that it was Captain Farfán de los Godos who had already
demonstrated his play-writing abilities at El Paso. At week's end, the
festival concluded with a thunderous volley of artillery.

The time had not been devoted entirely to frolic. On the day after
the church dedication, Oñate called a general assembly to announce
assignment of individual missionaries to the various Pueblo provinces
of New Mexico. He also used the opportunity to have visiting Indian
delegations render obedience to the king, in a ceremony much like
that held previously at Santo Domingo. Villagrá alleges that mixed
in the native crowd was a scattering of spies from distant pueblos,
on hand to learn the numbers and strength of the Spaniards. Conspicuous among them were representatives of Acoma, a village perched
on a towering and highly defensible peñol located some one hundred
air miles southwest of San Juan. These spies returned home and gave
a thorough report of what they had seen, including the information
that while Spanish harquebuses and cannon made a great deal of
noise, they seemed to cause no harm. That was a misunderstanding
destined to have serious consequences.

Sometime soon after taking up residence at San Juan, Oñate was
enjoying his midday meal when it was interrupted by Indians in the
plaza. They created such a clamor and frightful wail that the governor
and his aides thought perhaps the final Day of Judgment had arrived.
Upon inquiry, they learned the source of the commotion: Native
spokesmen explained that no rain had fallen in weeks, the prayers to
their gods having gone unanswered. Unless the drought was broken
quickly, maturing crops in the fields would fail and little or no harvest
could be expected.

The priests, led by Father Martínez, told the Indians to stop their
wailing. Then they offered up their own prayers and asked for abundant rains to revive the withering plants. At once the people of San
Juan began to scan the heavens, and on the next day, at the same
hour, the skies darkened, thunder boomed, and the clouds opened
to release torrents of rain. "The barbarians stood spellbound in awe
and mute gratitude at the unbounding mercy of God," avouched
Villagrá, whose story this is.

Very similar tales crop up throughout Spanish America: Indians are in some kind of trouble, traditional appeals to their gods go unheeded, missionaries intervene with effectual prayers, the Christian God saves the day, and the new religion triumphs over the pagan old. The theme is so commonplace that we are at a loss to know whether Villagrá simply bowed to convention in including it here, or whether, in fact, a drought did end after the prayers of Oñate's Franciscans. Twice on the expedition to New Mexico, the Spaniards sought supernatural aid to control the weather: once to bring them rain in the middle of the Chihuahuan desert, and later to quell a storm that caught them in its full fury along the Rio Grande. For Spaniards, who wore religion on their shirt sleeves, such incidents did not appear all that extraordinary.

Oñate sustained a severe shock on September 12. Four of his men stole horses and fled south toward Nueva Vizcaya. It was the first successful instance of desertion since arrival of the colony in New Mexico, and the betrayal left him shaken. The "evildoers," as he termed them, were identified as a pair of young brothers, Juan and Matías Rodríguez, together with Manuel Portugués and Juan González, both natives of Portugal. All had been a party to the conspiracy snuffed out three weeks before, so Don Juan naturally assumed their theft and flight was an outgrowth of that unhappy episode.

Since these soldiers had committed a crime, violated the laws of military conduct, and disregarded royal orders, Oñate determined to seize and punish them dreadfully. He informed the viceroy of his sending captains Villagrá and Gerónimo Márquez with instructions "to pursue and overtake them." But that was by no means all, as Villagrá revealed when he wrote: "Our orders were to execute the deserters promptly wherever we apprehended them."

That, indeed, was a harsh sentence, and it calls attention to the dilemma Oñate faced. The responsibility of command required him to display tact, fairness, and restraint, but balanced against that was the uncomfortable fact that he governed an impatient band of Spanish subjects who needed a strong hand to enforce some minimum of social discipline. He seems to have begun this whole enterprise with a certain largeness of spirit mixed with flexibility and enthusiasm for diplomacy. However, if our reading of the piecemeal records is correct, his early difficulties had the effect of souring his mood and pushing him along a path that led eventually to suspicion of underlings, showing of favoritism, and brutal retribution meted out to those who opposed him—in short, the behavior of a natural autocrat, or even petty despot. The emergence of this unflattering image of the governor first assumes recognizable form with his issuance of Villagrá's order to arrest and execute the fugitives.

Oñate claimed that their taking of horses injured others who were thereby prevented from fully serving the king, for which reason horse stealing, even in that early day, was a capital offense. On the other hand, the culprits apparently stole nothing else (other than possibly some food for the road), nor did they make any attempt to carry off Pueblo slaves. The best guess is that they simply wanted to get clear of New Mexico, and to keep others from having the same idea, Don Juan decreed that they pay with their lives.

Villagrá and Márquez, tapped for this merciless errand, were rated by Oñate as among the bravest and most loyal of his officers. That being the case, he assigned them only three soldiers to complete their party. Gerónimo Márquez, captain of artillery and a native of San Lucar in Spain, had joined the expedition with his entire household, including four sons and a daughter. He brought with him a complete set of armor, plus thirty-five horses, a significant addition to the expedition's livestock. Quite possibly, some of his mounts had been pirated by the deserters.

Gaspar Pérez de Villagrá remains the best known of all Don Juan's subordinates, owing to his having written and published at Alcalá de Henares, Spain, in 1610 an epic poem entitled *A History of New Mexico*. Composed in imitation of Virgil's *Aeneid,* the work recounts Oñate's efforts as a colonizer from 1595 to 1601, with plentiful mention of the part played by the author. Scholars have generally considered Villagrá's effort to be better history than poetry, for while he was an eyewitness to many of the events he describes, his verses are weighted with rhetorical flourishes, moral platitudes, and references to classical authors. Cervantes in his *Don Quixote,* a book he began writing the year Oñate entered New Mexico, makes fun of those literary devices, which cluttered popular writing of the day. Its deficiencies as literature notwithstanding, Villagrá's poem merits the distinction of being the first published history of any part of the future American nation, preceding by fourteen years Captain John Smith's *General History of Virginia.*

Born in Puebla near Mexico City, Villagrá attended Spain's renowned University of Salamanca, graduated as a bachelor of letters, and spent several years at the court of Philip II before returning to

New Spain. He joined the Oñate project at its inception and, according to his own statement, invested seven thousand pesos in it, probably the entire sum of his wealth. In 1596, upon recommendation of the expedition's officers, Don Juan appointed Villagrá to the position of *procurador general,* that is, chief supply-master for the New Mexican entrada, because, the governor noted, "he [is] a person of character and qualified for said post."

Originally, Oñate had planned to leave his supply-master behind to continue the process of assembling provisions for transshipment to New Mexico. In the end, however, he changed his mind and permitted Villagrá, who was craving adventure and eager to learn the art of soldiering, to join the march north. That decision put Captain Villagrá in the path of history and provided him the opportunity to become the expedition's poet-chronicler, a circumstance for which all later scholars have been grateful.

By the time the governor assigned Villagrá the task of tracking down the deserters, he was already a seasoned hand, having shown a flair for military life. At this date he was in his early forties and probably looked much as he appeared in an engraved portrait used as a frontispiece in his later book: a serious man of medium stature, with balding head, thick walrus mustache, and a pointed beard. Vicente de Zaldívar said that two deep wrinkles extended from eyebrow to eyebrow over his nose and rose to the forehead. Those are not evident in the portrait, which incidentally is the only surviving image of any person associated with Oñate's settling of New Mexico.

When Villagrá and Márquez set off on their chase, neither they nor the governor anticipated that it would last long. But the fugitives had a good start, and the pursuit turned into a lengthy one. They were finally overtaken on the Rio San Pedro far down in Nueva Vizcaya. Villagrá remarks with unusual brevity that he executed two of the men, while the other two escaped after abandoning the stolen horses. Another source, however, furnishes a more detailed picture.

Apparently, the men were seized through trickery, surrendering after receiving promises from Villagrá that their lives would be spared. When González and Portugués realized they were going to be executed, they begged to be allowed to confess to a priest at the nearby mines of Todos Santos. But Villagrá denied their last request and summarily beheaded them, also chopping off their right hands, which he pickled in salt to carry back to Oñate as proof of their deaths. Because the young Rodríguez brothers seem to have been his

Engraving of Villagrá from the frontispiece of his *Historia de la Nueva México* (1610)

friends, he permitted them to escape although they were the instigators of the horse stealing. All of this was done outside the jurisdiction of New Mexico, so Captain Villagrá had no legal authority for his acts. As a consequence, criminal charges would be preferred against him and his accomplice Márquez, later in Mexico City.

Since they were now so close to the outpost town of Santa Bárbara, Villagrá and his companions proceeded there to resupply and also to send a letter to Viceroy Monterrey giving him first word on conditions in New Mexico. In that document Villagrá took pains to exaggerate in high terms "the goodness, richness, and fertility" of the new land, and to claim for it a much larger Indian population than it actually possessed. In this we see an early indicator of a pattern soon to emerge: Don Juan and his chief supporters, upon realizing that New Mexico was a poor and sterile country, deliberately misrepresented the truth in reports to the king and viceroy. They did so in an effort to buy time, hoping that some dramatic silver strike, like the one made long ago in Zacatecas, would turn New Mexico's fortunes around. Already Villagrá must have concluded that the governor was in trouble, and his rosy letter to Monterrey was designed to hide that fact.

Back at San Juan, Oñate was struggling to keep his feet on the ground and at the same time give his restive men a sense of direction and purpose. Sometime in early September, an Indian named Jusepe arrived at the pueblo with an astonishing story, one that awakened Spanish interest in the eastern plains. Jusepe, an Aztec from the Valley of Mexico, had been a servant of Antonio Gutiérrez de Humaña who had accompanied the illegal Leyba de Bonilla expedition to New Mexico back in 1593. After spending several months living off the Tewas, this party had been lured eastward by intriguing reports of distant native kingdoms. In the central plains they encountered the earth blackened with buffalo and a great settlement, well populated and composed of innumerable domed houses the Indians had thatched with grass.

Beyond the great settlement, Humaña quarreled with the leader Leyba de Bonilla and stabbed him with a butcher knife. That so frightened Jusepe that he fled the camp, retracing the trail toward New Mexico. Falling in with Apaches, he was held captive until the day he heard other Spaniards had taken up residence with the Pueblos. That news led him to make his escape and find his way to Oñate's headquarters.

Don Juan eagerly listened to this tale, for what it revealed both about the geography and inhabitants of the plains and about the fate of Leyba de Bonilla. The viceroy had specifically enjoined him to find and arrest this man and his confederates, for launching an unauthorized entrada. Now it looked as if Gutiérrez de Humaña was the one to be apprehended, and on a more serious charge of murder.

Beyond that, Oñate was more interested in Jusepe's mention of the bountiful herds of buffalo. He desperately needed to replenish his dwindling foodstores, and a big-game hunt presented an easy way to accomplish that end. Therefore, he sent his nephew Vicente at the head of sixty men, half of the entire command, to bring in a winter's supply of buffalo meat. The task had the added advantages of keeping many soldiers occupied and, during their absence, reducing the drain on the commissary at San Juan. Further, the trip provided Vicente an opportunity to look for any sign of Humaña.

On September 15, with Jusepe serving as guide, the sargento mayor led his soldiers-turned-buffalo-hunters out of San Juan and rode down to Pecos pueblo, where he left Father Francisco de San Miguel and the lay brother Juan de Dios to begin missionary work. Then he moved eastward through the plains, finding occasional campfire remains and dried horse dung left by the Leyba de Bonilla party. The waters of several intersecting streams yielded huge numbers of fish when the Spaniards cast in their hooks and lines, and along the banks, tangled bushes were fruit-heavy with autumn plums.

The column met bands of Plains Apaches, or Vaqueros, "People of the Cows," as Coronado had originally termed them. They were roaming the open grasslands in search of buffalo, carrying their meager belongings by dog travois. They proved sociable enough, even a bit timid, except one brazen fellow who attempted to throw a fright into these strangers. He appeared in their midst dressed in a red suit with tail and a mask from which protruded a long snout and floppy ears. The soldiers, appreciative of good theater, feigned terror, when the Indian Satan made menacing gestures. Then they jerked off his mask and broke into peals of laughter. Another day they met an Apache chief of extraordinary complexion. "He had . . . whiter skin and bluer eyes than a Fleming," declared the chronicler, and "he was accompanied by a squad of bowmen." This white Indian, doubtless an albino, provided a guide to lead them to the buffalo.

Somewhere on the trackless plains, not far from where the western boundary of Texas would one day be drawn, the expedition was introduced to the first herd of "wild cattle," as the buffalo were then referred to. "Their shape and appearance are so amazing and amusing, or frightening, that one never tires of looking at them," wrote a companion of Zaldívar. The sargento mayor ordered an immense trap, in the form of a winged corral, to be built of stakes, but the animals proved so wild and unmanageable that none could be driven into it. Several calves were later captured, with the hope that they could be taken back to San Juan. But they fought their ropes furiously and died within an hour. The hunters went to work, slaughtering cattle, and within a few weeks an enormous quantity of meat and tallow was accumulated. In early November, Zaldívar set a homeward course, bearing sufficient jerky from his hunt to sustain the colony through that "rigorous winter" they had been told by the Pueblos to expect.

Meanwhile, in the absence of his youngest nephew, Oñate had wasted no time in idleness. Leaving Juan de Zaldívar in charge at San Juan, he resumed on October 6 his touring of the kingdom to receive the submission of pueblos not yet reached and to continue seeking for some trace of valuable minerals. First, he visited a series of pueblos strung along the east slope of the Manzano Mountains, far to the southeast. The area was known as the Saline Province because of briny lakes spotting the adjacent Estancia Valley. "These extend for many leagues and contain an infinite quantity of excellent white salt," observed the official journal of the expedition. Oñate knew the value of salt in world trade and more to the point its importance as one of the essential ingredients in the Spanish process of smelting silver. The lakes thus furnished a resource he could use in touting the worth of his New Mexico, even though he had no immediate prospect of profiting from it.

While among the Saline pueblos, Don Juan suddenly decided to march west to the discovery of the South Sea, that is, the Pacific Ocean. It was something that had been in his mind since the signing of his contract with Viceroy Velasco back in 1595—this locating of the sea on the western limits of the kingdom in hopes of establishing a port to receive supplies by ship. Just why he thought of it now is a bit of a mystery, although one contemporary source hints that because he found the Saline pueblos docile and cooperative, like the other Indians he had met so far, Don Juan concluded it was safe to undertake a new project that promised to carry him far afield. In any event, from here he sent a message to the Maese de Campo, Juan de

Zaldívar, who was still on duty at San Juan with a skeleton garrison. Wait until your brother returns from the buffalo hunt, Oñate told him, then bring a force of thirty men, follow my trail, and catch up with me on this quest for the South Sea.

Without further delay, Oñate crossed the mountains into the Rio Grande Valley, stopping briefly at Puaray, on the main north-south trail, and then angled sixty miles southwest toward Acoma, the famed mesa-top pueblo. Perched four hundred feet in the air, Acoma was accessible only by a treacherous succession of hand- and toe-holds pecked from the steep sandstone walls. Five hundred adobe apartments crowned the summit, their water supplied by several large depressions that served as natural cisterns. At the far end, the table top was cut in two by a deep chasm. The scene in all probability caused Don Juan to recall the tales of his father attacking the fortified peñoles of Indian rebels during the Mixton War of the 1540s. One of his men, assessing Acoma's defenses, rated it as "the best situated Indian stronghold in all Christendom."

When Oñate pitched camp at the base of the mesa, he had no way of knowing that the Indians above him were engaged in a stormy debate over the reception he should be given. The spies who saw the Spaniards at San Juan had brought back disturbing reports about their plans to stay in the Pueblo country, and that had sparked the formation of a war faction headed by a minor chieftain, Zutucapán. Cooler heads, nevertheless, argued for peace, and they were able to prevail. Subsequently, the Acomas swarmed down from the rock with gifts of food and water for the newcomers. They crowded around the Spanish camp to gawk at the bearded men in gleaming armor and to study the nervous neighing horses. To them, the animals seemed to be talking to one another, and Governor Oñate, according to informed reports, "encouraged them in this belief to inspire more fear and respect."

The visitors were invited to make the difficult climb to the village, and once on top they fired a salute with their harquebuses. Looking down they could see the camp, horse guard, and their own mounts reduced by distance to toy size. An Acoma warrior, one of Zutucapán's men, led Oñate apart and to the roof of one of the underground ceremonial kivas where a ladder protruded from an open hatchway that served as entrance. The Indian vigorously urged him to descend into it to view some astonishing treasure. But Don Juan, through long experience in the Chichimeca wars, knew enough to be suspicious of an invitation like that. He discreetly declined, quickly returned to his soldiers, and led them to the plain below. By a margin as thin as a sheet of parchment he had escaped with his life from the kiva. The darkness at the foot of the ladder had concealed twelve armed assassins placed there by Zutucapán, who planned to force a war by killing Oñate. The Spaniards did not learn of this until several weeks later. Before breaking camp, Don Juan assembled the Pueblo elders for his customary ceremony of submission. For them, the strange demands pronounced through an interpreter had little meaning. But the Spaniards, on the other hand, placed great store by their ritual formulas, particularly this: "And those who render obedience can never again withdraw their allegiance under penalty of death." Incomprehensible as those words may have been to the Indians, they would be used to justify a terrible retribution taken against Acoma in a sequence of events that shortly unfolded.

It was late October as Don Juan guided his expedition away from Acoma on its westward course. The sky turned slate gray and a raw wind whistled through the pines as the Spaniards worked their way toward the crest of the Continental Divide. At Agua de la Peña, afterward called El Morro, they filled their waterbags from a copious pool at the foot of a huge sandstone rock that towered above the valley floor like the prow of a ship. Just beyond this scenic place, heavy snowflakes began to swirl, the spare horses stampeded, and some of them were lost. Under a mantle of white, soaring cliffs backed by the ragged line of the Zuni Mountains held a savage beauty, but to the travelers, wet and shivering, no country could have looked more dismal.

They were considerably warmed, however, by their reception at the six pueblos of the Zuni Indians, which were clustered just east of the present-day New Mexico–Arizona boundary. The native people showered them with gifts—corn, tortillas, calabashes, beans, and braces of rabbits. In their villages, the Spaniards were surprised to find large devotional crosses dating back sixty years to Coronado's visit. The Zunis dusted the crosses with sacred cornmeal and tied prayer plumes to the arms in veneration. Oñate even met the son of an Aztec, now dead, who had been left here by Coronado. Impressed by the friendliness of the Zunis, the governor went into camp for a week.

Hearing that a salt lake lay nine leagues to the south, he sent Captain Farfán de los Godos and four companions to have a look.

El Morro, the soaring rock in Western New Mexico that figures promi-
nently in the Oñate chronicles. (Courtesy Archaelogical Institute of
America)

They returned in a few days agog over the marvel discovered. Captain
Farfán felt convinced he had seen the best saline in the world—a
league in circumference, and its surface encrusted with crystallized
salt so hard the men walked safely across the lake. "Nowhere in
Christendom or elsewhere can such a wondrous thing be found. Nor
does our King possess such salt," he testified. Oñate reckoned the
matter significant enough to have an official report of the discovery
drawn up for King Philip and the Council of the Indies.

During the week's stopover at Zuni, Don Juan ordered three of
his soldiers to retrace the expedition's trail in an effort to find the
horses lost in the snowstorm. The errand produced an unexpected
result. West of El Morro the search party chanced upon Captain
Villagrá, wandering afoot and near death from exposure. After a
campfire was kindled with flint and steel, and hot food was given
him, he explained his predicament. Returning to New Mexico from
pursuit of the deserters, he had left Captain Márquez and the others
to follow at a slower pace and had raced ahead, alone, to tell Oñate
the outcome of his assignment. At Puaray pueblo he learned that the

NEW MEXICO AND ARIZONA EXPLORATION

Routes of:

——— Colonizing Expedition by Oñate, 1598

- - - Arizona Exploration by Oñate, 1605

——— Farfan De Los Godos, 1598 expedition

New Mexico and Arizona Exploration

governor was not at San Juan but had passed through this village days before on his way to the South Sea. Villagrá, therefore, turned his swift purebred horse in that direction and commenced following the windblown tracks of Oñate's expedition.

Approaching Acoma, he came upon a war party under Zutucapán guarding both sides of the trail. "Like so many crouching tigers ready to pounce upon their prey," was the way he portrayed it. By bluff and skillful maneuvering of his mount, he got past them but carried with him a deep sense of foreboding. These Indians unequivocally were out for blood.

Before dawn the next morning, snow began to tumble from the

sky, the same storm that scattered Oñate's horses miles ahead at El Morro. In the gloom and teeth-rattling cold, Villagrá failed to see a trap the Acomas had placed in the trail. Suddenly man and beast plunged into a pit whose opening had been disguised with brush. The horse died instantly, but miraculously the captain escaped unscathed. (A similar incident in 1851 narrowly missed claiming the life of U.S. Army Colonel Edwin V. Sumner, who fell into a hole dug by the Zunis, meant to entrap their Navajo enemies. In that instance the bottom of the pit was lined with sharpened stakes. Villagrá neglects to mention stakes, but they well could have been what killed his horse.)

Afoot and suspecting the Acomas were closing in, the lone Spaniard faced a desperate situation. But a fear of capture, combined with resourcefulness, moved him to action. Stripping off armor and helmet and casting aside his heavy harquebus and shield, he prepared for flight armed only with a sword and dagger. Nor was that all he did, for as he remarked: "To avoid being tracked, I put my shoes on backward so that the heels faced to the front. Fortunately for me, the barbarians did not return while I was making all these preparations."

For four days Villagrá drifted in a westerly direction, keeping to the timbered ridges for concealment and suffering terribly from hunger and the weather. Then his luck saved him once again when he ran upon Oñate's three soldiers tracking the strayed horses. Without that chance meeting, he certainly would have perished. Indeed, he was so drawn and haggard from the ordeal that his comrades failed to recognize him and had to ask his name. Two days later, they all reached Zuni, and Villagrá promptly presented Don Juan a full recital of his adventures.

Somehow, incredibly, Oñate overlooked the significance of what he was hearing. His own encounter with the Acomas should have put him on the alert, and now he had confirmation, by the experience of Captain Villagrá, that they intended to do the Spaniards harm. Through hindsight we can say that he ought to have wasted no time in dispatching a messenger to seek out Juan de Zaldívar and warn him to give the peñol of Acoma a wide berth, as he moved west from the Rio Grande to join his uncle. There is no evidence at all that such a thought even occurred to him, possibly because he assumed that young Zaldívar, being an able soldier, could handle any difficulty that might arise. Whatever his thinking, Don Juan made an error of judgment destined to have far-reaching consequences.

While waiting for his nephew to arrive so that the journey to the
sea could be renewed, Oñate decided to keep the men active by
making a sidetrip to the last of the Pueblo provinces, that of the
Moqui (modern Hopi) centered on isolated mesas to the northwest
across the Painted Desert. On Sunday November 8, 1598, he departed
Zuni in a raging snowstorm. Although Oñate did not know it, on
the same day Vicente de Zaldívar made his belated return to San
Juan, concluding the buffalo hunt to the plains, and thereby releasing
his brother Juan from guard duty at headquarters. Oñate made his
way in improving weather through a sandy, desolate country, frightening in its vastness, to reach at last the scalloped mesas of the
Moquis. The Indians descended with gifts of tortillas and scattered
sacred cornmeal over the armored knights and their horses as a token
of peace.

Don Juan was pleased with their show of cordiality, and he led his
men through five pueblos so the people could render obedience to
the king. But the unrelieved poverty of the towns proved disappoint-
ing, and the hundred-mile viewscapes from the mesa tops, appeared
stark, windswept, and utterly depressing to European eyes. Although
Oñate found little of interest among the Moqui, he did acquire
valuable information. Remembering that Espejo, twenty years before, had claimed rich mineral finds somewhere hereabouts, he in-
quired of silver and other metallic ores. The Indians obligingly
pointed toward the southwest, saying that there lived the Cruzado
people who painted their bodies with colors from the earth. Perhaps
that might be a clue to what the strangers were after.

Oñate thought so. He instructed the reliable Farfán de los Godos
to take eight companions and explore the homeland of the Cruzados.
Meanwhile, he turned around and guided the main party back to
Zuni, to await the coming of Juan de Zaldívar and his reinforcements.

Traveling at a good pace, Captain Farfán crossed the Little Colorado River and threaded his way through a belt of pine forest on a
plateau south of central Arizona's lofty San Francisco peaks. In this
vicinity, he came across encampments of the Cruzado Indians (probably the modern Yavapai) who decorated their faces with bright paint
and wore seashells suspended from their noses and foreheads. The
tribesmen were easily persuaded to lead Farfán farther south to their
mines in the Verde Valley. There on an overhanging mountain, he
observed a deep shaft with a vein of ore from which the natives
extracted the brilliant yellow, blue, green, brown, and black ores

used for daubing themselves and painting their blankets. On the surrounding slopes, the Spaniards pried loose chunks of rock laced with virgin silver. Excitedly, they stalked claims, in their own names and the names of the men who had accompanied Oñate back to Zuni. The ore samples they carefully stowed in saddle bags, to be assayed at San Juan, for the governor had in his company men skilled in that metallurgical task, and he had brought to New Mexico the quicksilver (mercury) required to reduce the ore.

Farfán would tell Don Juan in the days to come that the staked claims "appeared to be the richest in New Spain!" Probably that was his honest conviction, but he knew too it was what the governor wanted to hear. Moreover, he was to disclose that according to the Cruzados the seacoast lay only thirty days' travel southwest of the mines, and it was rich in pearls, something else sure to please Oñate.

Captain Farfán retraced his path to the Moqui pueblos, where he left seven of his men to rest their jaded horses, and with one companion he hurried on to Zuni to present the account of his findings. The pair arrived back on December 11. Oñate in his log recorded that "they brought alluring reports of excellent mines . . . very fine samples of silver ores . . . and as a result, the men who were languishing for want of metals to smelt were reanimated." It was just the sort of promising news he needed.

That welcome word, unfortunately, was offset by Oñate's growing uneasiness over the failure of Juan de Zaldívar and his detachment to put in an appearance. The winter season was already far advanced, well into the second week of December, and the men's thoughts were turning to their families at San Juan and to Christmas. Oñate, therefore, concluded his best course lay in returning to the capital. He could discover what had delayed his nephew, let the men enjoy the holidays, and reorganize his forces for a new expedition to find the South Sea.

On December 12, the Spaniards left Zuni and by fast marching reached El Morro the following evening. Here, one of Oñate's officers from San Juan, Bernabé de las Casas, met them with a squad of men. His face grave, he saluted the governor and briefly delivered a somber announcement, one that scarcely seemed believable. Juan de Zaldívar was dead. Ten of his men were also slain and others injured. The Acomas had rebelled. And the Spanish kingdom of New Mexico teetered on the edge of disaster.

CHAPTER 8

Crises

"GOOD fortune can never be depended upon," philosophized Gaspar Pérez de Villagrá. "No matter how blessed one may be by fate, the good luck can turn at any time and one see himself sadly oppressed by a multitude of adversities." Those sentiments certainly must have been in tune with Oñate's thoughts upon receipt of the news that his senior nephew and men had fallen. Casas had been eyewitness to the tragedy and thus was able to give Don Juan a detailed summary of what had transpired. Dazed and grief-stricken, the governor retired to his tent, pitched in the shadow of El Morro, leaving word that no one was to disturb him.

After a time he summoned Captain Villagrá and had him make a simple cross of branches. With this planted in the floor of his tent, Oñate knelt before it and wept and prayed the night away. As a rule a Spanish caballero was expected to contain or hold back any revelation of deep inner emotion, in the manner of Philip II when he learned of the defeat of his Great Armada. But in actual fact, the sternest of the conquistadors on occasion gave themselves over unabashedly to sorrow. One recalls, for example, that night in 1520, the *Noche Triste,* when Cortés sat under a giant cypress tree and shed tears for all his men who had perished in fighting with the Aztecs.

At dawn Oñate pulled himself together. He was in trouble up to his beard and needed every ounce of iron resolve given him by his Basque blood and a strict upbringing. Another call went out to Villagrá, this time ordering him to assemble the men in front of the tent. They gathered slowly—morose, shaken, drooping in spirit—on the sandy ground below El Morro's bare and wind-worn face.

Juan de Oñate strode from the tent and stood before them: eyes swollen and red, face clouded by gloom, fists clenched; yet, withal, stolid and composed as a cardinal. He spoke as brave Spaniards were supposed to speak, and from his anguish came words to inspire and to kindle courage:

Men! Heaven knows my heart bleeds at the loss of our valiant comrades. In the deaths of the *Maese de campo* and his companions we have suffered an irreparable loss. They cannot be replaced, for they had no equals. We have heard how nobly they died in the service of their God and of their King. Their work is done. It is essential now that our labors should continue.

I know of no one present who is not worthy of the name of a true soldier of Christ. . . . We have heard from eyewitnesses who came to us, grievously wounded in body and soul, the terrible fate our comrades met. They were beaten and torn to pieces. And they died like martyrs. . . .

But, my soldiers, let us keep true Christian spirit. Whether death, hardships, or sufferings come, we shall meet them as behooves brave men . . . so let us lay aside our sorrow and place trust in the Almighty. . . .

It was a speech perhaps sounding melodramatic and overly formal to modern ears, but one thoroughly in character for a Spaniard in Oñate's plight. His fervid appeals to divine assistance and reference to militant Christianity were echoes of a battlefield rhetoric that stretched far back into Iberian history. For the troops, the governor's language had a calming effect and served to stiffen backbones. It also vividly reminded them that, adversity aside, Juan de Oñate remained firmly in control.

Preparations were begun immediately for the homeward march. Don Juan sent for his Indian interpreter, Tomás, and gave him a special mission: to return to Moqui, alert the seven soldiers left there by Captain Farfán, and advise them to make directly for San Juan, avoiding the hostile Acomas. His taking that prudent step indicates he had learned a lesson. Probably he was disturbed by the thought that a share of the blame for this tragedy rested upon himself. For after all, he *had* neglected to send his nephew any warning, and the result proved disastrous. From that experience came a newborn sense of wariness, a sudden attention to detail, a careful avoidance of unnecessary risk.

His caution was much in evidence during the seven-day journey back to the capital. The expedition was strung out from El Morro in full battle array, with advance and rear guards to protect against surprise attack. Scouts ranged ahead to reconnoiter the country and report any suspicious movements of the Indians. At each night's camp wide-awake sentries kept watch. Their haunting fear was that the rebellion might have spread beyond the confines of Acoma to other pueblos, and that a sea of foes was gathering to engulf them. They saw nothing along the way, however, to confirm that threat. Approaching San Juan, the governor sent a small delegation ahead to tell the colonists not to come forth and greet him, as they usually did, because this occasion was too solemn.

A vastly relieved Vicente de Zaldívar welcomed the appearance of these messengers, for he had received no word from his uncle since the catastrophe at Acoma. When the survivors of his brother's troop had first galloped into San Juan with their story, he had been stunned. According to the reports he heard, Juan de Zaldívar, riding at the head of thirty-one men, had paused at the foot of Acoma where he offered to trade hatchets and other articles for flour needed to supply his men on the journey west. But by this time Zutucapán and the war faction had gained complete control of the pueblo and laid plans for destroying any Spaniard who fell into their hands.

Upon being informed by the sullen Acomas that several days would be required to grind a large quantity of grain, Maese de Campo Zaldívar retired with his party a short distance and encamped near water to wait. On the appointed morning, he detached eighteen of the men and several Indian servants to go with him and collect the flour. The rest of the force was left in camp under command of Captain Gerónimo Márquez, who had returned from his long pursuit of the deserters just in time to be enlisted by Zaldívar for this new duty.

At the bottom of the peñol, the maese de campo ordered Lieutenant Bernabé de las Casas to keep three soldiers and guard the horses while he climbed to the pueblo. Once on top he allowed his followers to break into small groups so they could go about the village gathering the sacks of flour. Suddenly, they were attacked from all sides as men and women commenced hurling stones and war clubs from the terraced rooftops. At several points, the Spaniards rallied and made gallant stands before succumbing in frenzied hand-to-hand fighting. The Acomas quickly learned that Spanish firearms were indeed lethal. In one corner, Juan de Zaldívar drove back the attackers with his sword. Then, Zutucapán himself stepped forward and struck him a terrible blow on the forehead. To use Villagrá's words: "Zaldívar fell, delivered unto that eternal sleep to which we are all doomed someday." From his boyhood home in Zacatecas, he had marched north more than a thousand miles to die before his thirtieth birthday on this forlorn rock.

On the plains below, Bernabé de las Casas and the remaining horse guards heard the commotion and firing of harquebuses. Soon one of the servants escaped down the steep trail, bringing word of the deaths of many Spaniards. Casas looked up then and his blood chilled. Two of the youngest soldiers, Juan de Olague and Pedro de Robledo had fought their way to the edge of the stony mesa. And there, assailed and having no other choice, they jumped. Robledo struck a sloping spur of the wall and died instantly, but Olague landed in a sand dune blown against the base of the cliff. Casas discovered him unconscious and bruised, but alive. That prompted him to go in search of other survivors. He found two more soldiers lying senseless in a neighboring dune, and then Captain Gaspar López Tabora with another pair of men joined him. They had escaped from the rear of the rock soon after the melee started and were the last to turn up safe.

Mounting their horses, this remnant rode back to camp at the watering place and rejoined the rest of the command. The able Captain Márquez assumed charge in the emergency and wasted no time in issuing orders. First, he sent López Tabora with a small escort to search for Governor Oñate, somewhere in the west, to tell him of the massacre. And second, he dispatched messengers to the various Rio Grande pueblos with a warning for the defenseless priests stationed among them, urging that they hurry back to Oñate's headquarters. Márquez possessed plenty of experience in Indian warfare and knew how swiftly rebellion could sweep across an entire province. The colonists must be hastily prepared for that possibility, so with Juan de Zaldívar's fractured troop he retraced the trail to San Juan.

He had barely arrived back when Captain López Tabora rode in with a discouraging report. He had been followed and harried by the Acomas and, worse, he had lost the governor's trail and turned back leaving him unwarned. Vicente, therefore, summoned Bernabé de las Casas and ordered him to assemble a heavily armed squad and to find Oñate at any cost. It was that party, moving at breakneck speed, that encountered the governor at El Morro and accompanied his sorrowful procession on its return to San Juan.

Oñate rode into the plaza on December 21 to confront a colony in mourning. He first visited families who had lost men and delivered words of comfort. Then, together, they proceeded to the church where the priests sang the traditional hymn of thanks, the *Te Deum Laudamus,* for the safe delivery of the governor and his army. Afterward, Don Juan posted sentinels and retired to his quarters.

Of the frailty of the Spanish position in New Mexico, he no longer entertained any doubt. Should the rebellion spread from Acoma, his slender military forces held small chance of containing it. That dark thought, he well knew, was in the minds of his men who now waited to learn what action he proposed to take. A vigorous and decisive response on his part might yet prevent destruction of the shaky kingdom, but just how far could he legally go? Oñate was quite aware of the king's ruling that war with the Indians ought to be avoided whenever possible, and that stricture could not be lightly dismissed. Still, what was he to do? This weighty matter preoccupied him far into the night.

The Spaniards were not, as many writers would have us believe, a reckless people, given to headlong and unprovoked reprisals. They moved according to His Majesty's law and the church's doctrine, and this required cool deliberation. The justice of waging war against the Indians was a controversial issue in the sixteenth century, one over which Spanish jurists and theologians argued long and heatedly. Specifically, their concern focused upon the question of what conditions constituted a "just war," for given the resistance of many New World natives, some conflict was found to be inescapable. Gradually, there emerged a highly formalized and legalistic procedure that had to be observed by soldiers in the field before launching a full-scale war. The structure of that procedure is revealed in the pronouncements and acts of Juan de Oñate in the days that followed the Acoma uprising.

Just past dawn on the morning after his return, he asked the Franciscan fathers to examine the circumstances of the Acoma affair and render a judgment regarding lawful punishment. He framed his appeal in these words: "Don Juan de Oñate, Governor, Captain General, and Adelantado of the provinces of New Mexico requests an opinion as to what conditions are necessary in order to wage a just war. In the event of such a war, what steps may be taken against those warred upon and against their possessions."

Father Martínez, with aid from all the priests, agreed to undertake a reply, but preparation of the formal document had to wait a few days since the religious holiday was upon them. The colony's first Christmas in New Mexico, 1598, became fixed in memory as a time of deepest gloom and perplexity of spirit. For Governor Oñate, it marked another low point in his endless sea of troubles. But the pageantry of the Christmas Mass in the new church of San Juan Bautista exerted its power over the Spanish mind so that persons of both high and low degree left the service with at least a pinch of optimism and restored self-confidence. In this way grief was alleviated before it could become hopelessness.

On December 28, Don Juan, himself presiding, formally opened judicial proceedings, which would last more than two weeks and whose purpose was to determine the fate of Acoma. He took lengthy testimony from each survivor of his deceased nephew's troop and listened thoughtfully to the recommendations for action made by the officers. Captain Gerónimo Márquez, for instance, expressed the opinion that if Acoma "is not leveled and its inhabitants punished, there will be no security in all of New Mexico, nor could it be settled, as the natives of [other] pueblos are watching what we do at Acoma and whether we punish them." His harsh conclusion was shared by others.

Several of the men recounted the grisly details of how their companions had died on the rock. Their bodies, smashed with war clubs, had been tossed to the plains below, while Indians paraded along the rim wearing the helmets and brandishing the swords of their victims. Young Juan de Olague, who leaped for his life into the dunes, added that he felt certain the Acomas had "acted with treachery and premeditation in killing the Spaniards." That was exactly the kind of language useful in buttressing a case on behalf of waging just war. Olague's testimony and all the rest was made under oath and entered in the record, with the appropriate signatures and certifying formulas the occasion seemed to require.

Last in the proceedings, the friars submitted their opinion on the legality of a declaration of war. Oñate, they determined, possessed both the authority and sufficient cause to take such a step for "the purpose of attaining and preserving peace," but not for revenge or similar base motives. The Acomas, by earlier swearing fealty to the king and becoming his subjects, had placed themselves under royal laws, and therefore under the jurisdiction of the governor. Though guilty of crimes, as subjects they must be given an opportunity to make peace, and only if they refused could war be justified. Delinquents and their goods taken in just war, concluded the friars, are at the mercy of the victor. To an Englishman, perhaps, such an exercise in legal and moral self-vindication would have seemed unnecessary, even absurd. But to Spaniards, intent upon doing things by the book, their efforts to conform to the behavior a just war imposed appeared to be part of the natural order of things and eminently reasonable.

For the next stage, Don Juan issued a proclamation on January 10, 1599, summoning the army to assemble before his headquarters after the morning's high Mass for the purpose of allowing everyone the opportunity to voice an opinion on the best way to punish Acoma. According to what the royal secretary, Juan Gutiérrez Bocanegra, wrote: "The criminal proceedings previously drawn up were read word for word, and in addition the Governor discussed many other reasons both for and against carrying out the proposed punishment." From the ensuing general discussion emerged a decision by consensus to attack and vanquish Acoma as speedily as possible. The reason, entered in the record, was that any delay might encourage other pueblos to form a league with Acoma and, thus strengthened, wipe out the Spaniards. Underscoring this fear, the married soldiers proclaimed that unless the rebellion was crushed right away, they would ask permission to take their women and children back to New Spain, as there would be no security in the kingdom of New Mexico.

And so, by a sort of rudimentary democracy, a verdict was reached and sentence passed, sealing the fate of Acoma. If anyone in the assembly held doubts concerning either the wisdom or fairness of bringing this pueblo to its knees, he failed to speak up. With a clear conscience and all doubt removed from his mind, Juan de Oñate publicly declared "war by blood and fire" (*guerra de sangre y fuego*) against the hapless Acoma Indians. That was a phrase habitually used in the Moorish crusades and employed just as regularly by the Oñates and other frontier captains in their drawn-out conflicts with the Chichimecas. It meant, quite simply, a war of no quarter. Although by generating a great deal of legal paperwork, Don Juan attempted to show that soldier and cleric alike supported his severe penalty imposed upon the Acomas, subsequent events would reveal that he alone bore responsibility for the terrible happenings that soon unfolded.

The governor at first intended to conduct the war in person, but the priests and all his subjects convinced him not to risk his life in this hazardous undertaking. Should the attack upon Acoma fail, he would be needed to lead the colonists in flight from New Mexico. Reluctantly, Oñate yielded and turned command of the army over to his surviving nephew, the Sargento Mayor Vicente de Zaldívar. He also handed him a detailed set of instructions, outlining the steps to be taken in the campaign.

Zaldívar was to march to Acoma with seventy-two men, including the two Indian interpreters Tomás and Cristóbal. Speaking through them, he would order the rebels to submit to the authority of the king, lay down their arms, and surrender those persons responsible for slaying the Spaniards. Should they accept these terms, the population was to be resettled on the plains and the pueblo demolished so that it could never be reoccupied. But if they resisted, then Zaldívar was empowered to consult with a council of his officers and decide the best course for defeating the pueblo by force of arms. "Make more use of clemency than severity," his uncle told him, "if it should turn out that the Acomas had committed their crimes more from incapacity of reason than from malice." That seems a remarkable consideration on Oñate's part, given the fact that his struggling kingdom was threatened with extinction and he had already decreed a war of no quarter. But it was not at all unusual for sixteenth-century Spaniards to think in abstract terms and weigh complicated moral questions, even as they sifted their gunpowder and sharpened their blades in preparation for battle. That did not prevent them, nevertheless, from taking on occasion action that shocks modern sensibilities.

Governor Oñate, backed by a much stripped-down garrison and a worried body of colonists, watched Vicente de Zaldívar depart San Juan in the morning's bracing cold on January 12. The heavily armed column, though small for the job ahead, looked formidable. Flanking Zaldívar, in full armor, were such captains as Marcos Farfán de los Godos, Gaspar Pérez de Villagrá, Gerónimo Márquez, Alonso Sánchez (Oñate bookkeeper), and Pablo de Aguilar, the officer who twice before had narrowly escaped execution for disobedience and disloyalty. In addition to personal weapons, they bore two brass culverins—artillery pieces engraved with the Spanish crown that had been carried up from New Spain at the cost of prodigious effort.

The ride to Acoma consumed nine days. Reaching the foot of the peñol, Zaldívar circled it three times with his men, as much to get the pueblo's defenses clearly in mind as to let its people know that the time for reckoning had come. The Acomas who crowded to the edge of their great rock and peered down at the undersized Spanish army indicated that they were totally unimpressed. They jeered, uttered deep-throated yells, and shouted insults, which were dutifully translated by Tomás. Some of the impatient soldiers were eager to respond with words or bullets, but Zaldívar restrained them. With his interpreter, he called upon the Acomas to give up and accept the

The outline of Acoma Pueblo atop its peñol, as it must have appeared to Vicente de Zaldivar's attacking army in 1599. (Courtesy Museum of New Mexico)

terms of Governor Juan de Oñate. On his third and last call they responded by unleashing a cloud of arrows and spears, and for good measure tossing down stones and jagged chunks of ice that raised little geysers of dirt when they struck the ground. Not only did they intend to polish off these puny Spaniards, the war leaders cried, but afterward they planned to march east and annihilate those pueblos that had welcomed and fed them. Seeing nothing but deadly animosity in their words, young Zaldívar broke off communication and proclaimed the war of no quarter.

The Spaniards had come spoiling for a fight, and now they had it. Most of them likely knew stories from the Mixton War, which revealed the difficulties of attacking Indians entrenched on peñoles. But those tales could hardly have prepared them for the seemingly impossible challenge they faced here. Any military strategist viewing Acoma's high-altitude defenses would have had to say, practically speaking, that the pueblo was unassailable. The residents themselves thought so—their feeling of invincibility had led them to slay Juan de Zaldívar and his companions, in the first place. Some of Vicente's men now began to wonder whether that wasn't the case after all and the thought of defeating Acoma a mere pipe dream.

Whenever the morale of Spanish soldiers began to falter, invariably the leader would deliver an impassioned speech, designed to restore confidence, bolster courage, and nourish an esprit de corps. Oñate, as we have seen, resorted to oratory on not a few occasions to hold his beleaguered colony together during the long delay preceding his New Mexico entrada. Preparatory to his launching an assault on Acoma, Vicente de Zaldívar decided that some speech making of his own was in order. Therefore, late in the day of the twenty-first, he called a council.

Villagrá recorded, in rather stilted and high-flown style, the tenor of Zaldívar's exhortation. In essence, he urged the troops to stand and fight until achievement of a complete victory. Otherwise, it would be seen, he intoned, as "a serious blot upon our honor as Spaniards." To leave the Acoma affronts unpunished, Zaldívar warned, would cause the Spaniards to lose the obedience and respect of the remaining pueblos. And to turn aside objections that the fearsome peñol could not be taken, he said: "Let us use a little strategy and this task will not be so difficult as it seems."

In a few words, he laid before his listeners what he had in mind. The main army would deploy in full view of the Indians and launch a frontal attack, to create a diversion. Under that cover, Zaldívar with eleven men would steal behind the peñol, scale the steep cliff, and gain a foothold on the summit. Villagrá declares that "all applauded and approved this daring plan," and well they might, for it was just audacious enough to work.

On the following afternoon, Zaldívar fearlessly rode to the base of the rock and shouted to his foes to prepare themselves, as he was going to attack headlong. The Indians were astonished by his bold-ness and by his warning, but then this was their first encounter with Europeans in a formal war. Zaldívar's action was just the class of dramatic gesture, rendered with grand style, that noble Basques and Spanish knights held in high esteem. It was conduct reminiscent of the Moorish wars and the struggles with Aztec and Inca, and it also represented cunning strategy, especially for a leader who was only in his mid-twenties, since by his rashness he meant to distract the Aco-mas from the trap he was setting.

At three o'clock, with the winter's sun slanting in the west, the battle commenced by a blare of trumpets and an all-out assault against the chief stepway leading upward to the pueblo. Like a magnet, the action drew all the Indian warriors to that point, just as Zaldívar hoped. Accompanied by Villagrá, Aguilar, and nine others, he hurried to the far side of the rock and then, in the words of the soldier-poet, "we climbed the high walls of this immense mass of stone . . . for there were none to oppose us." Once on top, however, their presence was discovered, and four hundred warriors besieged them. In fierce stand-up fighting, the two sides grappled, and for a while it was touch-and-go for the Spaniards. Vicente saw one of the enemy garbed in his dead brother's clothes, and eyes ablaze he rushed forward and "cleft his skull asunder" with one mighty slash of the sword. At nightfall, the gory fighting broke off, but the Spaniards still held their beachhead on a corner of the peñol.

They expanded it the following morning by bringing up more soldiers from below, and with them a large beam to be used as a bridge over a deep but narrow chasm dividing Acoma's rock into two sections. Some of the men crossed on the timber and then picked it up, thinking to use it on ahead. Immediately, however, they were beset by a swarm of club-wielding Acomas and almost overcome. On wings lent by desperation, impulsive Villagrá made a flying leap across the chasm and replaced the bridge, allowing reinforcements to reach the advance party. His act of heroism became part of the saga of this extraordinary conflict, as related afterward in his own narrative poem.

Later in the day, Zaldívar ordered the pair of culverins hauled up on ropes, and the entire peñol shuddered when they belched and boomed. The slaughter was appalling, and as the volume of smoke deepened the constricted battlefield became odorous with the acrid smell of burned gunpowder. As the Spaniards pushed forward, they set on fire the houses and kivas, and many of the defenders died in these rather than surrender. Others committed suicide by jumping off the rock, and family members slew one another. At the close of the third day, Acoma surrendered. The remaining population—about five hundred in all, predominantly women and children—gave themselves up to captivity. Hundreds had perished, the exact number unknown, and a few others had managed to escape.

To the Spaniards their victory seemed miraculous. Only one soldier had died and he accidentally shot by another, although numbers had suffered wounds. The suspicion of aid from on high seemed confirmed when some of the Indian survivors spoke of seeing a Spaniard on a white steed who emerged from the bank of smoke in the thickest of the fray and with his flaming sword swept them before him like a whirlwind. Moreover, a maiden of great beauty rode at his side. Zaldívar's men were awestruck. Santiago, in fulfillment of his ancient role, had intervened on their behalf, for they believed the Indian accounts implicitly. In addition, the Virgin Mary must have come along to guarantee success. The entire campaign from first to last, they decided, was cause for elation. The remnant of the Acomas, on the contrary, viewed the events in an altogether different light, and even now their suffering was not ended, as they shortly would discover.

For Juan de Oñate, the waiting at headquarters during the long days his men were gone to war proved difficult to bear. The evening following Zaldívar's departure, the governor was in his lodgings when the San Juan Indians raised an alarm, claiming they had a report that neighboring pueblos were massing to destroy the weakened Spanish garrison. Oñate quickly posted his men at the four entrances to the central plaza and awaited attack. Soon the women of the colony appeared on the rooftops and led by Doña Eufemia, the indomitable wife of the junior officer Francisco de Sosa Peñalosa, announced their intention to join in the defense. Oñate swelled with pride at their show of bravery and refused to order them to seek cover. In fact, they stood their watch in the numbing cold, marching up and down in martial step, until word finally was passed that Spanish readiness had intimidated the Indian army and turned it back.

Time dragged for the governor as he awaited news from Acoma. On the twelfth day an aged woman of the pueblo, evidently a seer and clairvoyant, approached him with a startling story. In vivid detail she described a mighty battle on Acoma's rock, even indicating that the final outcome might be favorable to the Spaniards. Oñate was eager to believe her, but more days slipped by before he gained confirmation. The quartermaster Diego de Zubia rode in, as the personal messenger of Vicente de Zaldívar, and broadcast the Spanish victory. Oñate's people breathed a collective sigh of relief and then rejoiced.

For reasons not altogether clear, the governor adopted the idea of hurrying downriver and meeting the triumphant Zaldívar at Santo Domingo pueblo. There would be Acoma prisoners aplenty, and he had already decided to put them on trial. Since Santo Domingo was a large and commodious village, well known to him from previous visits, and also occupied a central location in the kingdom, perhaps it suited him as a convenient showcase for his court, by which he meant to make an unforgettable example of his rebel captives. On February 9, 1599, Vicente de Zaldívar arrived at the pueblo to be warmly greeted by his Uncle Juan, who promptly decreed that the trial should begin that very day.

Oñate appointed Captain Alonso Gómez Montesinos to serve as defense attorney for the accused Acomas, and the Indian Tomás once more filled the role of interpreter. As presiding judge, the governor called a series of native witnesses to explain why they had slain the maese de campo and his men and later disregarded Vicente de Zaldívar's demand to surrender. Most of those replying claimed that they had been away in their fields when the original killings occurred and only learned of them after their return. And some, they said, had wanted to surrender, but others refused, and so they fought. Defending attorney Gómez Montesinos entered a plea for clemency on their behalf because they were "uncivilized," that is, lacking in reason. The soldiers gave their testimony next, simply telling what had happened.

In three days it was over, Oñate closing the lopsided proceedings on February 12 and issuing his sentence, from which there was no appeal. While no one received a death penalty, the punishments were drastic nonetheless:

> Males over age twenty-five to have one foot cut off and condemned to twenty years of personal servitude. (That amounted to twenty-four individuals.)
> Males twelve to twenty-five years old condemned to twenty years of personal servitude.
> Women over twelve years of age condemned to twenty years of personal servitude.
> Two Moquis captured in the Acoma fight to have the right hand cut off and to be set free to take home news of their punishment.
> Children under twelve, whom Oñate ruled free of guilt, to be handed over to Father Martínez and Zaldívar for a Christian upbringing. (Sixty of the small girls were afterward sent to Mexico City for parceling among the convents there. None ever saw their homeland or relatives again.)

To ensure that the sentences of mutilation had the widest possible impact, Don Juan directed that they be carried out at Santo Domingo and nearby pueblos, where the condemned Indians lost their hands or feet over a period of several days. The rest of the prisoners were herded back to San Juan and distributed among the colonists, to begin their two decades of servitude. This retribution was reminiscent of the Spanish crusades and the practice of the Moors, but for the Pueblo Indians it represented something entirely new and shocking. Oñate wanted to nail down a message—that resisting the Spaniards by arms brought swift and iron-fisted retaliation. For the most part, he seemed to have succeeded. The Acomas, however, proved more resilient and slippery than he imagined, for within a year or two most of them escaped their servitude, fled back to the rock, and rebuilt a new pueblo that remains occupied to this day.

In the aftermath of the episode, Governor Oñate took stock of his position, trying to assess the best course of action. Although the Pueblos were cowed, the Spanish colonists had lost that sense of ease and security they felt before the Acoma troubles. Don Juan meant to resume his wide-ranging explorations, but now he worried that making up an expedition might leave his headquarters under-garrisoned and invite attack. The answer to that problem was to obtain reinforcements, which he needed under any circumstances if his kingdom was to expand and develop. That was one of the things he requested when on March 2 he sharpened his quill and wrote to the Viceroy, his first letter from New Mexico.

Oñate related at length the details of the grueling trip north, the settling-in at San Juan, the initial efforts to explore the land, and the uprising at Acoma. Then he grew eloquent describing New Mexico's potential riches. So extraordinary was this new realm that "none other held by his Majesty in these Indies excels it." Not content with his hyperbole, he predicted that he would add to the king's empire a domain far larger than that conquered by Cortés, and he extolled the value of the mineral specimens he had collected. To the letter he attached an assay report made by his man Diego de Zubía, showing that a large quantity of silver was obtained from a small sample of ore. He mentioned, as well, reports of pearls said to come from the distant shores of the South Sea, and referred to the ample salt lakes and available "wealth from the wool and skins of the buffalo." In plain fact, Oñate did his best to put the most optimistic face on his New Mexico entrada.

The reason could be found in the second half of his letter to the count of Monterrey. "I humbly beg and entreat you," he stated, "to

Acoma Pueblo (1885) rebuilt on the site conquered by Oñate's soldiers in 1599. (Courtesy Museum of New Mexico)

send me all the help possible." Clearly, the purse strings in Mexico
City could be loosened more quickly if the viceroy became convinced
the new kingdom was abundantly endowed with natural resources.
On the other hand, the urgency of Oñate's appeal ought to have
alerted his superior that all was not as rosy as he painted it in his
letter. Indeed, Don Juan's outright exaggerations would later come
back to haunt him.

Oñate put together a distinguished party to hand-deliver his letter
and other documents to the viceroy in Mexico City. It included
Father Martínez, who was to request more friars for New Mexico,
and Father Salazar, the governor's cousin and one of his closest
advisers, who could be counted upon to represent Oñate's accomplishments in glowing terms. (Unfortunately, Salazar died on the trip
south, depriving Oñate of his valuable services.) Heading the escort
were captains Pérez de Villagrá, Farfán de los Godos, and Juan
Pinero, loyal and good men chosen to address the count of Monterrey. Don Juan also asked Villagrá to take personal charge of recruiting
new soldiers, should the viceroy grant permission. And Villagrá carried a document drawn up and signed by nineteen of the leading
colonists, intended to be a vote of confidence in Oñate's leadership.
However, the praise was so fulsome and contrived that the viceroy
could not have failed to see through it. But Don Juan was missing
no opportunity in trying to advance his cause.

When Oñate sent his messengers off in March 1599, it was with the
hope that they would return quickly accompanied by new blood,
soldiers and friars, and bringing back supplies to nourish his hungry
colony. He might have been more than a little downcast had he
known then that more than a year and a half would pass before the
aid arrived. During that interval of waiting, several significant events
occurred, but information concerning them is extremely sketchy.
Either Oñate was keeping no day-by-day journal, or if he was, it
failed to survive. Nor did anyone else in the colony preserve a record
of events.

Sometime during this period, the governor presided over the
movement of his headquarters and capital across the Rio Grande one-
quarter mile to the facing pueblo of San Gabriel. It is puzzling that
in subsequent letters to the viceroy and king, he makes no reference
to this shift of residence. But the circumstances that forced the move
were not ones he would want to call attention to, so that may be a
sufficient explanation. As noted, his original intention was to build

a standard Spanish municipality, San Francisco, somewhere in the vicinity of San Juan. That obviously entailed a long-term building project, even with Pueblos joining in the labor. And it was a burden his colonists were unready to assume. They stated flatly their refusal to participate. Long afterward a soldier would testify that he thought "the reason for this was their dissatisfaction at remaining and their desire to abandon the land because of the great privations they were suffering."

In any event, Oñate elected not to press the issue and instead worked out an arrangement whereby the native residents turned over their pueblo of San Gabriel, with its plaza and some four hundred apartments, to the Spaniards and relocated elsewhere, most of them in San Juan. Quite likely the San Juans were only too glad to receive their own people in exchange for Oñate and his colonists. Actually, not all of the San Gabriel Indians left their pueblo. Some remained behind to work for the Spaniards at hauling wood and water, tasks that guaranteed them regular rations of corn. Already the Spanish presence was producing food shortages, since the delicate equilibrium by which the Pueblos had managed to sustain themselves was completely upset.

In time, the Spaniards remodeled San Gabriel, making changes that accommodated their own needs and producing a U-shaped village plan. They opened exterior doors and windows in the ground floors (which all pueblos, for defensive reasons, lacked at that period), cut interior doorways, and built outside dome-shaped adobe ovens, of the kind still to be seen in rural Spain. Moreover, work soon began in the opening of the U on a new church, with a cruciform floor plan, and with an attached *convento,* or friary. Traces of these architectural features were uncovered by University of New Mexico archaeologists who excavated portions of San Gabriel over several seasons beginning in 1959. They found a quantity of artifacts dating from the Oñate era, among them a cannonball, a religious medal, trade beads, a copper spoon, armor and harquebus parts, including a gunstock ornament, and mineral specimens, no doubt representing some of the ore samples Don Juan brought in for assaying. There was little in these twentieth-century finds to suggest that the first European settlers in western North America lived at San Gabriel under anything but the most primitive conditions.

During the remainder of 1599 and through the entire year of 1600, Don Juan did what he could do encourage the colony's two chief activities—the conversion of the Indians and the search for mines. Success in both areas, he knew, was of intense interest to the king. Perhaps still unknown to him at this time, Philip II had died on September 13, 1598, just as the kingdom of New Mexico was being established. But with the passing of the crown to his son and successor Philip III, nothing was to change in the reverence Oñate and other New World governors felt toward the monarchy. Stray reports indicate that the Franciscans scattered among the Pueblos were winning the Indians to Christianity, but later events would prove that the natives' acceptance of the new religion was mainly superficial.

The Spaniards continued to scour the hills for mineral traces, and Oñate persisted in claiming that important strikes were being made. But he had difficulty producing evidence that convinced anyone. He liked to tout the value of the silver lodes located near San Marcos pueblo, but his people were aware that, in fact, they were very low grade. Not so, insisted the governor. The San Marcos silver was just not as rich as mightier deposits farther on. One promising cluster of mines lay adjacent to the pueblo of El Tuerto, which probably was situated east of the Sandia Mountains. Don Juan sent his nephew there with mining equipment to build an ore crusher and smelter. On a visit to San Gabriel, Vicente de Zaldívar passed a small, gleaming piece of ore among the soldiers, exciting their interest. It was a fine silver specimen, commented a priest sarcastically, but had it been really unearthed in New Mexico? To that, Vicente made no reply. Indeed, nothing else appears in the record with regard to the operations at El Tuerto.

Sometime before mid-1600, Governor Oñate decided to send young Zaldívar with about twenty-five or thirty men on a trip to the far west, its aim to make another attempt at locating the South Sea. There is no ready answer as to why he launched this new exploration before arrival of his long-awaited reinforcements from New Spain. Presumably, though, he was hoping for some sort of quick discovery in that direction, which might bolster the fading spirits of his men. Gone for three months, Zaldívar penetrated as far as the southwestern corner of Arizona, where he became lost and then encountered hostile Indians. His misfortunes caused him to turn back only three days' march from the sea. An official report as well as a daily log of his expedition must have been written, but neither has come to light. So, nothing is known of the startling adventures this party surely experienced.

As prologue to this whole undertaking, Zaldívar had ridden down to the Jumano pueblos in central New Mexico to collect a levy of provisions he would need on the trail to the South Sea. The Indians closer to San Gabriel had already been relieved of their surplus corn, so the Spaniards were having to range farther afield to make their levies. At the largest of the three or four Jumano villages, the one now called Gran Quivira, Zaldívar issued his demands. But instead of handing over grain, the inhabitants gave him stones. As best we can determine, Zaldívar then turned west on his sea quest, but not before notifying his uncle of the Jumanos' act of insolence and bravado. Don Juan hastened southward from San Gabriel with fifty armed men to administer punishment.

At the offending pueblo, he drew up and demanded tribute in the form of cotton *mantas*, that is, the blankets commonly woven by New Mexico's Indians. Grudgingly, the Jumanos turned over a dozen or so, saying that was all they could spare. Oñate retired with his soldiers to a nearby water hole to camp, returning early the next morning. Through an interpreter who spoke the Jumano language (seemingly an Indian other than the faithful Tomás or Cristóbal), he told the villagers that he was going to chastise them for having given Zaldívar stones to eat. Thereupon, the governor ordered a corner of the pueblo set afire, and he had the troops discharge a harquebus volley into a crowd on the rooftops. Five or six Indians died, and others suffered wounds. Two men, identified as Jumano war leaders, were captured, and Don Juan promptly had them hanged. He spoke again to the residents, now mostly subdued, and a question arose as to whether the interpreter was rendering his words correctly or was, in fact, speaking against the interests of the Spaniards. Oñate could not be sure so, to play it safe, he had the interpreter hanged.

His uncompromising treatment of the Jumanos quieted them temporarily, but resentment simmered. Around Christmas of 1600 a party of five Spaniards passed through their country heading south for Santa Bárbara. Jumano warriors, out for revenge, pounced upon the group, slaying two. News of these deaths and word that the Jumanos were plotting a general uprising threw the San Gabriel colonists into panic. The Franciscans approached Oñate and urged him to take swift action to prevent spread of a rebellion. At a general war council, attended by all men under arms, the matter was discussed and a consensus reached to dispatch a punitive expedition under Vicente de Zaldívar, who had inherited his late brother's rank of maese de campo.

Delays followed, for reasons not known, and Zaldívar finally started for the Jumano district in the spring of 1601. Fighting men came forward and attacked him in the open with arrows and stones, but he soon drove them behind the walls of their largest pueblo. He besieged the place over the next six days and fought a series of bitter skirmishes, sustaining a severe wound in one of the engagements. When the village was taken, he burned it and distributed one adult Indian male to each of his soldiers as a servant. Later in that year, Fray Juan de Escalona wrote the viceroy that in the Jumano War more than eight hundred men, women, and children were killed and three pueblos burned with their supplies of corn. Whether that occurred during Zaldívar's expedition or in another campaign is difficult to say, since reports of the affair remain lost in Mexican and Spanish archives. The effect of this latest traumatic episode, however, was to further tax Oñate's strained resources and add to the growing impression that he still did not have a firm grip on his kingdom of New Mexico.

On Christmas Eve of 1600, which is to say, prior to Zaldívar's sortie against the Jumanos, the reinforcements and relief supplies at last reached Oñate and his subjects at San Gabriel. While not actually facing starvation, the people were hungry enough from short rations that the arrival was an occasion for celebration. The emissaries Don Juan had sent forth with his dispatches in March of the previous year had not reached Mexico City until the second week of June, when they were eagerly received by the viceroy and his advisers. When he subsequently wrote to the king, the count of Monterrey appeared fairly well disposed toward Oñate, saying that the persons who had come from New Mexico spoke positively of his conduct and management of the kingdom. But one matter that troubled the viceroy was the conflict at Acoma, which he characterized as a great cruelty. The battle forces were actually led by a nephew rather than Don Juan himself, he informed the king, and the Audiencia had decided not to initiate an investigation lest it discourage the people who had gone to New Mexico. His remark foreshadowed greater troubles for Oñate, who would yet have to answer for what happened at Acoma.

Captain Villagrá and others of Oñate's officers, upon appearing at the viceregal court, gave highly colored descriptions of New Mexico to match those provided in the dispatches of their commander. That persuaded the count to grant permission for recruitment of reinforcements, although he himself furnished little or nothing in the way of material support. Don Juan's brothers Cristóbal and Luís were still in Mexico City representing his interests, and now another brother,

This cross marks the place where Spanish colonists under Oñate built the first settlement in New Mexico in 1598. (Courtesy Museum of New Mexico)

Remains of the small rooms occupied first by Indians then by Spaniards at San Gabriel. (Courtesy Museum of New Mexico)

Alonso, taking letters for the king brought by Villagrá, took ship for Spain to play a similar advocacy role at the court of the sovereign.

Through the fall and early winter of 1599, Villagrá headed up the enlistment of new troops. As on the earlier expedition, the outpost of Santa Bárbara was designated as the rendezvous for men and supplies. Juan Guerra de Resa, Oñate's kinsman, was again providing almost unlimited funding, and his expenses in the present endeavor were said later to have amounted to one hundred thousand pesos. The relief expedition was of such magnitude that a government inspection proved necessary, the viceroy appointing for that purpose an officer stationed in Nueva Vizcaya, Captain Juan de Gordejuela. He reached Santa Bárbara by May 1600 before many of the recruits had drifted in. The captain encountered there a Mexican Indian named Lorenzo, one of Oñate's servants, who had recently abandoned New Mexico without leave. He told of the desperate conditions in the colony and the acute need for provisions and cattle. The colonists' plight so concerned Gordejuela that he summoned seven men, the only enlistments then on hand, and sent them with a priest, Fray Alonso de la Oliva, off to New Mexico bearing a small quantity of emergency supplies and notice that reinforcements were not far behind.

As summer lengthened, the number of soldiers and their dependents assembled at Santa Bárbara steadily grew. Gordejuela's muster records reveal a preponderance of young men in their late teens and early twenties, many of them Spanish born. Evidently, they had decided to chase fame and fortune in the New World, and upon arriving had heard, perhaps from Villagrá and his fellow recruiters, that New Mexico offered the latest opportunities for enrichment. Captain Gordejuela enrolled seventy-three officers and men, but several others are known to have joined the expedition after close of the inspection in late August.

Juan Guerra de Resa remained on hand throughout the summer's inspection, for he retained the title lieutenant-governor of New Mexico even though he had never entered the kingdom and was not planning to go now. Initially, Captain Villagrá was scheduled to lead the reinforcements northward, but shortly before the departure date of September 4, he suddenly announced his refusal to return to New Mexico and sought sanctuary in the nearby church and convent of Saint Francis. Guerra de Resa instantly preferred charges against him, for disobedience and violation of his military oath, but could not arrest him since Spanish law did not allow for the forced removal of fugitives from churches. Absolutely nothing is known concerning the circumstances that prompted Villagrá's unexpected defection. The most likely cause would have been a personal dispute arising in camp and grounded in some touchy point of honor. Whatever it was, the incident left Oñate without the services of a most valued subordinate.

Two other captains who had departed New Mexico with Villagrá, Marcos Farfán de los Godos and Juan Pinero, fail to reappear in the inspector's muster, indicating that they too somewhere along the way had relinquished their allegiance to Oñate and his enterprise. Hence, Guerra de Resa settled upon a junior officer, Bernabé de las Casas, now advanced to captain's rank, to assume command of the relief column. He had proved his mettle during the Acoma War, and in this his first major command, he performed commendably, delivering the soldiers, families, six Franciscans, supplies, livestock, and cart train safely to Governor Oñate on the propitious evening of December 24, 1600, in time to celebrate the first Christmas of a new century.

CHAPTER 9

Nadir

IN the years when the Spaniards were endeavoring to unlock the secrets of New Spain's far frontiers, the name Quivira became attached to the remote plains lying northeast of New Mexico and centering upon the modern state of Kansas. The word first occurs in the chronicles of the Coronado expedition, when a Plains Indian encountered at Pecos pueblo spoke of his native country to the east as a land rich in "gold, silver and fabrics." Somehow from this communication, quite imperfectly rendered, the eager Spanish listeners came up with Quivira as the name of that wondrous kingdom, whose wealth to their ears seemed unlimited.

Whether *Quivira* represented the mangling of some Indian word or a purely Spanish creation is difficult to say. One persistent explanation holds that Coronado selected as the motto, or watchword, for his exploration the challenging phrase *Quién vivirá, verá,* meaning "He who lives, will see." His men shortened that to *Quién vivirá,* then to *Qui'vivirá,* and in a final act of compression to *Quivira,* thereby inventing the term that was eventually applied to the rainbow's end on the plains. That story is unverifiable, as is the suggestion that Quivira has its root in the Arabic word *quivír,* signifying "great," which appears in Spanish place-names such as Guádal-quivír, the large river flowing through the southern Spanish city of Seville. Whatever the origin of the word, it lived beyond Coronado's day to become synonymous with the idea of illusive riches. The ruin of the chief Jumano pueblo attacked by Oñate's forces, for example, was long afterward called Gran Quivira by fortune hunters who mistakenly thought its tumbled walls might hide a golden treasure.

Don Juan must have initially heard of Quivira in connection with Coronado's wanderings, but it was from the Indian Jusepe, the servant lately attached to the Bonilla and Humaña party, that he garnered firsthand information on that faraway land and its people. Actually, there existed little in Jusepe's recital of his experiences to suggest that Quivira had much to offer the Spaniards, but still Oñate found something to pique his interest for he had firmly resolved to make a personal reconnaissance at the first opportunity. Perhaps in the back of his mind was the hope that he might stumble upon the Strait of Anián that had eluded all searchers before him. An accomplishment of that magnitude would unquestionably get his New Mexico project back on track and earn him the gratitude of viceroy and king. Whether moved by that motive or another, Don Juan eventually launched his march to Quivira in June 1601.

By that time six months had elapsed since the Christmas arrival of Captain Casas and the relief train with its reinforcements. During the first half of the year, enough unsettling events had occurred that Oñate ought to have had second thoughts about leaving his colony while he went upon a months-long journey to the plains. For one thing, the Jumano War took place, serving notice that the germs of rebellion continued to breed in the far corners of Puebloland. For another, the grumblings of soldiers and settlers assumed a new intensity.

Oñate had been counting on the relief supplies to still some of the complaints, but the needs of his subjects had grown so large that the cartloads of provisions, when distributed, seemed frightfully thin. And then there was the matter of those who had gone and failed to return: Fray Cristóbal, his cousin who had succumbed on the trip out; the captains Villagrá, Farfán de los Godos, and Pinero; and Father Martínez, once called by the governor, "the most worthy man he knew." Martínez had generally been supportive of Oñate, and indeed was asked to speak on behalf of his project upon reaching the viceregal court. Afterward, however, Martínez received an assignment other than New Mexico, but whether at his own request or at the order of his Franciscan superior is uncertain. In his stead, Father Juan de Escalona went north at the head of the new contingent of missionaries. Very shortly, he was to demonstrate his profound dislike for Oñate's conduct and methods of rule.

In partial compensation for the several supporters he had recently lost, Don Juan did gain one new confidant and advisor, Fray Francisco de Velasco, another cousin, who was a Mexican-born priest with a good education. Upon reaching San Gabriel in the company of Father Escalona, Velasco immediately moved into the governor's small inner circle and subsequently accompanied the expedition to Quivira as chaplain. With problems of supply and morale steadily mounting, Oñate relished all the backing he could get.

By early 1601 life in New Mexico had been reduced to a simple formula—fending off hunger and cold. This was not quite what the colonists had expected when they sold off their estates in Mexico, invested in the enterprise, and blandly rode forth behind Oñate's standard. The more affluent had packed clothing of velvet and Chinese taffeta, Cordovan slippers, and other finery into stout hide trunks for the trip north, expecting to use it when the silver-rich capital of their new kingdom rose in splendor on the banks of the Rio Grande. But now, less than three years later, both the garments and the dreams were in tatters, and the bulk of the settlers miserably disillusioned.

Most intolerable were the food shortages. It was the newly arrived Father Escalona who declared that, "Here, corn is God," while noting that "any Spaniard [in New Mexico] who gets his fill of tortillas feels as if he has obtained a grant of nobility." Oñate earlier had seen to the planting of wheat and other European crops in the valley of the Chama above its junction with the Rio Grande, but the initial harvests had thus far met no more than a small part of the Spaniards' requirements. As of 1601, they continued to remain dependent primarily upon the Pueblos for grain and beans, even while those aggrieved people bordered on starvation.

Severe winter temperatures furnished the second source of misery. Many of the Spaniards came from zones blessed with a Mediterranean or semitropical climate and thus lacked familiarity with harsh cold. Even Don Juan and his relatives who had been raised in the high, frigid uplands of Zacatecas found the bitter winters difficult to bear. "The cold is so intense," lamented a soldier, "that the rivers freeze over, and it snows most of the time during the winter, which lasts eight long months." The settlers shivered in the tiny vault-like rooms of San Gabriel, wrapped in the light blankets taken from the Indians and huddled over feeble fires whose wood had to be brought at great labor from a distance of five or six leagues. Overnight, drinking water froze in the *tinajas*, or pottery jars, and the sacramental wine became so cold the priests had to warm it before sunrise Mass. "May God grant us patience to bear all these hardships," wrote one man in a letter to Mexico City. But there were others among Oñate's followers who had run out of patience in the period immediately preceding his Quivira excursion.

One of them evidently was Captain Pablo de Aguilar, the man who twice before had committed acts serious enough to earn death sentences, both of which, as we have seen, were set aside by Oñate. The nature of Aguilar's last offense against his governor is not given in the documents, but that it was grave there can be little doubt. Captain Luís Gasco de Velasco later claimed he and others were in Aguilar's tent when Don Juan entered with his servants, all armed with swords and butcher knives. They attacked Aguilar, who begged to be allowed to confess since he was in a state of sin. His pleas were ignored, and Oñate delivered the final sword thrust to his body. Velasco refers to the victim as a truthful and honorable man, and an individual who had performed well up to this time. That does not square with other sources that paint his character in a sinister light, but still whatever crimes he may have committed could hardly have justified the brutal manner of his death. The historian George Hammond, usually sympathetic to Oñate, calls the act a dastardly killing, a judgment difficult to dispute. Yet, the sole account of the unseemly affair is from the pen of Captain Velasco, who shortly emerged in the role of mutineer and outspoken critic of Don Juan's conduct in New Mexico. Thus, we have to view the veracity of his statements with some suspicion.

He is the only source as well for the details surrounding another slaying, at about the same time—that of Captain Alonso de Sosa Albornoz, a man in his early fifties who had brought his wife and five children to New Mexico. When he asked Oñate for permission to return to Nueva Vizcaya, he stated as the reason that this kingdom on the Rio Grande was too poor to support his family. After the governor appeared to acquiesce and gave his consent, Captain Sosa began the process of packing up his cart. Before he could depart, however, he was sent into the countryside with other men to round up horses. Two leagues from camp, the captain was attacked by Vicente de Zaldívar and several accomplices who stabbed him to death and then hid the body under a pile of stones. "In view of this incident," comments Velasco, "the relatives of Captain Sosa did not again ask for permission to leave."

The plain truth was that the colony, into which Oñate had poured so much of his energy and treasure, was a shambles and so near to complete disintegration that he found himself compelled to condemn as a traitor anyone who spoke of giving up and returning to the southern provinces. That transformed him from a leader into an oppressor, a metamorphosis that may well have occurred over time without his quite being aware of it. In a desperate effort to retain control, he probably was able to justify in his own mind the use of high-handed tactics—even murder—as necessary for survival of the colony. But why he could not see that such behavior merely compounded his problems remains inexplicable. In a letter of denunciation addressed to the viceroy and smuggled out of New Mexico at great personal risk, Velasco declared that here, "we are all depressed, cowed, and frightened, expecting death at any moment." To the degree that his complaint actually represented the state of affairs at San Gabriel, it provides a sad commentary on the collapse of Oñate's dream.

Although fortune seemed determine to withhold her favors, Don Juan appeared just as determined to rebound from his endless chain of reverses. If indeed morale had collapsed and hope faded among the men, the governor persisted in speaking as if some great triumph lay just around the corner. He might have been approaching the end of his tether, but if so he artfully disguised that fact from the colony as a whole. To demonstrate his optimism and self-confidence, he began planning, just as soon as the December reinforcements were gathered in, another full-fledged expedition. Initially, Oñate announced his intention to march again for the South Sea, to follow up Zaldívar's recent attempt in that direction. And he went so far as to ready arms, outfit carts, and hold an assembly of the entire army in April 1601. But then he changed his mind, for reasons that remain obscure, and informed the soldiers that their journey would take them east instead of west, to Quivira rather than to the sea.

The official chronicle of the Quivira expedition says that it was composed of more than seventy picked and well-equipped men, plus guides (among them, Jusepe) and servants to handle the baggage, eight carts, and artillery—in short, a formidable force to accompany the governor of Spain's newest frontier kingdom. We possess evidence that Oñate had carefully combed the muster roll of his army to identify the names of potential troublemakers, and these he drafted for the journey, intending to keep a close eye upon them. By various strategies, however, several officers who were already scheming to desert managed to slip through Oñate's net and get assignments to remain on guard duty at San Gabriel.

Vicente de Zaldívar, Don Juan's right arm and firmest ally went, of course. And so did the lately arrived kinsman Fray Francisco de

Velasco, along with enough others of proven loyalty so that Oñate felt comfortable in embarking upon this long and probably hazardous undertaking. Lieutenant-governor and captain-general Francisco de Sosa Peñalosa, a man of property but scant leadership ability, was left to rule in his absence. Those staying behind listened as Don Juan delivered an impassioned parting speech in which, with tears in his eyes, he implored them to protect and maintain San Gabriel in the service of His Majesty. Then he gave the signal, and the Quivira-bound cavalcade lurched into motion. It was the twenty-third day of June, the eve of the feast of San Juan Bautista.

Oñate's route led him past Galisteo pueblo, across the Pecos River, and over the plains to the Canadian River, which he struck just above the point at which it made a sharp bend to the east. As the expedition followed its course through the Texas panhandle, one of the men remarked: "We found it green and delightful, bordered everywhere by vines and fruit trees, whereupon we came to realize that it was one of the best rivers that we had seen anywhere in the Indies." They pressed on, feasting upon wild plums and fish and meeting small bands of smiling Apaches whose women and children honored them with simple gifts. One afternoon thin black streaks of rain collected in a veil on the skyline then moved forward to drench the Spaniards in what they described as "a terrible cloudburst such as often falls in those plains."

Near the Texas-Oklahoma boundary line, the expedition encountered rough going for the carts, namely, a patch of sandhills and dunes. Therefore, Oñate decided to change course, leaving the river and striking out at an angle to the northeast, the direction in which lay Quivira according to his guides. The army now emerged upon the flat plain whose immense emptiness astonished the men, just as it had awed members of the Coronado party sixty years earlier when they braved this same country. One of them, Pedro de Castañeda, had likened the circular horizon to the rim of a bowl so that when a man sat down he seemed to be in a bottom with the ground rising around him. Flat, yes, but the plains were not utterly empty, as Oñate's cavaliers discovered a few days later. Numberless hordes of "monstrous cibola cattle," or buffalo, moving mounds of dark fur, blocked their path, "so tame that unless chased or frightened they stood still and did not run away." Hunters brought down four or five bulls, and the soldiers gorged on savory steaks they pronounced tastier than beef.

Traveling steadily on course, Oñate forded the North Canadian and Cimarron rivers, both of which carried little water in late summer, and as he approached south-central Kansas he sent Zaldívar scouting ahead. His nephew soon reported a sprawling tipi village with five thousand inhabitants. It was tenanted by Escanjaques, a warlike people who at once made preparations to fight. Speaking by signs, the Spaniards explained they were there on a peaceful mission and convinced the warriors to put aside their weapons. From them, Don Juan learned details of the massacre of the Humaña party, which the Escanjaques swore had been carried out by their northern neighbors and enemies, the Quivirans. When Oñate directed his march toward Quivira, some of the Escanjaques insisted on going along, which he could not prevent for fear of antagonizing them.

Advancing just a few leagues, the expedition came upon the waters of the Arkansas River whose filigreed surface, shining under late summer's sun, was painful to the eye. The banks were clothed in dense forests, while the bottoms back from the river nourished grasses that reached above a horse's belly. Here was the beginning of Quivira. The first bands of Indians the Spaniards saw formed themselves in battle array and threw handfuls of dirt in the air, the sign of war universally recognized on the southern plains. But again the Spaniards succeeded in conveying their friendly intentions, so the would-be attackers removed strings of beads they were wearing and placed them around the necks of the bearded newcomers.

The handsome and prosperous Quivirans dwelled in large towns of round houses thatched with bundles of prairie grass. Oñate's followers marveled at the surrounding fields, fertile and heavy now with crops of corn, beans, and calabashes ready to harvest. The contrast with agriculture they knew in New Mexico was startling, for there farm size was strictly limited by the amount of land fit for irrigation. In this country, on the other hand, plentiful rains through the growing season watered cropland naturally. The largest of the Quiviran centers contained twelve hundred houses and was the one Jusepe, upon escaping to New Mexico, had described as the "Great Settlement." These people, it can be stated with fair certainty, were the Caddoan-speaking Indians known in later times as the Wichita.

From the talkative dwellers in the Great Settlement, Don Juan learned that the lands farther on were even more thickly populated and that the multitudes there were hostile and would surely overwhelm his little army. Balanced against that disturbing news were

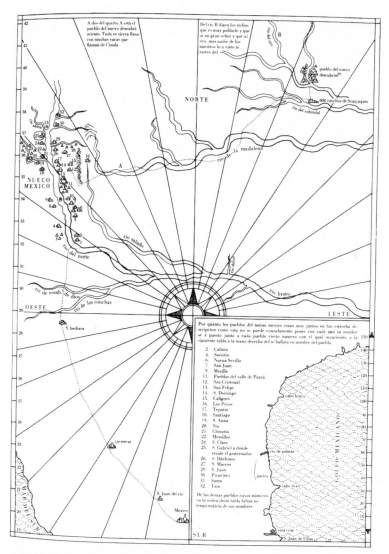

The Enrico Martínez Map of 1602, showing Oñate's Kingdom of New Mexico at upper left and the Rio del Robredal (Arkansas River) and the Great Settlement of the Quivira Indians at upper right. (From Hammond and Rey, *The Rediscovery of New Mexico, 1580–1594*, courtesy University of New Mexico Press)

seashells he observed ornamenting the foreheads of some of the Indians. They could only have come from the North Sea, which he mistakenly concluded must be close, and perhaps also he wondered if the continental strait might not be at hand. Those prospects stimulated him to press forward in spite of the warnings of danger.

Oñate coaxed his ranks on another three leagues, at which point the expedition ground to a halt. The soldiers had had enough, and almost to a man they petitioned their commander to turn around. Better their lives be spared, they said, so that word could be carried back to His Majesty of the richness of this new land, the thousands of souls awaiting conversion, and the wealth in meat, tallow, and hides furnished by the herds of wild cattle. "It was a hard decision for the Governor to accept and he expressed strong feeling against ending the expedition," declares the official log. Under the circumstances, he had no choice but to defer to his men, and so he gave the order that started them all on the homeward trail. They had covered 220 leagues from the Rio Grande, that is, nearly 600 miles.

Recrossing the Kansas plains under the hard blue of an October sky, the Spaniards reached once more the territory of the Escanjaques who by now had abandoned their pretense of friendliness and elected to challenge their passage. Oñate instructed his troops to put the armor on their horses, which was carried in the carts until needed, and they rode against a massed formation of fifteen hundred warriors. The battle boiled furiously for more than two hours, as arrows rained down on the horsemen. Most of them sustained minor wounds, but their body armor and shields prevented any fatalities. When the conflict became stalemated, Don Juan ordered a withdrawal, and his army left the field and eventually the high plains without experiencing further trouble. By the time he again entered the precincts of the Rio Grande Valley, five months had passed and in that troubled interregnum, unknown to him, the structure of his large and expensive project had been fatally bushwhacked.

Juan de Oñate had scarcely departed San Gabriel the previous June when the colonists' smoldering dissatisfaction with him and his misplaced optimism burst to the surface. At first they met in small, informal groups to air their grievances, real and imagined, against the iron discipline of the governor, the stinginess of the land, the poverty of the Pueblos, and the scarcity of silver. Few there were who did not claim to have entered into extravagant expense, selling off valuable properties in New Spain, often at sacrifice, to outfit themselves and families in hopes of reaping vast rewards in serving the king on the Rio Grande. But those rewards had not been forthcoming; only hardships existed in plentiful supply. New Mexico would never meet their unrealistic expectations.

Oñate himself had grown up listening to the heart-thumping story of how his father's business partner Juan de Tolosa had made the sudden and spectacular silver strike at La Bufa Mountain, the one that had given rise to the opulence of Zacatecas and created the Oñate family fortune. With such a tale to stir the imagination, it is not hard to believe that Don Juan was fully conditioned to expect that his New Mexico explorations would rapidly yield up some new bonanza, maybe even larger than La Bufa. He must have communicated that conviction to potential recruits as early as 1595.

When no second Zacatecas materialized in Oñate's kingdom, the soldier-colonists could find nothing else to support them, at least in the style they had anticipated. The governor had not been able to distribute encomienda grants as promised, mainly because the tribute, in the form of bushels of corn and cotton blankets, was so meager that he had to make all the collections in the name of his government and then ration out the take to the neediest of his settlers. Most irrigable cropland was already preempted by the Pueblos, meaning that large-scale or commercial agriculture was an impossibility, even had the colonists wanted to turn farmer, which they did not. Nor did there seem to be in those first years much to recommend the raising of cattle. Indeed, it was descendants of the founding pioneers who would discover that the short grasses of semiarid New Mexico were better suited to a sheep industry. So all that the disgruntled colonists could see on the horizon as payment for their huge and painful efforts was the title of hidalgo. But what use a title when a man's children cried with hunger?

That was the sort of question asked at San Gabriel as the spirit of rebellion grew and casual gatherings gave way to public meetings in the church attended by the entire community of Spaniards. On September 7 the elderly Fray Francisco de San Miguel delivered a speech from the altar urging the colonists to leave, on grounds that the Spanish presence was inflicting so many injustices upon the Pueblos that the church could no longer win converts. Father Escalona, because of his official position as head Franciscan in the kingdom, was not in attendance, but from the wings he encouraged and supported San Miguel's call. In fact, all of the friars quickly joined in the movement to desert, a rather astonishing turnabout since their order had long been a major advocate of settlement in New Mexico. In a letter, Escalona told the viceroy that the colony should not actually be abandoned, because the numerous baptized Indians ought to be served, but he was releasing the friars under him since conditions had become intolerable. He severely criticized Oñate, blaming him for all their woes, and implied that he should be replaced.

While the friars emerged as the most vocal spokesmen of the disaffected faction, several veteran officers who had been with Don Juan from the start acted as the wirepullers. They were headed by the treasurer Alonso Sánchez and his son-in-law, the supply-master Diego de Zubía, and included the able captains Bernabé de las Casas, Gregorio César, and others. They argued that this beleaguered outpost was not worth defending, for in four years of exploration nothing worthwhile had been found that could possibly benefit the crown. Because of the suffering caused by food scarcity, abandonment was a legitimate remedy, "in accordance with human and divine law," as one of them loftily phrased it. There at the church of San Gabriel in the waning summer, a majority of the colonists fell in step with the leaders, who now drew up elaborate documents in hopes of justifying their actions. No question about it, they were treading on perilous ground, for despite appeals to higher law, the action proposed bore all the earmarks of a mutiny.

By no means all of the San Gabrielites were prepared to go along. Oñate still retained a diehard corps of backers. Though small in numbers, they worried the conspirators since a solid front was needed to convince authorities in Mexico City and Madrid of the futility of maintaining the settlement. The rebel captains went among the holdouts and told each in private that he was the only one willing to stay behind. Upon hearing that, quite a few caved in and signed an agreement to leave. But when they learned that, in fact, others were staying, and that lies had been told them, they decided to remain. The conduct and motives of the deserters suffered additional stains when, prior to their leave-taking, they rifled the personal possessions and stole the horses of their comrades who were absent with Oñate in Quivira. The loyalist faction tried to prevent the thefts, but failed owing to the weakness of their numbers.

As the rift in the capital had widened, finally producing an open rupture, Lieutenant-Governor Sosa Peñalosa made no effort to preserve order. To all appearances, his sympathies lay with the people proposing flight, and probably he would have accompanied them had not his office securely bound him to New Mexico. His great perplexity is evident in a report to the viceroy sent out with the departing colonists. Therein, he claimed to be at an utter loss to know who was responsible for the calamitous situation. It would be unjust to blame Governor Oñate, he said, since he was away exploring in the name of the king. If he blamed the friars for fomenting desertion, they would bury him under an avalanche of quotes from the Holy Scriptures by way of defense. And if he accused the officers and soldiers of disrupting the peace by stealing grain and blankets from the Indians, they countered that their survival demanded it. Wanly, he concluded that all the colonists' troubles must be attributed to bad luck.

Oñate's handful of partisans saw things in a different light: cowardice, treachery, and disloyalty, not ill luck, had brought the settlement program to ruin. Knowing they were helpless to prevent the deserters from carrying out their plans, they nevertheless refused to sit idly by. Their side of the case must be presented to the viceroy, and to do that in person, they selected the faithful Captain Gerónimo Márquez. From a dozen of the governor's most articulate supporters, he took written statements repudiating charges that Oñate's administration was inept and the kingdom devoid of wealth.

Strongest censure fell on the shoulders of the friars, who were condemned for loafing about San Gabriel instead of attending to the hard work of conversion in distant pueblos. As to charges that starvation stalked the land, witnesses declared that the harvests of European crops had steadily increased each year so that the one being then brought in would prove the best ever. The natives, too, asserted one soldier, "have good fields where much will be gathered," a claim that contrasted markedly with critics who said the Indians were reduced to eating dirt, ashes, and twigs to stay alive. And in opposition to the missionaries' complaint that the Pueblos had been completely alienated by bad treatment, the pro-Oñate men stated that, on the contrary, they were content and pleased with the Spanish presence because it had put a stop to the wars between villages that had formerly taken place. In summary, this was the content of the documents Captain Márquez was delegated to deliver into the hands of the count of Monterrey for the purpose of vindicating the performance of Don Juan de Oñate.

By early October the mutineers had decamped, pushing south toward Santa Bárbara as rapidly as slow ox carts would allow. Besides Sosa Peñalosa and Father Escalona, about twenty-five soldiers, some with family and servants, remained behind to occupy the capital. This bare-bones garrison might have been easily overcome by the surrounding Pueblos, had the Indians shown an inclination to resistance. But perhaps they were, after all, still disposed to be friendly to the Spaniards. Or, as seems more likely, any warlike impulse they may have harbored would naturally have been held in check by the certain knowledge that Oñate, his seventy men, and cannons, were due back soon from Quivira.

As it developed, Don Juan did not return from his protracted circuit until November 24. He was exhausted, and some of the men were still suffering from battle wounds, yet he had reason to be pleased. Quivira had proven to be prodigal in human and natural resources. He continued to believe it bordered on the sea. And like Coronado he had heard wispy tales suggesting gold might exist farther on, in margins he had left unexplored. But whatever good feelings he carried instantly evaporated when he rode into San Gabriel and met the glum remnant of his colony.

This is another of those occasions when we sorely regret that Don Juan kept no personal diary, which might have revealed his innermost thoughts upon receipt of the thunderous news of the mutiny. That he felt anger, despair, and a sense of betrayal seems indisputable. Basques held firmly to the supremacy of loyalty, and this breaking of faith by so large a number of his subjects could only have left Oñate profoundly shaken. Had he been able to hold his rancor in check long enough to examine his dilemma, he might have been able to assess the causes behind this latest and deepest plunge in his fortunes.

Reduced to a single denominator, the governor's problem did not lie in his lack of zeal or inability to lead, but rather in the near impossibility of finding a way to reward his men in their efforts to explore and settle the poor, isolated, cold, and unlovely kingdom of New Mexico. When the colonists became convinced that no wealth was forthcoming, they escaped at the first opportunity. And the friars defected because Oñate's brutal rule made conversion of the Pueblos unfeasible, or so they claimed. The governor, on the other hand, undaunted and undiminished in his dedication to the assignment of colonization, could not see past their ingratitude, violation of trust, and dereliction of duty.

With scarcely any delay, Oñate instituted legal proceedings against the traitors, as he now termed those who had fled. In his capacity as chief magistrate of the colony, he tried the case and passed sentence. The papers generated by this litigation have been lost, but according to what Fray Francisco de San Miguel later told a fellow missionary, Don Juan condemned the captains of the mutineers to beheading. To carry out that sentence and to bring back the other fugitives, he sent Vicente de Zaldívar with a highly mobile escort on a lightning pursuit. But the errant colonists had too much of a start, and they coasted safely into Santa Bárbara where they immediately composed a flurry of letters and reports to the viceroy, denouncing Oñate's governorship and painting his character in the blackest terms. These attacks were meant to serve as a justification for desertion of their posts in New Mexico.

When Zaldívar reached Santa Bárbara twelve days later, he learned that the men he was chasing were securely under the protection of the king's officers and, in any case, he had no authority here in Nueva Vizcaya to make arrests or conduct beheadings. At this point, he must have sent a letter back to his uncle, informing him of his sudden decision to continue on south to Mexico City, and even Madrid if necessary, in an attempt to repair the considerable damage Oñate's reputation and government had incurred.

Meanwhile, the count of Monterrey was having a very difficult time sorting out the sharply conflicting reports that were reaching his desk. Whose version of the truth was he to trust? The pro-Oñate faction, filled with righteous indignation, accusations of treachery, and demands that the disloyal settlers be forced to return? Or should he give credence to the grave charges of the fugitives from New Mexico who now wished to be shielded from their governor's wrath? "The matter is greatly complicated," he explained in a message to the king.

As a move toward disentanglement, the viceroy convened a council of theologians and jurists and handed it the delicate task of judging whether the runaway New Mexicans should be punished and returned as Oñate demanded. After solemn deliberation, the councilmen ruled that the accused were primarily settlers and only secondarily soldiers (a view that challenged established custom), and hence ought not to be charged with military desertion. Nor should they be compelled to return to New Mexico. Finally, the councilmen concluded that the allegations of wrong-doing on Oñate's part merited investigation by a higher tribunal. All this was in line with the viceroy's own thinking, not unexpectedly, so the net result was that Don Juan never got his colonists back.

A historian of that day, Fray Juan de Torquemada, wrote that the deserters tried to throw the blame for their failings on others, just as Adam attempted to blame Eve for his fall from grace. And even the superiors of the Franciscan Order in Mexico City went so far as to suggest that their brethren who abandoned New Mexico might be unworthy and cowardly individuals. But notwithstanding, men of authority in New Spain, starting with the count of Monterrey, were left with the notion that the greatest fault for the unraveling of the New Mexico venture rested squarely on the shoulders of Don Juan de Oñate. That view was not wholly accurate, of course, but neither was it completely wrong.

Upon reaching Mexico City, Vicente de Zaldívar in May 1602 appeared before the viceroy and Audiencia. To them he imparted a first-hand report of the desperate state of affairs on the Rio Grande and underscored the need for substantial royal help. Specifically, he asked the government to provide and pay for three hundred soldiers and a new set of missionaries, and to furnish the supplies required to sustain them on the long journey north. His Uncle Juan, he pledged, would fund another one hundred soldiers, and the total force of four hundred men "will be sufficient to complete what has been started." The viceroy did not believe that for a moment, but he was content to defer the decision to Spain since Zaldívar had already announced his intention of going there in a bid to win the ear of the king.

Alonso de Oñate, Don Juan's brother, was still at the Spanish court where for the past couple of years he had been bombarding the crown with petitions and requests for favors. He managed to win a few minor concessions and two others of some importance. For one, the king agreed to go ahead and confer upon Oñate the highly prized title of adelantado, which had originally been promised by his contract. For another, Oñate's government was made independent of the viceroy and Audiencia in Mexico City. That action incensed the count of Monterrey when he learned of it, and he contrived by adroit bureaucratic maneuvering to evade the royal decree and keep Oñate under his jurisdiction during the months that remained in his own term of administration.

Zaldívar arrived in Spain, evidently sometime in the second half of 1602, armed with reports on New Mexico and letters from the viceroy urging the king to give him a speedy hearing. Soon afterward, he made a presentation at court requesting the three hundred men and supplies, and seeking permission to recruit musketeers, shipwrights, and two ships' pilots to serve at the port Oñate intended to found upon the coast of the South Sea. By now, however, full disclosure of the scandals in New Mexico and the poverty of the land had reached the king, counteracting the glowing picture Vicente de Zaldívar tried his best to paint.

His Majesty, upon advice of the Council of the Indies, threw the question of the soldiers and supplies back in the lap of the viceroy, with instructions not only to make a final decision but also to launch a full investigation, as quietly as possible, into Oñate's fitness to continue in office. The council, perhaps as a token of support, did recommend that Zaldívar be extended a modest loan and permitted to recruit his musketeers, shipwrights, and pilots. That was all that could be reaped from the long trip to Spain. In 1603 Vicente set sail for America, leaving Alonso to continue representing the Oñate interests at court.

During the period his nephew was abroad, Don Juan de Oñate set about reconstructing the edifice of his rule over the threadbare handful of settlers still at San Gabriel and over the widely dispersed villages of the Pueblo Indians. He received one welcome boost, which must have cheered his mood, with the arrival of four new Franciscans, probably in late winter or early spring of 1603. They were sent by the count of Monterrey, as answer to the one request Zaldívar had made that he was able or willing to act upon immediately. As a gesture of conciliation, the viceroy selected friars, in his words, "who are good friends of . . . Oñate, in order that there may be greater harmony than heretofore." Fray Francisco de Escobar, who was said to have a gift for learning Indian languages, headed the little band.

The quartet of priests may have been escorted to New Mexico by the unwavering Captain Gerónimo Márquez, who had gone south at the time of the desertion to counter charges hurled at Oñate. At least we know that the officer was back at San Gabriel about this time, placing his arms once more in the service of the governor. So many of the early captains were either dead or gone that Don Juan looked gratefully upon the steadfast few who continued at his side.

Of events over the next year and a half, only brief mention occurs in the records. At some point during 1603 a serious disturbance shook Taos pueblo, a village that for the next three centuries would launch bloody revolts against intruders. Oñate carried out a punitive campaign, in the course of which he was reputed to have killed a young Taos chief by throwing him from an upper terrace of the pueblo. That act was included in the list of criminal charges brought against him long after he had left New Mexico.

In the forepart of 1604, the governor dispatched a peace mission to the newly reestablished Acoma pueblo, where memory of the terrible battle a half decade before remained vivid. The three most prominent missionaries in the kingdom—fathers Velasco, Escalona, and Escobar—went as emissaries. Their overtures met with some success, so that the chasm war had opened there began to be bridged.

Acting on orders, Father Velasco left his companions at Acoma, and taking a twelve-man escort under Captain Márquez he commenced his own mini-expedition to the west. His trail led to Zuni and Moqui and thence southwestward to the land of the Cruzado Indians in central Arizona. There he collected more stories of the South Sea and gathered up mineral specimens from the same native mines visited by Captain Farfán de los Godos in December 1598. Then he backtracked to San Gabriel.

The motive behind Velasco's junket remains puzzling since he covered no new ground and, so far as is known, discovered nothing that might benefit the colony. On his return, Oñate did package up some of his ore samples and ship them off to the viceroy for assay, no doubt with the hope that they might prove rich and excite the count's interest. But Don Juan's uncanny bad luck still held, for when assayed in Mexico City the specimens produced one-eighth part copper, without any trace of silver. The viceroy reported this to the king and remarked laconically: "All other communications from [Oñate] express nothing but hopes, which, even if not realized, always leave the possibility that they may turn into realities."

The best that can be said about Father Velasco's trip is that somehow it served as a prelude and preparation for Oñate's last significant effort at exploration, for in the third quarter of 1604 he began the march that would finally carry him to the South Sea. Two years before, the mariner Sebastián Vizcaíno had sailed the California coast and described the Bay of San Diego as "the best port to be found in all the South Sea." Quite probably word of this reached Don Juan, through persons coming from New Spain, and if so it would have fueled his long-held desire to find the coast and locate his own port that could receive supplies and reinforcements for New Mexico. Then too he was beguiled by old rumors of pearl fisheries in California waters. Should that lure prove to be real, it might aid in convincing skeptical royal officials that New Mexico was worth maintaining. Whether Oñate realized it or not, this expedition west was a last, desperate grab at straws.

Leaving about fifty people to hold San Gabriel, Governor Oñate set forth on October 7, 1604. Accompanying him were Captain Márquez, Father Escobar, a lay brother named Juan de San Buenaventura, and thirty soldiers, the majority of them raw recruits who had entered with the latest contingent of friars. There was even a man who had sailed on one of Vizcaíno's earlier voyages, Oñate perhaps thinking his knowledge of the sea might prove useful. In contrast to other expeditions he had fielded, this one was small, drab, and unspectacular. Truly, Don Juan had fallen on hard times.

The route taken was the by-now-well-marked horse trail that unwound its familiar leagues through the distant Zuni and Moqui pueblos, dropped off the edge of the Colorado Plateau, and entered Arizona's Verde Valley and the home of the Cruzado people. From there, the Spaniards' way ran west to the later-named Bill Williams River and down that stream to its confluence with the mighty Colorado. Descending the latter river, they passed through the thickly populated country of Yuman-speaking tribes. At one camp they heard of a lake called Copalla on whose banks dwelled people wearing gold bracelets and other golden ornaments. Continuing south, Oñate and his men in late January 1605 reached the head of the Gulf of California and beheld the thrilling sight of open water.

Fray Alonso de Benavides, writing thirty years after the event, declares that Governor Oñate waded into the foamy brine, waist deep, and striking the water with his sword, proclaimed: "I take possession for the King, our lord." Brother Juan de San Buenaventura followed and elevating a crucifix took possession in the name of the church. They were at the estuary of the Colorado, which emptied into a spacious bay, forming "one of the best sites he had ever seen for a port," or so stated the Vizcaíno sailor. The party had no instruments for taking soundings but one of the soldiers, Juan Ruíz, dived into the water and said it was of good depth. Oñate thought that he was claiming a portion of the South Sea coast, unaware that he was in the upper end of an attenuated gulf and hundreds of miles from the ocean. This error derived from a mistaken belief of the day that the narrow peninsula of Lower California was an island,

Letter of Fr. Francisco de Escobar, January 25, 1605, to Oñate, regarding his arrival at the Colorado River, on the expedition to the South Sea. (Courtesy University of New Mexico Library) something that would not be corrected by geographers until long after Oñate was dead.

The expedition lingered only a few days before starting homeward. By one report, Father Escobar had such a phenomenal memory and talent for languages that he mastered a working vocabulary of the native tongues almost overnight. As a result: "On this return journey, he spoke with all the nations, and they all understood him." Among the things he heard were tales of beings, "monstrous and never seen in our time." They included persons, said to live farther on, who had large ears that dragged on the ground, others who were born with one foot, another tribe that always slept standing up, and a neighboring one whose people slept under water. The Spaniards must have smiled at these fanciful yarns, when Father Escobar made his translations, for their great-grandfathers had listened to almost identical stories when they first landed in the Caribbean.

Severe hardships beset the expedition on the journey home. The animals grew thin from a scarcity of grass, supplies dwindled, and at one point the men ate horsemeat to survive. In mid-April the haggard party encamped at El Morro, under the shadow of its enormous fin of rock. Oñate, or one of the soldiers acting for him, seized the opportunity to incise the following inscription in the smooth-faced sandstone:

Paso por aqui el adelantado don juan de onate del descubrimiento de la mar del sur a 16 de April de 1605.

[Passed by here the Adelantado Don Juan de Oñate from the discovery of the South Sea on the 16th of April 1605.]

By his reference to "discovery" Don Juan surely meant that he was the first to discover the sea by marching overland from New Mexico. His inscription, carved fifteen years before the Pilgrims' landfall at Plymouth Rock, is preserved to this day and stands as the most specific and authentic physical memento of Oñate's presence in the Southwest. Nine days later, on April 25, the expedition entered San Gabriel with "all sound and well, and not a man missing," according to a contemporary account.

For all of his exertions, Don Juan again could only show minimal results. He had found a good harbor, wide enough so "a thousand vessels can anchor," and encountered vast numbers of peaceful Indians on the lower Colorado who seemed ripe for conversion. But he had turned up no pearls or new evidence of silver, nor had he heard

Oñate inscription at El Morro, carved in 1605 on his return journey from the Gulf of California. (Courtesy L. A. Mitchell)

any whisper of a clue about the Strait of Anián. Still, he moved to make the most of the expedition's paltry accomplishments. Initially, Father Escobar was selected by all the settlers in New Mexico to visit Mexico City and furnish a complete report to the new viceroy, the marquis of Montesclaros, who had recently replaced Monterrey. Now, however, Oñate himself decided to accompany the priest and seek government backing for the development of his seaport. He got only as far as the vicinity of Santa Bárbara, when he decided to return to San Gabriel, possibly because of health problems. But Escobar with a horse guard went on to complete the mission.

Viceroy Montesclaros, who had been reviewing a lengthy file of documents on Oñate, received the friar and four of his companions at the government palace. He interrogated them closely on conditions in New Mexico and expressed pleasure over discovery of the South Sea harbor. Nevertheless, his common sense led him to the conclusion that Oñate's conquest had become a fairy tale, as he informed the king in precisely those words. And he added that the string of reports extending back through the years demonstrated that nothing of real substance had come from the new land. It had turned into an albatross and one that threatened to drain the royal treasury of large sums.

The viceroy acknowledged a weighty fact that he must have known the king clearly understood: New Mexico in good conscience could not be abandoned, no matter the size of its liabilities, as long as it contained one lone Christian Indian needing the services of church and state. But as a start toward a remedy for the situation, Montesclaros recommended that Don Juan de Oñate be removed from office.

The taking of such a drastic step could not work itself through the ponderous bureaucracy overnight, yet, once the viceroy had unloosed his suggestion, the wheels commenced grinding in that direction. Months would elapse before Oñate, who had imagined himself unstoppable, was brought to the realization that the text and footnotes of his Rio Grande adventure were moving toward an obituary. For him, it was to prove a bitter draught to swallow.

CHAPTER 10

Retreat

THE count of Monterrey, in accordance with orders of the crown, had for some time been quietly investigating the charges of misconduct leveled against Governor Juan de Oñate. At an early stage he had told the king that he did not wish to take any legal action because it would discourage the colonists and prevent the New Mexico venture from succeeding, which then still seemed a possibility. However, after the mass desertion of 1601, Oñate's credibility declined precipitously, and he became increasingly vulnerable to removal. When the next viceroy, Montesclaros, made that recommendation, it ultimately pushed the vacillating king and Council of the Indies to action.

On June 17, 1606, Philip III dispatched a directive to New Spain's viceroy requiring him to recall Oñate from the Rio Grande on some plausible pretext, detain him in Mexico City until his alleged excesses and crimes could be formally investigated, and appoint a new governor—a discreet and Christian one—to assume charge in New Mexico. With the interminable delays of the day, this order did not reach Mexico City until early 1607, by which time the marquis of Montesclaros was no longer viceroy. Don Luís de Velasco had returned from Peru to take his place, the same man ironically who had approved Don Juan's original contract back in 1595.

In the meantime, Oñate with his slender means and reduced garrison had been doggedly hanging on at San Gabriel. By 1606 Apaches and Navajos on the fringes of New Mexico had turned aggressively hostile, assaulting and burning outlying Pueblo towns and slaying numbers of their residents, whom they regarded as allies of the Spaniards. The raiders ran away with Spanish livestock and eventually attacked San Gabriel itself. In response the governor and his captains led a series of retaliatory campaigns that appear to have had little effect. This development simply heaped another burden upon the weary shoulders of the colonists.

In the autumn of that year, the Maese de Campo Vicente de

Zaldívar returned to the fold, after a four-year absence that had taken him to Mexico City and Madrid. The aging of his uncle during that extended interval, accelerated by hardship and disappointment, must have been readily apparent. For his part, Don Juan, while delighted to have his dependable nephew back in harness, was disheartened beyond measure by the scanty results of his drawn-out mission. Zaldívar brought from the king no ringing endorsement or pledge of large-scale material support, which was what Oñate so fervently desired. Nor was he escorting new legions of volunteers or carts groaning under the weight of supplies. The insignificant party of recruits accompanying him, together with several more friars and a modest assortment of provisions, was so inadequate an answer to their repeated pleas for aid that the long-suffering populace of San Gabriel was almost overcome with discouragement.

When later he wrote to the viceroy, Oñate underlined the sad fact by saying that his soldiers were so dejected, hard pressed, and exhausted, he had to employ every ounce of his ingenuity and effort to hold them in place. Those words were preamble to the stunning capitulation that followed: "Finding myself helpless in every respect, because I have used up on this expedition my estate and the resources of my relatives and friends, amounting to more than 600,000 pesos, . . . I find no other means . . . than to renounce my office, which resignation I am sending Your Excellency." So there it was—the dissolution of the vision, the end of the dream, laid plainly upon the table and inscribed for the record in ink, August 24, 1607, at San Gabriel, capital of the kingdom of New Mexico. On that date, Oñate still had not learned of the king's order recalling him from his governorship.

The immediate reason for his surrender, as he unabashedly admits, was an economic one. But another, we can surmise, lay in the disintegration of his expectations for the future. Nothing had panned out as he had hoped, and Zaldívar's return virtually empty-handed confirmed that no relief could be anticipated from the outside. Perhaps on the lean chance that something from inside the realm might still be found to cushion his pending fall, Don Juan had sent Zaldívar with a skeleton expedition, in the first part of 1607, to retrace the trail leading to the head of the Gulf of California. Of what occurred on that pointless ramble, we are left totally in the dark since the official log, sent afterward to Mexico City by Oñate, has been lost. But it seems likely that a failure of the expedition to produce any tangible results may well have contributed to the governor's decision to resign.

Moreover, Oñate informed the viceroy ruefully that he, the soldiers, and friars were all painfully aware that no one in authority had ever bothered to acknowledge their monumental sacrifices in this distant land or "encourage them by good words." And added to that, he explained that his feelings were greatly hurt because the deserters of 1601 had gone entirely unpunished. Indeed, they had used their liberty to spread falsehoods, justify their treason, and sully his reputation. By stepping down now, he said, he was unburdening his conscience and also providing the king a chance to reevaluate the status of New Mexico, which in his own informed opinion ought not to be abandoned. Notwithstanding, Don Juan declared pointedly that he would hold the colonists at San Gabriel only until the following summer, 1608, and if by that time he had not received definitive instructions he would release them from any obligation to remain.

The late Professor France V. Scholes suspected that Oñate's resignation was more in the nature of an armistice than a capitulation, and that actually he hoped it would force the crown to assume financial support of the kingdom, converting its status from a proprietary to a royal colony, and retaining him as royal governor by way of reward for his past services. In that event, Oñate could see himself freed from the heavy monetary obligations that he had assumed under his contract. If that in reality was his wish, it was a wish formulated without a complete understanding of how deeply recent events had undermined his superiors' confidence in him.

Viceroy Velasco received Oñate's letter of resignation sometime in the last quarter of 1607. Apparently, he had been sitting on the order from Spain that mandated the governor's recall, as it would not be a pleasant task for him to execute. After all, he had been a friend and supporter of Don Juan and had encouraged the New Mexico project at its inception in 1595. Now he was faced with presiding over its demise. Thus, Oñate's letter, in which he relinquished his office, spared Velasco an unpleasant chore. After consulting with members of the Audiencia, the viceroy on February 27, 1608, sent Don Juan a reply, accepting the resignation, but commanding him to remain at San Gabriel until further orders. Whether to maintain New Mexico at government expense or give the kingdom back to the Indians had not yet been determined by the king. And until it was decided, everything must remain on hold.

New Mexico in the interim, however, needed someone in charge, so Viceroy Velasco appointed one of Oñate's officers, Captain Juan Martínez de Montoya, to sit as temporary governor. Spanish-born Martínez, now in his middle forties, had first come to New Mexico with the relief column of 1600 and served admirably thereafter in various offices and on several campaigns and expeditions. Oñate, when he finally started making grants of encomienda, gave Martínez one of the Jemez pueblos, from which he was privileged to collect tribute, and he also certified him for the title of hidalgo. In addition to filling the office of secretary of government, Martínez was selected to be an *alcalde ordinario,* or magistrate, on the town council (*cabildo*) of San Gabriel. From missionaries and other persons coming out of New Mexico, Velasco had learned of Martínez's services and honors, and on the basis of that named him to succeed Don Juan. In the letter of appointment, the viceroy instructed him to stay on good terms with Oñate as long as he remained in the kingdom, and to consult the former governor in all matters where his experience might prove valuable. Ordinarily, instructions like that would have furnished a sure formula for conflict.

As it happened, no problem, jurisdictional or otherwise, arose simply because Juan Martínez de Montoya never took office as governor. He had not sought the position, and, in fact, when the Viceroy's certificate of appointment reached him at San Gabriel in mid-1608, he must have been more than a little startled. In any case, the cabildo refused to accept his governorship, and exercising prerogatives and a spirit of independence that traced back to Roman antecedents, it appointed Don Juan's young son, Cristóbal, to carry on as interim governor. This was done, following tradition, during a *cabildo abierto,* or open town meeting, at which all adult males of property participated and had their say.

It requires no great stretch of imagination to conclude that the rejection of Martínez and the elevation of Cristóbal were engineered by Oñate himself. The cabildo had come into being by 1605, if not before, and was purely his creation and ready, therefore, to do his bidding. The councilors went so far as to ask him to resume office, but Don Juan prudently declined, since to do so was hardly proper or expedient. Election of his son, nevertheless, would keep the governorship in the family until the crown came to a decision about New Mexico's future.

To this point, Cristóbal's name appears only rarely in the official documents. We know that during the previous eleven years, when he was coming to manhood, he accompanied his father on most of the major expeditions, but his presence receives no more than passing mention. By his middle teens, he was leading forays against the Apaches, as Don Juan had once done against the Chichimecas, and it was he who commanded the punitive force that pursued the enemy after an attack upon San Gabriel. While the youth might claim to be well trained in the military arts, he was barely able to read and write, a not-unexpected deficiency since formal education of any sort was unavailable on the Rio Grande. Notwithstanding, at age eighteen he became the unofficial governor of New Mexico, carrying out the functions of that office for the next year and a half.

It was about this same time, 1608, that the city of Santa Fe seems to have had its beginnings. Stray references point to some of the San Gabriel settlers moving twenty miles south, perhaps even as early as 1607, and establishing themselves in a narrow valley and at a place that was called, from the start, Santa Fe (Holy Faith). Did Oñate give it that name? And did he choose it to honor the historic town of Santa Fe near Granada, Spain? Those questions cannot be answered at present. What appears certain is that Don Juan, still de facto in charge, had approved this move. In dispatches sent to Mexico City, which arrived there in December 1608, the viceroy was informed of plans under way to establish a new villa and provincial capital. No reasons were given, but one may have been that Oñate foresaw little future for San Gabriel, obliged to compete with nearby San Juan pueblo for limited resources. The little valley at Santa Fe, on an affluent of the Rio Grande, by contrast was unoccupied by Indians. The viceroy suggested later that it was the colonists and friars who were behind the transfer of the capital, but still Oñate would have had to acquiesce, at the very least.

When Viceroy Velasco in 1609 appointed a royal governor, Don Pedro de Peralta, to succeed Oñate, he stipulated that one of his first duties ought to be the foundation and populating of the new villa then being attempted. In 1610 Peralta seems to have fulfilled his instructions, formally establishing Santa Fe, probably with the customary ceremonies. Unfortunately, no written evidence of such events has been brought to light. For the past half century, scholars have offered 1610 as the official year of Santa Fe's birth and have credited Peralta as the founder. Nevertheless, it is plain that Juan de Oñate had a larger role in the founding than has heretofore been acknowledged—something of more than academic interest since this oldest state capital in the United States, as it now appears, can be claimed as part of the Oñate legacy.

Two years of dithering on the part of the crown, its advisers, and colonial officials lay behind the appointment of Peralta. Upon reclaiming the viceregal chair, Velasco had studied the New Mexico reports and come away pessimistic about the kingdom's chances for survival. The missionaries there, from what he could tell, were eager to leave, saying they had made only about four hundred real converts in eleven years, mainly because the natives showed little desire for the gospel. When to that he added the remoteness and poverty of New Mexico, Velasco advised the king in March 1608 that it would perhaps be best to put a stop to the whole thing, withdraw the Spaniards, and have them bring out the few Christian Indians. "This plan," he said, "would put an end to the great expense to the royal treasury, both now and in the future, which will always tend to increase."

Months later the viceroy's letter reached Spain, and the Council of the Indies, which reviewed all colonial correspondence, attached its recommendations and then submitted the documents to King Philip for final action. In the case of New Mexico, the council recommended abandonment. The king, who seldom made hasty decisions, pondered and wavered, with the result that on the far Rio Grande circumstances changed and the entire matter assumed a new complexion.

What seems to have happened is that the Franciscan Order belatedly awoke to the realization that it might actually lose its rich missionary province of New Mexico. True, the friars had not acquitted themselves very well to this point, many of them complaining of the dangers and discomforts in the kingdom and the difficulty of mastering the many Pueblo languages. And, as demonstrated, those in the field had sometimes argued for quitting, and even done so. But that was never the policy or desire of the Order's superiors, headquartered in Mexico City. When they learned that Viceroy Velasco was calling for the closing down of Oñate's struggling enterprise, they must have experienced something akin to panic.

The exact nature of the order given is not known, but seemingly a call to action was conveyed from Mexico City northward to the missions of New Mexico. At long last, we are told, the friars bestirred themselves and during the summer of 1608 performed mass baptisms among the Pueblos, to the number of seven thousand. As soon as these impressive figures were tabulated, one of the missionaries, Fray Lázaro Ximénez, went hurrying down the eighteen-hundred-mile Camino Real to place them before the viceroy. Velasco was delighted. Ximénez insisted that other thousands were suddenly clamoring for conversion and suggested that the Lord Himself had intervened to keep New Mexico from being written off. Anyway, said the friar, the kingdom was not the worthless place others had pictured it, and the possibility remained that silver might still be found.

The week before Christmas, 1608, Viceroy Velasco relayed the details of Ximénez's report to the king, exhorting him to reconsider New Mexico's fate in light of this new and more promising information. The spectacular claim of seven thousand recent converts greatly impressed Philip. Acting with uncharacteristic celerity he decreed that New Mexico should be taken under the patronage of the crown and converted to a royal colony, its expenses henceforward to be met by his treasury. The chief purpose in maintaining New Mexico would be as a missionary field.

This, in effect, was what Juan de Oñate had been seeking for almost two years, while he languished practically in limbo at San Gabriel. In anticipation of the creation of a royal colony, he had placed two requests on the viceroy's desk: one, that his son Cristóbal be retained as governor of New Mexico and, two, that he be permitted to seek compensation from the government for his largely unrewarded services in carving out the kingdom. Velasco's legal adviser quickly vetoed keeping Cristóbal as governor, saying because of his age and lack of education, he was unqualified for the post. As to the other matter, the adviser suggested that Don Juan might be offered a governorship elsewhere to compensate him, if his merits warranted it.

In the first part of 1609, Velasco notified Oñate that he had named Don Pedro de Peralta to be governor and captain-general of New Mexico, and that as soon as the new official reached the Rio Grande and effected an orderly transfer of power, Don Juan and his son should promptly leave for Mexico City. In sum, that notice drew the final curtain on Oñate's frontier adventure.

The old hand Captain Gerónimo Márquez was in the viceregal capital on courier duty from New Mexico and was drafted into a force of fifteen other soldiers to escort Governor Peralta to his distant assignment. There were the inevitable delays in making preparations for the long journey, and the party did not reach its destination until late 1609 or, as seems more likely, early 1610. Shortly afterward, Don Juan, his son, and some of his closest associates bid their final good-byes and began the trip out of New Mexico. A dozen years before, Oñate had marched up this same trail gloriously optimistic and expansive in his enthusiasm for the grand task ahead. Now with a cartload of sobering experiences behind him, he was returning in a very different mood, not defeated perhaps, but certainly chastened, and also a good deal poorer for his efforts. After a brief stopover, we presume, at his home in Zacatecas, he reached Mexico City on April 30, 1610, just a few months short of fifteen years from the date he had signed his New Mexico contract in the viceregal palace.

The whereabouts of Juan de Oñate during the next three years cannot be pinpointed with certainty, but the most plausible guess is that he took up residence in the capital. His health had not been good for some time, owing largely to the mental and physical stresses he was under, and now as he neared the age of sixty, he might have decided that a period of recuperation in Mexico City was in order. Besides, proximity to the seat of colonial power afforded him the opportunity to press his case for compensation. This is strictly conjecture, since the next definite word of him does not turn up until 1613 when he is reported to have returned to his old home at Las Minas de Pánuco, outside Zacatecas.

Predictably, he found that his mines, suffering from his absence and neglect, were in such poor condition that they were on the verge of being shut down. Indian miners in those days were in the habit of stealing chunks of ore and selling them to local merchants, a practice that cost owners heavily. They even took ore from the pillars left to support the tunnel roofs, thereby contributing to cave-ins. To put things right, Don Juan went zealously to work and through reorganization and the introduction of new machinery he had his mines on a paying basis in a matter of months. Over the next decade, they produced 137,510 marks of silver, on which Oñate paid 129,454 pesos tax, the royal fifth, into the treasury. Those figures alone ought to disprove the statement, sometimes made, that the New Mexico débacle left Don Juan permanently impoverished.

The speedy financial recovery of his nephew Vicente de Zaldívar proved even more dramatic. Soon after returning from the Rio Grande, Vicente had taken over management of the Zaldívar mining properties in and around Zacatecas, and by all accounts began to wring staggering profits from them. In time, he was credited with accumulating a fortune of three million pesos. That allowed him to develop a baronial estate, the Hacienda de San Pedro, located near Sombrerete, north of Zacatecas, where he bred cattle and fine horses and cultivated grain. He also contributed heavily to the construction and endowment of a large Jesuit college and church at Zacatecas in 1616, his donation reputedly reaching one hundred thousand pesos. Don Juan himself would later make a significant bequest to the Jesuits in his will. The founder of the Order, Saint Ignatius de Loyola, was a Basque from Guipúzcoa, the native province of some of Oñate's and Zaldívar's ancestors, perhaps explaining in part the two men's generosity.

In the risings and ebbings of his fortunes, did it occur to Don Juan how much better off he would have been, economically speaking, had he never subjected himself to the New Mexico affair? Possibly not. The Spanish captains of industry and arms during the early colonial era were so eager to distinguish themselves under the royal banner and in the service of the church that they eagerly accepted long odds and risky challenges. The grand play, the spectacular gesture was what they hungered for, and the theater of their activity seemed to furnish innumerable opportunities. If the twists of fate led them to fail, then that abiding Spanish fatalism came to their rescue. The best of them always bounced back and simply made a try in another direction. Oñate, conditioned to accept the military and individualistic values of experience, opportunism, and personal resourcefulness, was not likely to have sat by the hearth and lamented his many losses in the country of the Pueblos.

Unhappily for his reputation and peace of mind, New Mexico had not finished exacting its toll. Very soon after launching his northern entrada, Don Juan had come under suspicion of serious crimes, but the strict censorship he imposed on his colonists at first prevented full disclosure of the details. The flight of two-thirds of the settlers in late 1601, however, permitted authorities in Mexico City to acquire eyewitness testimony regarding Governor Oñate's conduct. Although the complaints were serious and damaging, no legal action followed.

For one thing, the testimony could not be thoroughly credited, inasmuch as it came from deserters, and further it was at variance with the statements of loyal men who had faithfully remained at San Gabriel. For another, the wide and powerful connections of Governor

Oñate's family throughout the upper level of colonial society were doubtless sufficient to give any viceroy pause when considering legal proceedings. And finally, as the count of Monterrey had indicated to the crown, as long as Oñate was in New Mexico no action ought to be taken against him, lest it so dispirit the remainder of his people that they give up what little had been won. For these reasons, several directives from His Majesty calling for quiet investigations of Oñate had not been vigorously pressed in New Spain.

For almost two years after Don Juan's return, his old friend and mentor, Don Luís de Velasco, continued to rule as viceroy. It is a reasonable assumption that he shielded Oñate from prosecution, not a difficult feat since his executive powers were matched by authority over the judicial branch of government. But in 1612 Velasco was succeeded by Diego Fernández de Córdoba, marquis of Guadalcázar, who was a kinsman of the king and a strict interpreter of the law. On June 1, 1613, the crown issued a royal decree instructing the marquis to initiate the long-delayed case against Oñate, carrying it "to its conclusion, passing sentence, and imposing punishment." The clarity of that language left no room for waffling, even had the viceroy been so inclined.

Subsequently, Oñate was summoned from Zacatecas, and he installed himself, probably with family members, at his residence in Mexico City. There he was arraigned on thirty separate charges linked to alleged acts committed during his governorship. Until the completion of his trial, he was ordered held under house arrest. He may have considered that the greatest indignity he had suffered to date although it was the usual procedure in such cases.

The trial, presided over by the marquis of Guadalcázar, took place sometime before mid-May 1614 and by all indications was a lengthy one. The voluminous record of the day-to-day proceedings has escaped discovery in the archives by modern historians. What little is known has to be drawn from the sentence and Oñate's appeal that came afterward, two documents that are now available. The large number of charges was not out of the ordinary in a serious case of this kind, since the prosecuting attorney expected a certain percentage of them to be disproved. The chief witnesses were men who had been on the New Mexico expedition, and those who most eagerly offered testimony were from the ranks of the deserters. Don Juan's defense was that his accusers bore him malice and were his bitter enemies because he had sentenced them to death for deserting the army and other offenses. Therefore, their version of events in New Mexico contained deliberate distortions and lies.

Some of the charges sound trivial or even ridiculous by today's standards, for example, the accusation that Oñate in his arrogance allowed his nephew Zaldívar to address him as "Your Majesty." Don Juan won acquittal on this and seventeen additional charges, but was found guilty on twelve others. His crimes included unjustly hanging two Indians; using excessive force in putting down the Acoma rebellion; living immorally at San Gabriel by committing adultery and thus setting a bad example for his soldiers; executing Captains Pablo de Aguilar and Alonso de Sosa de Albornoz; ordering Captains Villagrá and Márquez to put to death two deserters; and so on.

In pronouncing sentence on May 13, 1614, the viceroy condemned Oñate to perpetual exile from New Mexico and to exile from Mexico City for a period of four years. Further, he levied a fine of six thousand Castilian ducats and ordered him to pay court costs. Others of Don Juan's officers, soldiers, and servants who were tried at the same time as accomplices received a variety of penalties. Given the magnitude of his misdeeds, it would appear that Juan de Oñate was treated rather leniently. Again, we must suppose that the reason lay in the prominence of his family name and the outstanding record of services he and his forebears had rendered to the crown.

No sooner had he retired to his home at the Pánuco mines than Oñate launched a campaign for exoneration and vindication of his name. The fine of six thousand ducats was easily paid and occasioned little remorse, but the stain left upon his honor was another matter, something that he could not bear gracefully or with resignation. Spaniards, it has been claimed, cultivate the world's most austere definition of honor, and Don Juan demonstrated that by the strenuous efforts he exerted over a span of years to reopen his case.

We know little of his personal life in Zacatecas following the return from New Mexico. Within two years, the son Cristóbal married Doña María Gutiérrez del Castillo and by her had a boy, who was named Juan in honor of his grandfather. However, Cristóbal de Oñate died in 1612, at age twenty-two, the cause yet to be identified. The loss of his only son and chief heir devastated Don Juan, and indications are that he never fully recovered from it. Years later he would commission one of Spain's eminent poets, Francisco Murcia de la Llana, to compose a tribute in verse, by way of honoring Cristóbal's memory. He had the poem published at Madrid in 1622.

Sometime prior to 1620—the specific date still eludes us—Don Juan's remaining child, his beloved Mariquita, Doña María de Oñate y Cortés, while still in her teens married her cousin, Vicente de Zaldívar. Now, in addition to being Don Juan's nephew and second cousin, Vicente became his son-in-law as well. His mines were far out-producing those of his uncle (in one five-month period they yielded one hundred fifty thousand pesos of silver), and he was accepted among the pillars of colonial society. Vicente de Zaldívar's prosperity failed to last his lifetime, however. During the 1630s, in one of the cyclical declines of the Zacatecas mines, his far-flung estate became encumbered with debt, and much of it had to be sold. By 1650 Vicente was dead, and his widow, María de Oñate, found herself in humbled circumstances. According to accounts, straw (*zacate*) was being sold from a cart on the streets of Zacatecas for her maintenance. Her son, Don Nicolás de Zaldívar y Oñate, who evidently inherited his grandfather's treasured title of adelantado, noted in his will of 1679 that the family had fallen into great poverty.

Juan de Oñate in the final years of his life, of course, had no inkling of his descendants' subsequent fate. Through diligent improvements made to the Pánuco mines, he had managed a respectable recouping of the financial losses sustained in New Mexico and was able to retire the debts left over from that disastrous misadventure. With María married to the then flourishing Vicente and her future seemingly assured, Don Juan could focus his dwindling energies on the one cause that overshadowed everything else: the clearing of his name and personal record.

In 1617, he filed a formal appeal with the king, asking for a lifting of the orders of banishment and suspension to which he had been sentenced. With the request went supporting documents, including excerpts from the original trial record in which Oñate had rebutted all charges and had introduced defense witnesses who supported his claims of innocence. Some of his remonstrances appear genuine, among them the denial that he had lived immorally with married and single women at San Gabriel. Don Juan called the accusation absolutely untrue, saying that "he had always lived a chaste life . . . without committing adultery." His witnesses concurred, noting that they had never heard or seen that the governor was living in sin, and since San Gabriel was such a small place it would surely have been common knowledge and impossible to keep secret.

Others of Oñate's disavowals are unconvincing, even lame: for instance, his assertion that captains Aguilar and Sosa had not been murdered but had been executed upon conviction of treason and in accordance with standards of military justice. While at this late date, it is practically impossible to gauge Oñate's culpability on any single charge, nevertheless, upon the cumulative strength of the case against him, we are left with the firm suspicion that in New Mexico he resorted to grave abuse of his powers. The king may have arrived at the same conclusion, for so far as can be told he made no response to Don Juan's 1617 appeal, which turned out to be merely the first of many.

About 1619 or 1620, Oñate's wife of thirty years, Doña Isabel, died at their home in Pánuco and was buried there. Her passing left him badly shaken, but it also freed him to carry out a plan that soon afterward formed in his mind. He would travel to Spain and personally press his case before the Council of the Indies and perhaps even His Majesty. The timing seemed particularly auspicious.

On the continent, Spain was involved in the Thirty Years' War and thus in urgent need of funds. A mining magnate like Oñate whose family over the years had contributed significant tax revenues to the royal treasury might well expect to get a sympathetic hearing. Further, Philip III, who had assumed the throne in the year Don Juan began his New Mexico entrada, died in 1621 and was followed by his sixteen-year-old son Philip IV. The new king was well intentioned and tried to interest himself in matters of government, so it appeared he could review the Oñate appeal with fresh perspective.

When Don Juan took leave of his family, home, and native city of Zacatecas in the summer of 1621, it must have been with the expectation that he would return within a year or two to finish out his days. But that was not to be. Probably he left the ancestral residence, his mines, and other property under the custody of his daughter's husband, Vicente de Zaldívar, who remained as devoted to him as he had been in New Mexico. Departing by ship for the voyage to Spain, Oñate could not have helped feeling keen anticipation at the prospect of seeing for the first time the land that had cradled his forebears. Ninety-seven years before, his father Cristóbal had made the transatlantic crossing that brought him to the New World and started the cycle that Don Juan was now completing by his maiden trip to Spain. In that near century, the Oñates had lived grandly and blazed their mark conspicuously upon the pages of colonial history.

It was December when Don Juan, after a journey overland, reached

Madrid, the seat of the empire to which he had given a lifetime of service. He was so widely connected and well known in New Spain that he had no trouble linking up with others from the colony who like himself had come to the capital on business, or had retired there. Wasting no time, he assembled a portfolio of documents, representing the substance of his appeal, and early the next year, 1622, submitted it to the Council of the Indies. Therein was a petition asking that the sentence of perpetual banishment from New Mexico be lifted, the only one still in force since his four-year term of exile from Mexico City had already expired. In addition, he sought to have the titles—not offices—of governor and captain-general of New Mexico returned to him, since their original revocation by royal order had left a blot on his record.

To justify what, in effect, would amount to a pardon, Oñate cited his many contributions, the expenses he had incurred in the conquest and exploration of New Mexico, and the fact that the original charges against him had been trumped up and he was blameless; he ended with reference to his advanced age and the hardships he had endured, which ought to entitle him to mercy. The council, at least, came away convinced and on April 6 urged the king to favor the petitioner from New Spain by raising the banishment and suspension of titles. Philip, however, responded with the terse statement: "Postpone this for the time being."

Dissatisfied with postponement, Oñate later in that same year renewed his petitioning and begged the king not to let him die grief-stricken, without receiving justice. Again the Council of the Indies endorsed his appeal and submitted it to the crown, together with papers on the original sentence, saying, "May your Majesty favor him as you deem best." In late November, the king sent the petition back to his advisers with these words and his rubric inked at the bottom of the page: "I am amazed that in such ugly cases the Council annoys me regarding a decision that I have already taken." In other words, he saw no reason to grant Juan de Oñate exoneration.

That would seem conclusive—the case was closed. Nonetheless, the remarkably persistent Don Juan refused to accept it. In 1623 he drew up a formal summary of his lifelong services to Spain and had it printed, as was the custom of those seeking rewards or favors from the government. For reasons not clear, whether through a softening of the heart or for more practical considerations, the king relented enough to grant Oñate, by a royal order of August 11, 1623, reimbursement of the six-thousand-peso fine he had been obliged to pay upon conviction of the New Mexico offenses. Even though the perpetual banishment from New Mexico still stood—and that was more symbolic than anything else—Don Juan could regard the new action as a partial vindication and a cause for celebration. Indeed, from that point forward he appears to have considered himself once more in the good graces of his monarch.

That may have emboldened him to press for new concessions. Not long after returning to Mexico City from the Rio Grande, he had sought the title of marquis and applied to have his honorific title of adelantado granted in perpetuity, that is, to be held forever by his heirs. Now, in what Don Juan may have regarded as a more favorable climate, he reintroduced both those requests. But again they went nowhere, the Council of the Indies this time turning him down flat. The formal refusal of its members read: "There is no reason or obligation to grant him the favors he seeks." That left Oñate without his marquisate and with the right, as initially conceded, to pass his adelantado title to one heir only, his grandson, upon whose death it would terminate.

In spite of that setback, the shift in Oñate's fortunes and the swing toward rehabilitation of his reputation still had momentum. In 1624 the king offered him the post of mining inspector for all of Spain, an unsalaried position, but one that carried prestige and authority. The country's gold, silver, and mercury mines had long been in decline, neglected because official attention was focused upon the huge mining operations in the colonies. In hopes of boosting home production, the crown directed Inspector Oñate to visit and examine the major mining regions and prepare a status report containing recommendations for their development. It is doubtful that any man in Spain at the time possessed better credentials for the job than Juan de Oñate, who since boyhood had been closely associated with every phase of mineral assaying, extraction, smelting, and refining. To assist him in this work, he said he needed to bring six Indians, experienced in mining, from the Indies, by which he probably meant from his own mines at Zacatecas. The king readily acceded.

During 1625, Don Juan moved from one mining center to the next, across the face of Spain. One trip took him to Burgos, north of Madrid, not far from the beginning of the Basque provinces. It can be wondered whether he did not extend his travels to include a visit to the birthplace of his father and grandfather and a meeting with distant relatives he had never seen. Another of his tours brought him south to Granada, the native city of his mother and her family. Through inheritance he owned interest in property there, the Belicena hacienda located a league into the countryside. It was then being managed by a nephew, Fernando de Oñate, who was son of Don Juan's brother of the same name. In the family chapel, Don Juan viewed with pleasure the Oñate coat of arms on the wall.

Back in Madrid, he finished and submitted his report and set of recommendations to the king. On the basis of that, updated regulations were published at Madrid in September under the title *Nuevas Leyes y Ordenanzas . . . de las Minas (New Laws and Ordinances . . . on Mines)*. It represented Don Juan's final accomplishment. His secretary, Andrés de Carrasquilla, wrote a flowery introduction to the printed laws, citing Oñate's distinguished background, characterizing him as one of the wealthiest men in the Indies, and referring to the special love he had for his grandchildren left in the New World. That same year of 1625, Don Juan won appointment to the exclusive and highly prestigious Military Order of Santiago, further proof that he had fully emerged from the shadow that so long clouded his name.

Oñate got a personal audience with the king, at which time he reiterated a point made in his earlier report, to wit, that the country's mines ought to be developed by way of supplementing the gold and silver from America. Afterward, he mapped out the route of another inspection tour, this one to take him from Cartagena on the Mediterranean coast to the silver mines at Guadalcanal, situated in the Sierra Morena north of Seville. Perhaps when he departed Madrid in late summer of 1625, he had a premonition of death, for he provided that should he fail to complete this inspection of mines, his nephew and son-in-law Vicente de Zaldívar ought to be summoned from Zacatecas to complete the work.

He reached Cartagena safely, conducted the required business, and then started with his party on the two-hundred-fifty-mile journey westward to Guadalcanal. Along the way Don Juan fell seriously ill, but managed to arrive at his destination. In lodgings at the silver mines, he rallied and filed his will on October 4, 1625. For the next several weeks he was bedridden and appeared to be near death, although remaining lucid. Then Don Juan's iron will, which had served him so well in New Mexico, reasserted itself, and he began a modest recovery. Regaining his feet, he was even able to resume some of his duties. On or about June 3, 1626, he went into one of the mines that was experiencing flooding problems and while underground collapsed and died. For a man whose life had been so closely identified with mining, it was perhaps a fitting death.

By bequest, Oñate left one-fifth of his vast estate to the Colegio Imperial, a Jesuit institution in Madrid. In his will, he specified that ten thousand ducats must go for a chapel within a new church then under construction at the Colegio, and that his remains should be transferred there from Guadalcanal. His interment was to be inside the chapel, under the Oñate coat of arms, with burial places reserved beside him for his heirs and descendants. Life thus closed for Don Juan de Oñate y Salazar, a man who in the course of his years labored to build a personal fortune and serve his Maker and his sovereign. If he died regretting any part of his long and action-packed career, it has failed to be recorded.

In life, Juan de Oñate was never the hero of his own story, but rather the victim of his personal catastrophes. "What a terrible thing it is to go and discover new lands . . . and endure their excessive toils," wrote Cortés's garrulous soldier Bernal Díaz. That was a truism Oñate easily understood, owing to his New Mexico experience. George P. Hammond characterized that fifteen-year episode as a personal disaster for Oñate, brought on by vacillation and dalliance of royal officials, by the jealousy of rivals, and by the poverty of New Mexico. He might have added also, for the sake of completeness, that some of the blame doubtless could be traced to Don Juan's own flaws.

It is tempting to suggest that Oñate, in the work of creating his kingdom on the Rio Grande, ought to be judged a failure, simply from the fact that he accomplished virtually nothing that he had set out to do and went home at last in disgrace. Oddly, however, Don Juan did not see things in that light, and in fact we have every reason to believe that while he was disappointed with the way events in New Mexico turned out, he did not view his efforts there as a failure. Even at the end, when every one of his projects had soured and his funds were exhausted, he was eager to stay on the Rio Grande and continue trying to develop the new but floundering realm he had hewn from the northern wilderness. Such dogged persistence was a hallmark of the conquistador's irreducible individualism.

Seen from the long perspective afforded by history, Juan de Oñate's performance seems more accomplished than it did at the time. The foundations he established proved solid and were built upon by others, often in ways that Don Juan could never have anticipated. He was the godfather of the Franciscan missionary program on the northern frontier, which within two centuries stretched from the Texas gulf to coastal California. He can be credited with launching the livestock industry in the Southwest, for the herds of horses and cattle and flocks of sheep he brought in 1598 furnished a foundation for ranching. He inaugurated mining and the first processing of ores. And he made a notable contribution, through his wide-ranging explorations, toward an understanding of the true geography of western America.

Oñate's grandest achievement, of course, resided in his establishment of a new kingdom (afterward downgraded to the status of a province) within the Spanish empire. At the time, he set great store by the titles of governor and adelantado, but he would probably have been pleased to know that four hundred years later he was still remembered and considered deserving of another title, Father of New Mexico. That realm of which he was the architect, while not evolving into the viceroyalty he had hoped, did grow to become the chief anchor and most populous province in the Spanish Borderlands.

By now it also appears fairly certain that Oñate deserves partial and perhaps even primary honors for the founding of Santa Fe, which exists today as one of the oldest cities in America and the first surviving municipality erected in the West. His accolades, moreover, include the designation of roadblazer, since he was the man who opened and marked the Camino Real from the Chihuahuan mining settlements to northern New Mexico. That was the first established thoroughfare laid out by Europeans within a portion of the present limits of the United States. In various categories, then, New Mexico's founding governor left an enduring and memorable legacy.

In the career of Juan de Oñate, we find a summation of the motives, aspirations, intentions, strengths, and weaknesses of the Hispanic pioneers who settled the Borderlands. For a dozen years, between 1598 and 1610, he lived at the center of his own small, isolated kingdom, thwarted by circumstance and human limitations, humbled by repeated misfiring of his plans. But the disappointments and setbacks never extinguished the compulsive drive that propelled him onward. To the end, the Last Conquistador remained true to his vision.

Sources

This biography was written almost entirely from published sources, both primary and secondary. While there are no footnotes or endnotes, the text does contain indirect citations, that is, brief reference to sources, at a number of points. The titles that follow furnished most of the information I have used in my book.

The foundation of any study of the life of Oñate must necessarily be the monumental work of George P. Hammond and Agapito Rey, who collected, translated, and edited all available reports, letters, decrees, contracts, and ancillary documents dealing with the New Mexico phase of Oñate's career. They published the documents as volumes 5 and 6 in the Coronado Historical Series, under the title *Don Juan de Oñate, Colonizer of New Mexico, 1595–1628* (Albuquerque: University of New Mexico Press, 1953). Much earlier Hammond had written a narrative summary, *Don Juan de Oñate and the Founding of New Mexico* (Historical Society of New Mexico Publications in History; Santa Fe: El Palacio Press, 1927), which was also printed serially in the *New Mexico Historical Review (NMHR)*, beginning in volume 1, number 1, January 1926, and concluding in volume 2, number 2, April 1927.

A pair of articles serve as a starting point in comprehending the complicated Oñate genealogy. The first, now dated, is Beatrice Quijada Cornish's "The Ancestry and Family of Juan de Oñate," in *The Pacific Ocean in History*, ed. S. Henry Morse Stephens and Herbert E. Bolton (New York: Macmillan, 1917), 452–64; and the second, Donald Chipman's "The Oñate-Moctezuma-Zaldívar Families of Northern New Spain" *NMHR*, 52 (October 1977), 297–310.

A biography of Don Juan's father, Cristóbal de Oñate, is long overdue. Scattered pieces of information concerning his early life appear in volume 2 of Hubert Howe Bancroft's *History of Mexico* (5 vols.; San Francisco: A. L. Bancroft & Co., 1883); in Arthur Scott Aiton's *Antonio de Mendoza, First Viceroy of New Spain* (Durham, N.C.: Duke University Press, 1927); in George P. Hammond and Agapito Rey's, *Obregon's History of 16th Century Explorations in Western America* (Los Angeles: Wetzel Publishing Co., 1928); in Jose López Portillo y Weber's *La Conquista de la Nueva Galicia* (Mexico: Talleres Gráficos de la Nación, 1935); in Peter Gerhard's *The Northern Frontier of New Spain* (Princeton, N.J.: Princeton University Press, 1982); and in Herbert E. Bolton's

Coronado, Knight of Pueblos and Plains (Albuquerque: University of New Mexico Press, 1949). For coverage of Cristóbal's later activities as a silver baron, two works by Peter J. Bakewell are extraordinarily useful: *Silver Mining and Society in Colonial Mexico: Zacatecas, 1546–1700* (Cambridge: Cambridge University Press, 1971); and "Zacatecas: An Economic and Social Outline of a Silver Mining District, 1547–1700," in *Provinces of Early Mexico,* eds. Ida Altman and James Lockhart (Los Angeles: UCLA Latin American Center, 1976). Useful also is Lesley Byrd Simpson's *Many Mexicos* (Berkeley: University of California Press, 1959).

General descriptions of Zacatecas that help us picture the city developed by Cristóbal and in which Juan spent his youth are contained in Elias Amador's *Bosquejo Histórico de Zacatecas* (Zacatecas: Tipografía del Hospicio de Niños, 1906); José Ignacio Dávila Garibi's *La Sociedad de Zacatecas en los Albores del Régimen Colonial* (Mexico: Antigua Librería Robredo, 1939), which also includes charts of the Oñate family tree; and Alonso de la Mota y Escobar's *Descripción Geográfica de los Reinos de Nueva Galicia, Nueva Vizcaya, y Nuevo León* (Mexico: Editorial Pedro Robredo, 1940).

Vivid depiction of the north Mexican frontier, in whose expansion the Oñates played a stellar role, is a major feature of these volumes: François Chevalier, *Land and Society in Colonial Mexico: The Great Hacienda* (Berkeley: University of California Press, 1970); J. Lloyd Mecham, *Francisco de Ibarra and Nueva Vizcaya* (Durham, N.C.: Duke University Press, 1927); Philip Wayne Powell, *Soldiers, Indians & Silver* (Berkeley: University of California Press, 1952); and Philip Wayne Powell, *Mexico's Miguel Caldera* (Tucson: University of Arizona Press, 1977). The letter written by Lansing B. Bloom from the archives in Seville, November 26, 1938, in which he cites a document giving Juan de Oñate's birth year and identifies him as a twin, is printed in *NMHR,* 14 (January 1939), 115–20.

A basic source on Oñate's rivals for the New Mexico contract, Urdiñola and Lomas y Colmenares, is the biography by Vito Alessio Robles, *Francisco de Urdiñola y el Norte de la Nueva España* (Mexico, 1931). See also J. Lloyd Mecham's "Francisco de Urdiñola, Governor of Nueva Vizcaya," in *New Spain and the Anglo-American West,* comp. George P. Hammond (2 vols; Los Angeles: privately printed, 1932), I, 39–65. Extensive documentation on Pedro Ponce de León's efforts to displace Oñate is published in Spanish, with English translations, in the first volume of Charles Wilson Hackett's *Historical Documents Relating to New Mexico, Nueva Vizcaya, and Approaches Thereto, to 1773* (3 vols.; Washington: Carnegie Institution, 1923–37). In this same volume are included the original Spanish versions of other Oñate documents, all of which are given new translations in Hammond and Rey's collection. Another gathering of Oñate materials occurs in Herbert Eugene Bolton's *Spanish Exploration in the Southwest, 1542–1706* (New York: Barnes & Noble, 1946), useful mainly for the introductory material and notes. An essential book for understanding the events that led up to the Oñate expedition is George P. Hammond and Agapito Rey's *The Rediscovery of New Mexico, 1580–1594* (Albuquerque: University of New Mexico Press, 1966). Valuable too on the entire entrada is Fray Juan de Torquemada's *Monarquia Indiana* (facsimile reprint, 3 vols.; Mexico: Editorial Porrua, 1975), first published in 1615, while Oñate was alive, and preserving details not available elsewhere. Several periodical articles treat specific aspects of the early enterprise: George P. Hammond, trans., "Oñate's Appointment as Governor of New Mexico," *NMHR*, 12 (July 1938), 241–54; George P. Hammond, "Oñate's Effort to Gain Political Autonomy for New Mexico," *Hispanic American Historical Review*, 32 (May 1952), 321–30; George P. Hammond, "Oñate a Marauder?" *NMHR*, 10 (October 1935), 249–70; and Agapito Rey, "Missionary Aspects of the Founding of New Mexico," *NMHR*, 23 (January 1948), 22–31. Data on the career of Oñate's Franciscan adviser, Fray Diego Márquez, appears in a manuscript by Juan de Villagutierre Sotomayor, published by Alfred Charles Herrera as *Historia de la Nueva México* (Madrid, 1953). Gaspar Pérez de Villagrá also provides sidelights on this interesting missionary in his *History of New Mexico* (Los Angeles: The Quivira Society, 1933), the book that most completely describes the caravan journey to New Mexico, the blazing of the Camino Real, and the colony's first troubled months.

While the founding and early development of the Villa of San Gabriel (variously referred to as San Gabriel de los Españoles and as San Gabriel de la Paz) remain obscured by a shortage of information, two recent books dealing with the archaeology of the site clarify at least a few points: Herman Agoyo and Lynnwood Brown, eds., *When Cultures Meet: Remembering San Gabriel del Yunge Oweenge* (Santa Fe: Sunstone Press, 1987); and Florence Hawley Ellis, *San Gabriel del Yunge, as Seen by an Archeologist* (Santa Fe: Sunstone Press, 1989). See also Marjorie F. Tichy, "New Mexico's First Capital," *NMHR*, 21 (April 1946), 140–44. The common assumption that San Gabriel was abandoned about 1610 with the formal founding of Santa Fe is probably erroneous. Settler Francisco García in 1665 indicated he was born in San Gabriel de Iunque in 1615 (Hackett, *Historical Documents*, III, 254.) The community may have gradually withered away after that date, for in 1620, the viceroy informed the king that "there are no other Spanish towns [in New Mexico] except the villa of Santa Fe" (Hammond and Rey, *Don Juan de Oñate*, II, 1140).

On the explorations of Oñate and his captains, consult: Katharine Bartlett, "Notes upon the Routes of Espejo and Farfán to the Mines in the Sixteenth Century," *NMHR*, 17 (January 1942), 21–36; David Donoghue, "Coronado, Oñate, and Quivira," *Mid-America*, 18 (April 1936), 88–95; Albert H. Schroeder, "A Re-analysis of the Routes of Coronado and Oñate into the Plains in 1541 and 1601," *Plains Anthropologist*, 7 (February 1972), 2–23; Susan C. Vehik, "Oñate's Expedition to the Southern Plains: Route and Destination," *Plains Anthropologist*, 31 (February 1986), 13–34; Herbert E. Bolton, trans. and ed., "Father Escobar's Relation of the Oñate Expedition to California," *Catholic*

Historical Review, 5 (April 1919), 19–41; and George P. Hammond and Agapito Rey, trans. and eds., *New Mexico in 1602* (Los Angeles: The Quivira Society, 1938).

In his book *Apache, Navajo, and Spaniard* (Norman: University of Oklahoma Press, 1960), Jack D. Forbes includes a narrative of the Oñate episode in New Mexico that is strongly anti-Spanish and uncritically accepts the validity of all charges and criticisms leveled against the governor. For more on Oñate's misconduct and legal problems, see George P. Hammond, "The Conviction of Don Juan de Oñate, New Mexico's First Governor," in *New Spain and the Anglo-American West,* ed. Hammond, 1, 67–69; and Lansing B. Bloom, "Oñate's Exoneration," *NMHR,* 12 (April 1937), 175–92.

The widely held belief that Governor Pedro de Peralta laid the foundations for Santa Fe in early 1610 traces back to Lansing B. Bloom's "When Was Santa Fe Founded?" *NMHR,* 4 (April 1929), 188–94. Father Benavides, admittedly not always a reliable source, does state categorically that Oñate founded Santa Fe, which squares with the reference presented in this book that the town had its genesis about 1608. On that issue, see France V. Scholes, "Juan Martínez de Montoya, Settler and Conquistador of New Mexico," *NMHR,* 19 (October 1944), 337–42; and Frederick Webb Hodge et al., *Fray Alonso de Benavides' Revised Memorial of 1634* (Albuquerque: University of New Mexico Press, 1945).

On the end of the Oñate regime in New Mexico, two brief articles are helpful: George P. Hammond, "The Date of Oñate's Return From New Mexico," *El Palacio,* 4 (May 1951), 112–14; and, Agapito Rey, "Cristóbal de Oñate," *NMHR,* 26 (July 1951), 197–203.

Information on Oñate's admission to the Military Order of Santiago, together with some genealogical data, is contained in Guillermo Lohmann Villena's *Los Americanos en las Ordenes Nobiliarias* (Madrid: Institute Gonzalo Fernández de Oviedo, 1947). Finally, Oñate's twilight years in Spain and his death are described in Eric Beerman's "The Death of an Old Conquistador: New Light on Juan de Oñate," *NMHR,* 54 (October 1979), 305–19.

Index